The Complete Guide to Photoshop Native Filters

Sherry London

Hayden Books

Hayden Books

President
Richard Swadley

Associate Publisher
John Pierce

Managing Editor
Lisa Wilson

Director of Marketing
Kelli S. Spencer

Product Marketing Manager
Kim Margolius

Acquisitions Editor
Rachel Byers

Development Editor
Beth Millett

Copy/Production Editor
Kevin Laseau

Technical Coordinator
Catherine Benante

Publishing Coordinator
Karen Williams

Cover Designer
Aren Howell

Book Designer
Ann Jones

Manufacturing Coordinator
Brook Farling

Production Team Supervisor
Laurie Casey

Production Team
Maureen Hanrahan, Linda Knose, Elizabeth SanMiguel, Scott Tullis

Indexer
Chris Barrick

The Complete Guide to Photoshop Native Filters

ISBN: 1-56830-453-6

Printed in the United States of America 1 2 3 4 5 6 7 8 9 0

Warning and Disclaimer

This book is sold as is, without warranty of any kind, either express or implied. While every precaution has been taken in the preparation of this book, the authors and Hayden Books assume no responsibility for errors or omissions. Neither is any liability assumed for damages resulting from the use of the information or instructions contained herein. It is further stated that the publisher and authors are not responsible for any damage or loss to your data or your equipment that results directly or indirectly from your use of this book.

TRADEMARK ACKNOWLEDGMENTS

ABOUT THE AUTHOR

Sherry London, author of *Photoshop Textures Magic* and contributing author of *Photoshop 4 Complete*, has been working with computer graphics applications since the days of "Paint" on the Atari 800. She has used Adobe Photoshop since version 1.0 appeared.

Since 1989, Sherry has been reviewing graphics software and writing how-to articles for a number of publications. She is currently a contributing editor for *Computer Artist* magazine and is quite active on CompuServe as one of the Mac Photoshop Section Leaders in the Photoshop forum. She has also been a Section Leader on the CompuServe Crafts form and a sysop on Ziff's Download and Support forum.

Professionally, Sherry has used Photoshop both as a graphic artist and as a fiber artist. She has been doing needlework desing since 1973, and has used Photoshop as the basis for several needlepoint works that are currently in a traveling exhibit sponsored by the Embroider's Guild of America.

Sherry's background is in education and she has worked as an instructional systems designer. She has taught classes in management information systems at Drexel University in Philadelphia, PA, and now teaches Photoshop and Pre-Press at Moore College of Art and Design. She is the author of *Photoshop Special Effects How-To* and *A Certified Course in Photoshop*, both published by the Waite Group Press.

HAYDEN BOOKS

The staff of Hayden Books is committed to bringing you the best computer books. What our readers think of Hayden is important to our ability to serve our customers. If you have any comments, no matter how great or how small, we'd appreciate your taking the time to send us a note.

You can reach Hayden Books at the following:

Hayden Books
201 West 103rd Street
Indianapolis, IN 46290
317-581-3833

Email address **hayden@hayden.com**

Visit the Hayden Books Web site at **http://www.hayden.com**

CONTENTS AT A GLANCE

TABLE OF CONTENTS

USING PHOTOSHOP'S FILTERS

Filters are one of Photoshop's most versatile tools, enabling the user to edit an image with an astounding range of effects, a range that goes from Accented Edges all the way to Zigzag. And they're all covered in this book. The filters in this book are organized by type: The Artistic filters are grouped together, the Blur filters are grouped together, and so on. If you're not sure what category to look under for a filter you're interested in, the following page has a table of contents listing each filter and the page it is on. Enjoy!

Sample images used in this book are on the CD-ROM that accompanies this package. Look in the Filters folder.

USING FILTERS—A GENERAL APPROACH

Photoshop uses filters to change image data in a variety of ways. Instead of using the Blur tool, for example, on a large portion of your image, you can use one of the Blur filters and change all of the pixels in your selection at one time. You can alter the lighting in your image by using the Lighting Effects filter. You can add tiny bits of random color to your image using the Add Noise filter...You get the idea!

There are ninety-seven filters in Photoshop 4.0. While some are more useful than others, this chapter describes them all. You really need to work with them, however, to discover their full potential. Filters are one area where "playing by the rules" is not always the best idea. Although each filter has something it was designed to do "best," your most creative uses often occur when you use the filter "wrong."

Tip

Take the time to play and experiment with the filters. Then put comments about how you created the effect you like in the Caption field of the File➡File Info command. These comments stay with your image to help you remember what you did.

Principles of Filter Use

No one can give you "rules" for using filters. The "filter police" are not going to shut down your business if you violate one. Nevertheless, there are more effective—or less effective—ways to approach the use of filters. Here's a list of suggestions:

- **Know your filters.** Play with them enough to get a good sense of what they can do. You will find that you have a number of "favorites."

- **Master a new filter every week** (That will take you close to two years!). Experiment with a new filter first using the default settings. Next, try setting the controls to the lowest and then the highest settings. See what the middle settings will do. If there are multiple controls, drag one high and one low. Reverse the settings. See how the results change. Instead of using the Undo command, work on a relatively small image and keep copying the original. This lets you compare the results. Make note of any settings you really like.

- **Apply a Filter to a Layer.** Before you apply a filter, place your selection on a layer and apply the filter to that layer. This enables you to blend the filter into the image if you do not want it at full strength, or change the Blending mode. It also enables you to change your mind at any point in your design process.
- **Experiment with the Fade... command** (even if you have applied a filter to a Layer). The Filter➥Fade command is new in Photoshop 4.0. It enables you to keep only a percentage of the filter you applied and to change the Blending mode as well. This is a wonderful new feature! It does everything for you that filtering a layer does except that after you are done, you are done. You cannot change your mind past the original Undo.
- **Filter in a single channel for a special effect.** Some filters (any filter that works on a grayscale image) can be applied to a single channel at a time. You can get some very interesting effects by applying a filter to only the green channel, for example.
- **Filter an alpha channel and use that channel as a selection mask.** You can get some really exciting results by applying a filter to data in an alpha channel (a grayscale version of your image, perhaps). Then, use that channel as a selection and apply another filter to the whole image through that selection. The Crystallize filter is especially effective for this technique.
- **Misuse the filters.** See what happens when you break the rules. You can get wonderful special effects—sometimes—when you apply a filter using what might otherwise be inappropriate settings (a too large Unsharp Mask setting or a Dust & Scratches Setting that smoothes the image much too much for color correction).

- **Think "multiple applications."** Another good special effects technique is to reapply the same filter to the same selection a few times. This is particularly good with One-Step filters (see discussion on categories). It can, however, work with many of the filters. You can also try re-filtering the selection with the same filter, different settings, or a completely different filter.
- **Make the filter effect your own.** This one is just my Puritan work ethic showing! I almost feel as if using a single-effect filter, such as the Colored Pencil filter (or most of the old Gallery Effects filters) is cheating. To just filter an image and say "OK, now it's art," is not only inaccurate, it doesn't seem right. And if it is art, it isn't your art. You can make it your own by changing Blending modes, adding your own textures, and combining effects. Of course, if you are on a tight deadline and the canned effect is just what you want, use it. That's what it is there for. But you will grow artistically if you find a way to incorporate the filters into your own style rather than just letting the filter be the artistic statement for you.
- **Use a little restraint.** Some filters are very distinctive and a little goes a long way. Especially with filters that were part of the original Adobe Gallery Effects collection (Artistic, Brush Strokes, Sketch, Texture), you need to make sure that they do not fight with one another visually in the filtered image. An over-filtered image is like a sampler. Samplers were wonderful devices for teaching needlework, but they were rarely good art. Don't use "one-of-each" just because you can. Let the filter support the artistic purpose of the image.

FADING A FILTER

4.0

After you apply a filter, a new menu item is enabled near the top of the Filter menu: Fade… This item enables you to incrementally "un-apply" the last filter used to the image—or to change the blending mode. This is a very powerful command.

In Photoshop 3, you could duplicate your image into a new layer and then filter the new layer. If you were not happy with the results, you could either throw the whole layer away or cut its opacity to mix it with the unfiltered layer beneath. You could also change the blending mode for the layer to change the result of the filter. In 4.0 you still can. The Fade command, however, which is new to Photoshop 4.0, can do exactly the same thing without the added overhead in RAM and file size. The only thing you lose is the ability to change the image later in the design process.

Try it.

1. Open the image "FallFlwr.Psd."
2. Apply the Glowing Edges filter by selecting Filter➥Stylize ➥Glowing Edges using the settings in Figure 1.

Figure 1

The Glowing Edges dialog box.

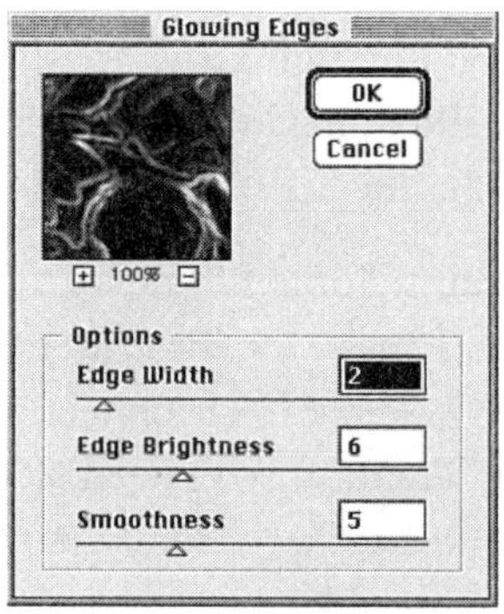

3. Select the Fade... command (Filter➥Fade Glowing Edges). The dialog box shown in Figure 2 appears. Set the Opacity of the filter to 70% and change the Blending mode to Hard Light.

Figure 2

The Fade Glowing Edges dialog box.

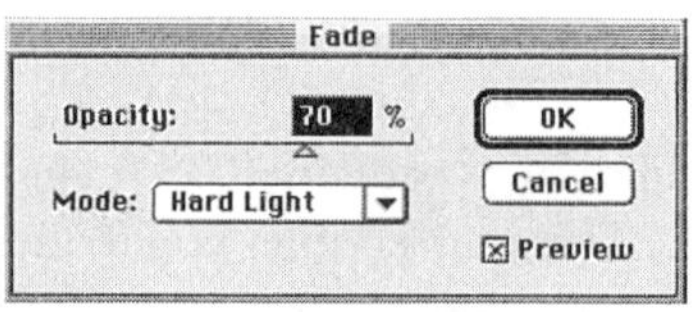

4. Click OK. Figure 3 shows the final, faded image.

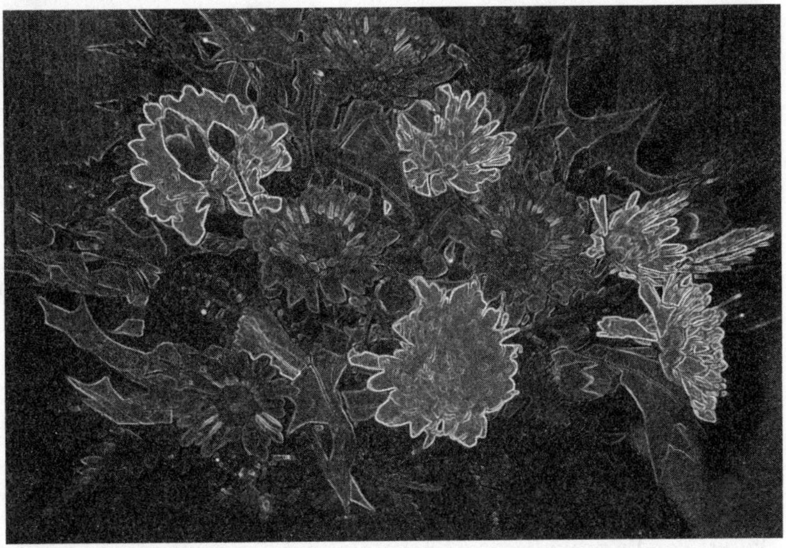

Figure 3

The faded Glowing Edges filtered image.

Interpreting the Chart

At the end of each filter description is a chart summarizing the main characteristics of that filter. Here's a brief explanation of each category.

Filter type	Category	Supported Color Modes	Preview type	Data Dependent	Color Dependent
Parameter	Stylizing Filter	RGB, Grayscale	Small Filter Preview	Yes. A blank image produces a blank filtered image.	Yes. Back-ground colors is the "bright-ness" color.

Filter Type

There are three main types of filters.

- A **One-Step filter** applies the filter with no user control. The Blur filter, for example, softens the pixels in an image so that the color in each pixel becomes a little bit closer to the color of the pixels nearest to it. You cannot specify *how* soft you want the pixel to be. You select the filter name from the menu, the filter does whatever it does, and you are done. You can apply it multiple times, but you cannot change the amount by which it filters the image. These filters can be spotted in the Filter menu because they do not have ellipses (...) after their names.

- A **parameter filter** gives you choices. You need to set sliders or controls to specify what the filter will do. Most of the native filters that come with Photoshop are of this variety.
- A **mini-application filter** is a filter that enables you to save and recall settings and creates its own environment inside of Photoshop. Many third-party filters (ones not created by Adobe and which you need to purchase separately) are mini-apps; none of the Photoshop native filters are.

Category

Filters can be broken up into several general categories. The two most basic ones are Production and Special Effects. A production-oriented filter is used for color correction or focus correction to help prepare an image for print. A special effects filter changes the image in a non-realistic way. The categories are further broken down in this part of the chart as follows:

- Pre-Press—Filter is used to help prepare an image for printing.
- Special Effects—Purpose is to change the image for an artistic, rather than realistic, purpose.
- Color Change—Filter alters the color values in an image.
- Deformation—Filter alters the geometry of the image by bending, warping, stretching, or otherwise misshaping it.
- Displacement—Uses another image or a built-in algorithm as a map to control the distortion of the original image. Makes the image look as if it is being viewed through some type of other surface, such as water or glass.
- Destructive—Filter replaces the image with its own effect; original image does not affect the filter results.
- Distressed—original image alters the effect of the filter, but the filtered image is not readily recognizable.

- Focus—Filter alters the focus of the image, making it either sharper or softer in some manner.
- Stylizing—Filter creates a slightly abstract and stylized version of the original
- Texture—Filter creates surface interest
- 3D—Filter appears to create a third dimension in the image

A filter can belong to more than one category. The "Special Effects" and "Pre-press" categories are intentions (as in *why* you want to filter the image) rather than results. They are likely to be used in combination with other categories on the charts.

Supported Color Modes

A filter may work on RGB, Grayscale, CMYK, or Lab colors modes—or only in some of them. This place on the chart tells you which color modes work for a specific filter. Images in Bitmap or Indexed Color modes cannot be filtered at all.

Preview Type

It is always helpful to be able to see the effect of a filter before you add it to your image. This is particularly important when you are using a parameter filter, because it helps you to select the desired settings and shortens the time it takes to "get it right." Many of Photoshop's filters have preview—areas in the filter dialog itself that allow you to see what will happen when you apply the filter. None of the One-Step filters have previews. There are a few different types of filter previews:

- None: the filter has no preview.
- Small Filter Preview: There is a small area in the dialog box that shows a tiny section of your image with the filter applied.
- Full Image Preview: in addition to the small box, you can see the results on your original image. Both the small preview and your image are updated as you change the parameter settings.
- WireFrame Preview: a schematic shows the deformation path that will be used to filter the image. You do not see any image data or color at all.

Data Dependent

This is a "Yes/No" category on the chart. A filter that is data dependent ("Yes"), needs something other than a blank image in which to work. Filtering a blank (solid colored) image with a data dependent filter will cause no change to the image. A data-independent filter ("No") will produce a result of some kind even if the image is totally blank. Some of the data-independent filters only work if the image is not white; the Clouds filter is the only filter that will produce results on a totally transparent (empty) Layer. Every other filter must at least have pixels on which to work (and will give you an error if you try to apply it to a transparent Layer).

Color Dependent

This is another "Yes/No" category. A "No" means that it does not matter what colors you have selected in the Toolbox as your Foreground or Background colors. A "Yes" means that the filter uses either the Foreground or Background color or both as part of the effect. Changing the color changes the effect of the filter.

The Filter Menu

Photoshop's native filters appear on the Filters menu in thirteen categories. Let's discuss them in the order in which they appear:

- Artistic
- Blur
- Brush Strokes
- Distort
- Noise
- Pixelate
- Render
- Sharpen
- Sketch
- Stylize

- Texture
- Video
- Other

PHOTOSHOP'S NATIVE FILTERS—ARTISTIC

The fifteen filters in the Artistic category are new to Photoshop 4.0. They were part of the three Aldus (later—Adobe) Gallery Effects series of third-party plug-ins. They have been added to Photoshop's native filter list for the first time.

These filters are used to apply a specific "art style" to your image. While they can be used in conjunction with other filters or on a selection, they make strong enough statements individually that they are hard to combine. Use these filters on an entire image for the best "intended" results.

The filters in this category can filter images that are in RGB or Grayscale modes only. They do not work on images in CMYK or Lab colorspace. In addition, none of them will work on an empty Layer. They are all parameter filters—that is, they have specific parameters (controls) that you can set for different results. All of the filters in this category have small previews in the filter dialog box, but none of them use a full-image preview.

Colored Pencil

The Colored Pencil filter takes an image or selection and stylizes it to resemble, supposedly, colored pencils on neutral (black-to-white) paper stock. In reality, the filter uses the predominant colors in the image and removes areas that it changes to the "paper color" depending upon the parameter settings. This filter leaves a type of cross-hatching that is attractive but not especially reminiscent of Pencil strokes. If anything, it almost looks like oil paints applied with a palette knife and feathered at the edges.

Try it:

1. Open the image "Fallflwr.Psd." Duplicate the image (Image➡Duplicate➡OK).
2. Open the Colored Pencil dialog box (Filter➡Artistic➡Colored Pencil) (see Figure 4).

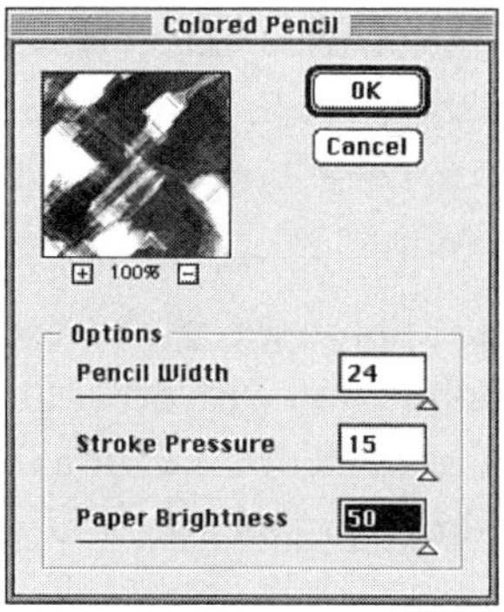

Figure 4

Colored Pencil dialog box.

3. Drag the Pencil Width to 24.

   The Pencil Width setting varies from 1-24. This parameter controls the size of the background color that shows through the image. At 1 the image is almost solid, and scratches of the background color show through. At 24 the image is broken up into roughly equal areas of original image and background color. It is as if the Pencil color used is actually the "paper" color setting, and you specify *its* width using the Pencil Width setting. You can set the slider anywhere along the length, though your detail will reproduce better on a large image (one with a high dpi setting and large number of pixels) if you use a slightly higher Pencil Width setting (above 3 at least).

4. Set the Stroke Pressure to 15.

   The Stroke Pressure can vary from 0 to 15. This parameter controls the intensity of the color in the image. When Stroke Pressure is 0, no image is produced—regardless of the other settings. When it is at 15, the original brightness of the image is preserved. A Stroke Pressure of 1 shows some color in the brightest areas of the original image and no color at all in the darkest areas of the original.

5. Finally, set the Paper Brightness to 50.

   The Paper Brightness varies from 0-50. A brightness of 0 makes the "paper color" black, and a brightness of 50 makes it whatever color is set in your Background color in the Toolbox. A Paper Brightness of 25 is a mixture between the two. If your Background color is white, my advice is to use a Brightness of either 0 or 50, as the in-between settings tend to muddy up the image.

6. Click OK. Figure 5 shows the result, which could be suitable for a Thanksgiving greeting card.

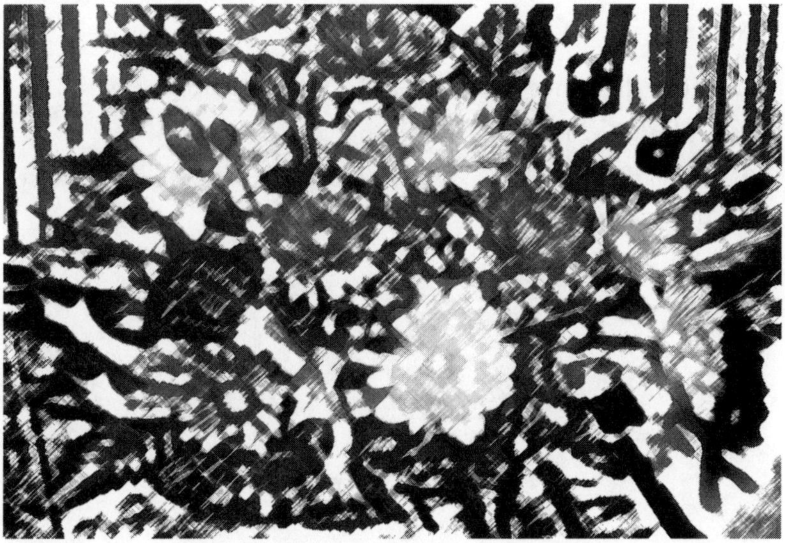

Figure 5

The Colored Pencil filter applied.

Filter type	Category	Supported Color Modes	Preview type	Data Dependent	Color Dependent
Parameter	Stylizing Filter	RGB, Grayscale	Small Filter Preview	Yes. A blank image produces a blank filtered image.	Yes. Back-ground colors is the "brightness" color.

Cutout

The Cutout filter, an enhancement of the Posterize command, simplifies the colors of your image into the number of levels that you request. But the Cutout filter uses colors from the original image—rather than colorspace "primitives" (RGB or CMYK) as does the Posterize command. It is a "smart" filter in that it looks for shapes to simplify, and it creates anti-aliased edges where the colors meet. The Cutout filter is computationally intensive and the preview is very slow. The filter, however, delivers a look that ranges from so-abstract-that-you-can't-figure-out-what-it-is (at 2 Levels, Edge Simplicty of 0, Edge Fidelity of 1), to a paint-by-numbers look (at 8 Levels, Edge Simplicty of 0, and Edge Fidelity of 3). You get the most detailed results from this filter by using a high contrast image as your original. In certain limited situations, the Cutout filter could be helpful in trying to make a mask.

Try it:

1. Open the image "FallFlwr.Psd." Duplicate the image (Image➡Duplicate➡OK).
2. Open the Cutout dialog box (Filter➡Artistic➡Cutout) to see the dialog box shown in Figure 6.

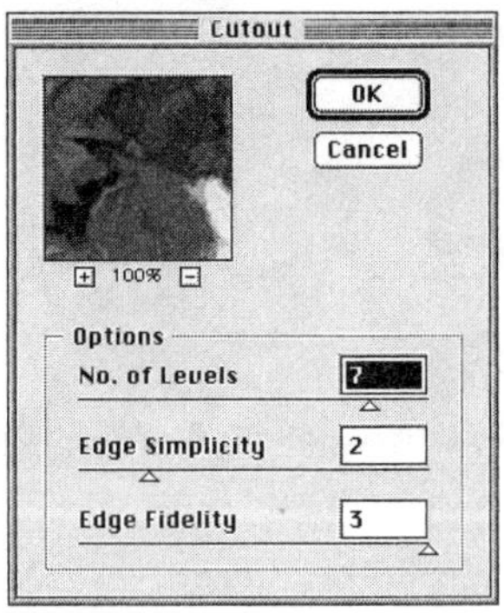

Figure 6

The Cutout dialog box.

3. Drag the Number of Levels to 7.

   The Number of Levels setting varies from 2 to 8. This parameter controls the number of colors in the filtered image. At its lowest setting, the parameter finds two levels in the original image. This still translates into a significant number of colors, however, though it greatly simplifies the image.

4. Set the Edge Simplicity to 3.

   The Edge Simplicity varies from 0 to 10. At the higher settings, the edges are so "simple" that there are none; the filter produces a solid colored block. The best settings for this parameter seem to be from 0 (the highest detail in the edge) to about 5.

5. Finally, set the Edge Fidelity to 2.

   The Edge Fidelity can vary from 1 to 3. This parameter does not seem to affect the image if the Edge Simplicty is set to 0. If, however, the Edge Simplicty is set to 5, you see a big difference in the edges of the shapes by varying the Edge Fidelity slider. A setting of 1 produces the most abstract edge (similar to selecting a loose autotrace setting in a vector program). A setting of 3 tries to capture the actual edge of the area as best it can.

6. Click OK. Figure 7 shows the result.

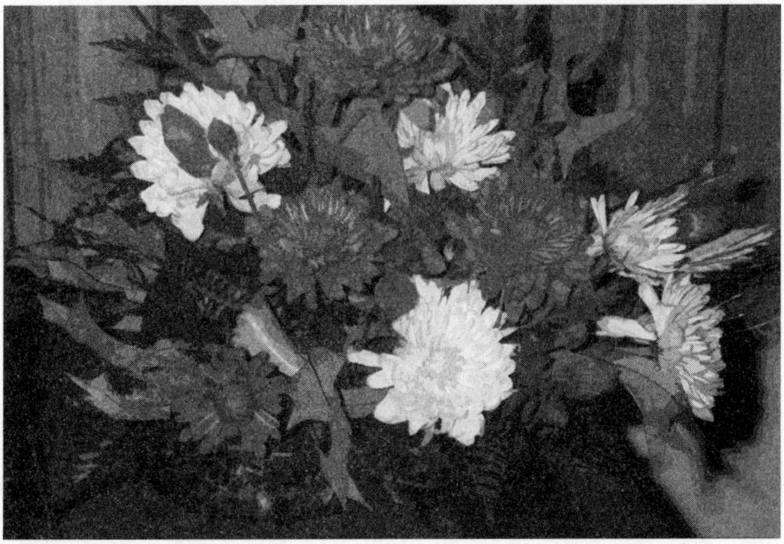

Figure 7

An example of the Cutout filter applied.

Filter type	Category	Supported Color Modes	Preview type	Data Dependent	Color Dependent
Parameter	Stylizing Filter	RGB, Grayscale	Small Filter Preview	Yes. A blank image produces a blank filtered image.	No. The Foreground/ Background settings have no effect.

Dry Brush

4.0

This is one of the rare filters that seems to produce good results at every setting—although what you get varies widely. I like this filter a lot. It imitates the traditional dry brush technique of dragging a loaded Paintbrush until it runs out of paint. The edges then fracture and fray across the canvas. In this electronic version, that means the edges are aliased and hard, though the internal shading still retains the variations and soft shading.

There are no settings in this filter that produce a blank image. With the settings of Brush Size = 0, Image Detail = 0, and Texture = 1, you get an almost lace-like effect with aliasing at all of the edges in the image. Change the Image Detail to 10 and you get a softly abstracted oil painting that is close in detail to the original but different in "feeling," as it is no longer photographic. If the settings are Brush Size = 10, Image Detail = 10, and Texture = 3, you get a very chunky oil painting that looks like it was done by patting down various colors.

Try it:

1. Open the image "FallFlwr.Psd." Duplicate the image (Image➥Duplicate➥OK).
2. Open the Dry Brush dialog box shown in Figure 8 (Filter➥Artistic➥Dry Brush).
3. Drag the Brush Size to 2.

   The Brush Size varies from 0 to 10. It controls the size of the strokes, with 10 as the largest.

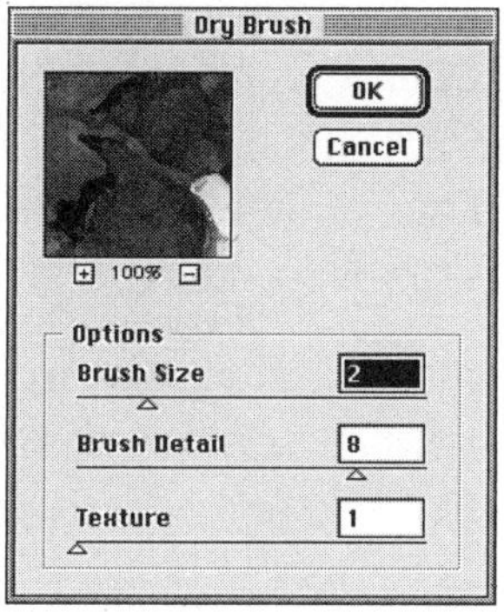

Figure 8

The Dry Brush dialog box.

4. Set the Brush Detail to 8.

   The Brush Detail can vary from 0 to 10. It determines how much detail will be captured from the original image. A setting of 10 captures the most detail.

5. Finally, set the Texture to 1. The Texture setting varies from 1 to 3. A setting of 1 produces a smooth image. A setting of 3 produces an image that contains bits of color that were not in that location in the original image. It adds flecks of pixels to the image.

6. Click OK. Figure 9 shows the result.

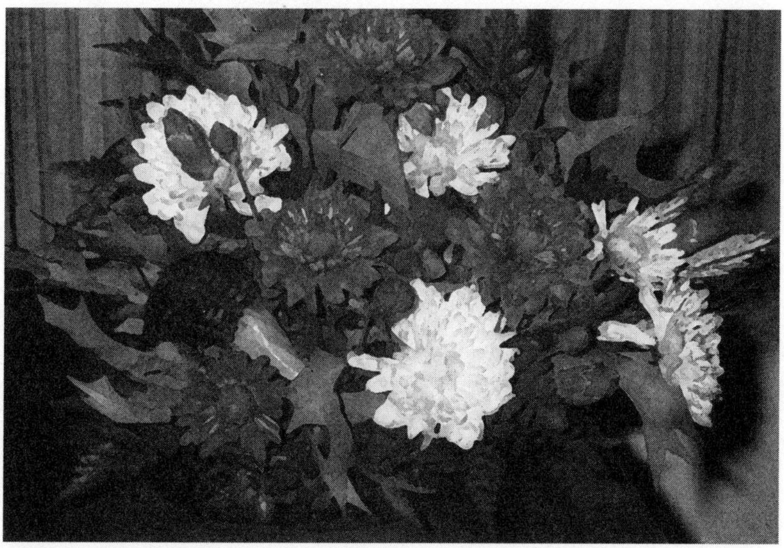

Figure 9

An example of the Dry Brush filter applied to an image.

Filter type	Category	Supported Color Modes	Preview type	Data Dependent	Color Dependent
Parameter	Stylizing Filter	RGB, Grayscale	Small Filter Preview	Yes. A blank image produces a blank filtered image.	No. The Foreground/ Background settings have no effect.

Film Grain

The Film Grain filter is a Noise filter combined with logic to lighten and intensify parts of the image. The Add Noise filter can obliterate an image with noise. This filter, even at its highest setting, does not. In addition, the Film Grain filter enables you to specify a highlight and intensity amount that adds more noise to the darker areas of the image than to the highlighted areas. This filter looks good when used on text, but I don't find this an especially attractive special effects filter. You might want to use it for pre-press where you would use the Add Noise filter.

At the lowest settings, the Film Grain filter does nothing. The filter seems to flatten the colors in the image—the higher the Grain setting, the flatter the colors get.

Try it:

1. Open the image "FallFlwr.Psd." Duplicate the image (Image➥Duplicate➥OK).

2. Open the Film Grain dialog box shown in Figure 10 (Filter➥Artistic➥Film Grain).

3. Drag the Grain to 20.

   Grain controls the amount of noise added and varies from 0 to 20.

4. Set the Highlight Area to 1.

   Highlight Area varies from 1 to 20 and controls the amount of the image that is lightened. The lightening occurs on the areas of the image that were lighter and more saturated in the original.

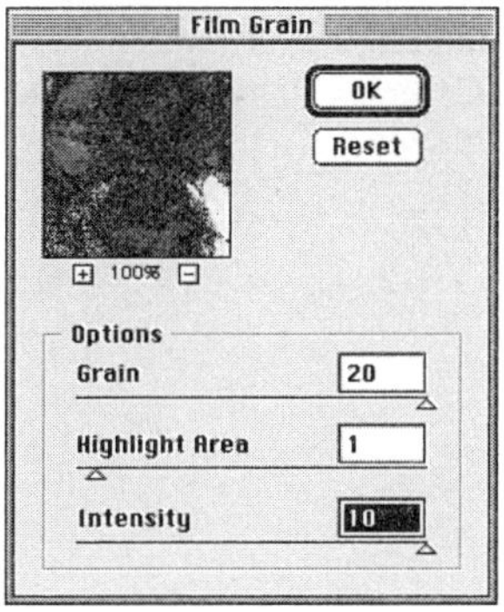

Figure 10

The Film Grain filter dialog box.

5. Finally, set the Intensity to 10.

   The Intensity varies from 0-10 and controls the amount of highlighting that occurs. If the Intensity is set to 0, it does not matter where you set the Highlight area. With the Intensity at a high setting, the film grain is noticeably less in the intense areas.

6. Click OK. Figure 11 shows the result.

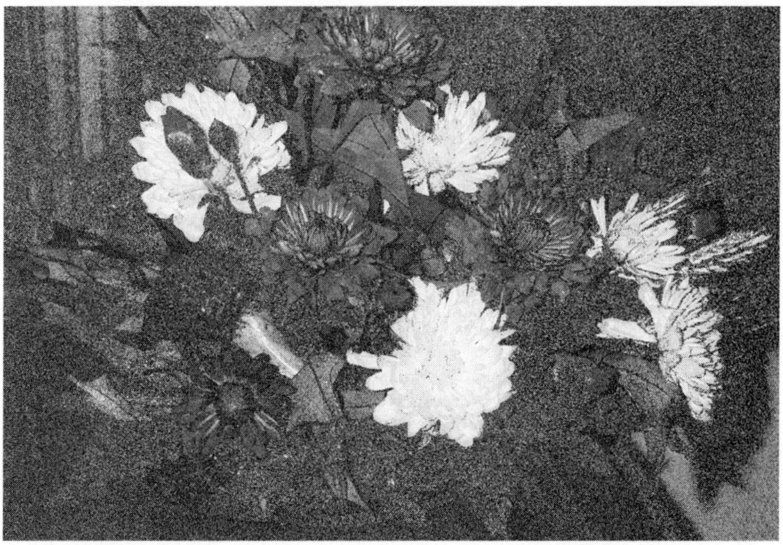

Figure 11

An example of the Film Grain filter applied.

Filter type	Category	Supported Color Modes	Preview type	Data Dependent	Color Dependent
Parameter	Stylizing Filter	RGB, Grayscale	Small Filter Preview	No. If you filter a solid-colored image at high settings, you will see film grain.	No. The Foreground/ Background settings have no effect.

Fresco

This filter is very similar to the Dry Brush filter, but it intensifies the contrast in the image and makes the darks much bolder. The Fresco filter has exactly the same controls as the Dry Brush filter. All settings in this filter produce a usable image.

The Fresco filter is good for abstracting an image and sharpening the contrast. The colors become very intense.

Try it:

1. Open the image "FallFlwr.Psd." Duplicate the image (Image➡Duplicate➡OK).
2. Open the Fresco dialog box shown in Figure 12 (Filter➡Artistic➡Fresco).

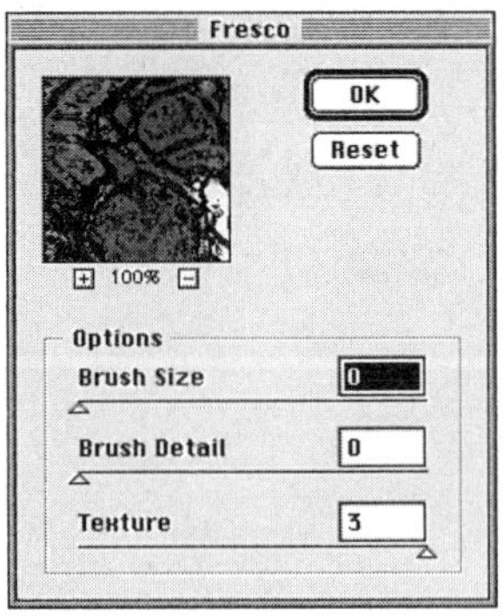

Figure 12

The Fresco filter dialog box.

3. Drag the Brush Size to 0.

   The Brush Size varies from 0 to 10. It controls the size of the strokes, with 10 as the largest.

4. Set the Brush Detail to 0.

   The Brush Detail determines how much detail will be captured from the original image. It varies from 0 to 10. A setting of 10 captures the most detail.

5. Finally, set the Texture to 3.

   The Texture setting varies from 1 to 3. A setting of 1 produces a smooth image. A setting of 3 produces an image that contains bits of color that were not in that location in the original image. It adds flecks of pixels to the image.

6. Click OK. Figure 13 shows the result.

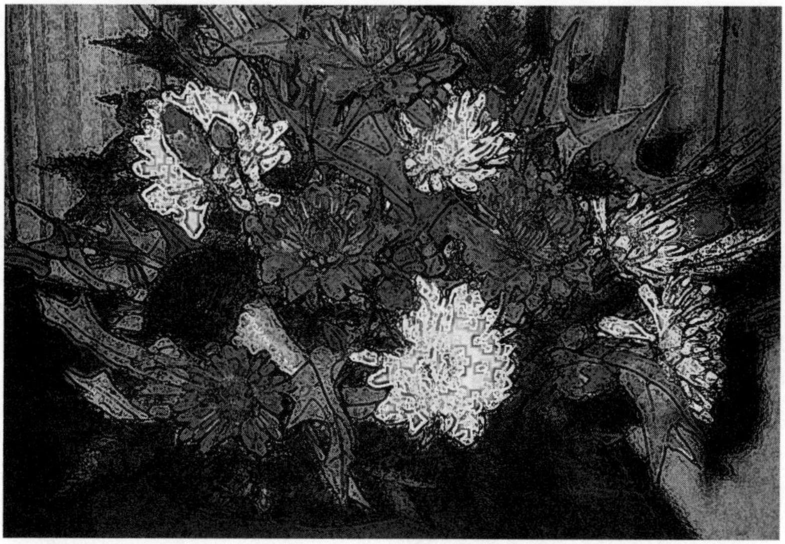

Figure 13

An example of the Fresco filter applied to an image.

Filter type	Category	Supported Color Modes	Preview type	Data Dependent	Color Dependent
Parameter	Stylizing Filter	RGB, Grayscale	Small Filter Preview	Yes. A blank image produces a blank filtered image.	No. The Foreground/ Background settings have no effect.

Neon Glow

The Neon Glow is a very odd filter. I'm not very fond of it at any setting. It makes a strange duo or tri-tone from your image, depending upon your color choices.

Unless you want a strange negative image or an odd-colored one, I'm not sure this has any major uses. It can give an other-worldly feel to an image given the right color choice, and could also be effective when used on a selection or on text. If black and white are your foreground/background colors you will get a grayscale image with the "Color" color as your glow. Make sure that the selection has some very bright values in it, however, if you are going to use positive values in the Size slider. This filter is extremely color dependent. It reacts to the settings of the Foreground and Background colors and to a third color selected in the filter itself. Pick contrasting colors for the most noticeable results.

Try it:

1. Open the image "FallFlwr.Psd." Duplicate the image (Image➥Duplicate➥OK).
2. Pick a deep orange from the image as your foreground color, and a light yellow as the background color.
3. Open the Neon Glow dialog box shown in Figure 14 (Filter➥Artistic➥Neon Glow).

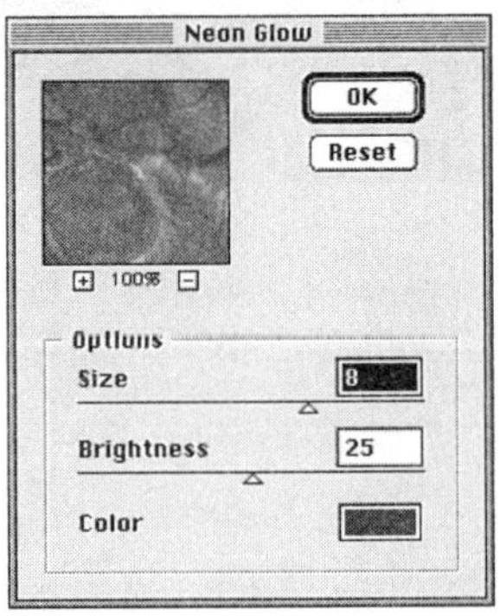

Figure 14

Neon Glow dialog box.

4. Drag the Size to +8.

   The Size setting runs from -24 to +24.

5. Set the Brightness to 25.

   The Brightness goes from 0 to 50. With a Brightness of less than 7, you get no results regardless of the Size setting. When the Size is in the negative numbers, you get a negative image.

6. Click the color icon to select a bright blue as your Color setting.

   The Color setting interacts in an odd way with the Brightness and Size settings. When Brightness is 50 and Size is -24, the darkest areas show the Color, the highlights show the Foreground color, and the midtones shows the mixture of Foreground/Background. When Brightness is 50 and Size is +24, the lightest areas show the Background, the highlights show the Foreground color, and the midtones shows the mixture of Foreground/Background; the Color is not used. At a Size setting of 0, the lightest areas in the image show up in the Color setting.

7. Click OK. Figure 15 shows the result.

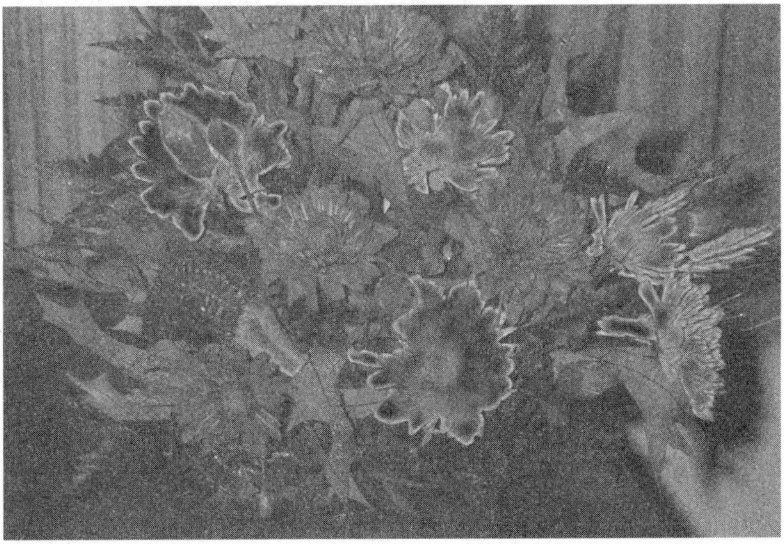

Figure 15

The Neon Glow filter applied.

Filter type	Category	Supported Color Modes	Preview type	Data Dependent	Color Dependent
Parameter	Stylizing Filter	RGB, Grayscale	Small Filter Preview	Yes. A blank image produces a blank filtered image.	Yes. Foreground/ Background settings have a profound effect.

Paint Daubs

This filter is supposed to look like spots of paint. It doesn't. There are, however, many settings here that give pleasing results—even if they don't match the filter name. The logic of this filter seems to be a cross between the Dust & Scratches filter with a Radius of 16 and a Threshold of 0 (that is, blurry areas of color) and the Unsharp Mask filter. It is as if you can select the amount of sharpening that you want after the image has been divided into color regions. The Paint Daubs filter can also select a brush that performs further mathemagic on the filter. This works nicely on an entire image to stylize and abstract it.

When the Brush Size and Sharpening are each about halfway, the Sparkle brush seems to give the same effect as if you had used the Gaussian Blur filter and the Find Edges filter and then sharpened these edges. It is an interesting look.

The middle ranges of the Brush Size and Sharpness settings seems most useful. If you set both Brush Size and Sharpness very low, you will see no change in your image.

Try it:

1. Open the image "FallFlwr.Psd." Duplicate the image (Image➡Duplicate➡OK).
2. Open the Paint Daubs dialog box shown in Figure 16 (Filter➡Artistic➡Paint Daubs).
3. Drag the Brush Size to 8.

   The Brush Size setting varies from 1-50. The Brush Size controls the size of the color-block regions.

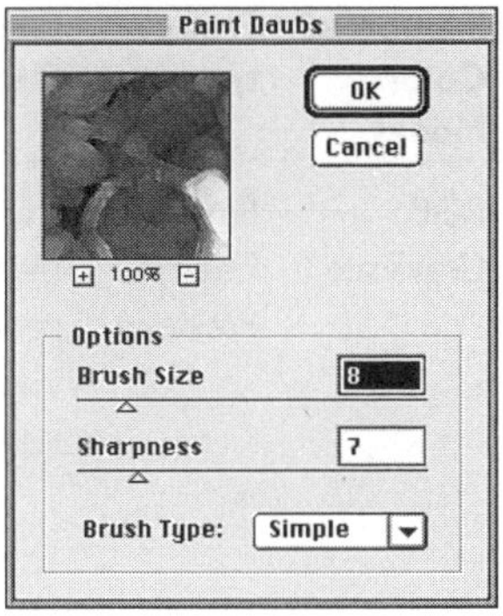

Figure 16

The Paint Daubs dialog box.

4. Set the Sharpness to 7.

   The Sharpness can vary from 0-40. The Sharpness controls the amount of sharpening applied (surprise!).

5. Finally, set the Simple brush.

   There are a number of brushes: Simple, Light Rough, Dark Rough, Wide Sharp, Wide Blurry, and Sparkle. The Rough brushes are noisy.

6. Click OK. Figure 17 shows the result.

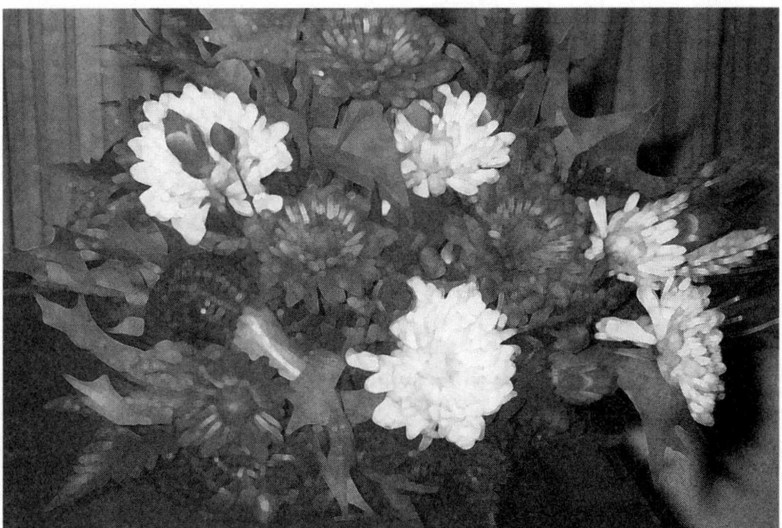

Figure 17

An example of the Paint Daubs filter applied.

Filter type	Category	Supported Color Modes	Preview type	Data Dependent	Color Dependent
Parameter	Stylizing Filter	RGB, Grayscale	Small Filter Preview	Yes. A blank image produces a blank filtered image.	No. The Foreground/Background settings have no effect.

Palette Knife

The Palette Knife filter can make your image look as if it had been painted using a palette knife—if you select the correct settings and *want* to use a palette knife that leaves paint perfectly flat on the canvas. The flatness is the only thing that I do not like about this filter. It is unnatural given the name of the filter.

The filter looks as if you are placing strokes of color on a canvas that was underpainted with black. The darkest shadow areas turn solid black, and the image seems to gain in saturation. The filter can help to enhance a simple line art graphic. The filter is good for an entire image or wherever you might wish to use the Crystallize filter. This could be a good filter for texture creation at large Stroke Sizes. It is also good combined with the Emboss filter.

Try it:

1. Open the image "FallFlwr.Psd." Duplicate the image (Image➡Duplicate➡OK).
2. Drag the Background Layer icon to the New Layer icon at the bottom of the Layers palette to duplicate it. Turn off the Eye icon so that you can see the Background layer.
3. Click on the Background Layer to make it the active Layer. Apply the Emboss filter (Filter➡Stylize➡Emboss) to it with any setting that you like.
4. Click on the top Layer and turn the Eye icon back on.

5. Open the Palette Knife box shown in Figure 18 (Filter➡Artistic➡Palette Knife).

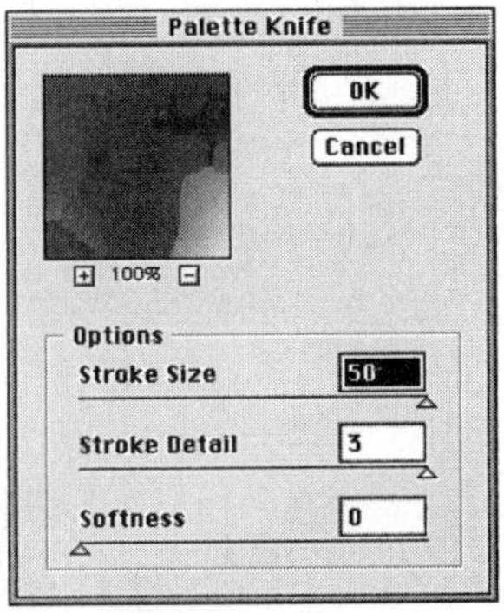

Figure 18

The Palette Knife dialog box.

6. Drag the Stroke Size to 50.

   The Stroke Size ranges from 1-50, but at the larger sizes you lose all of the detail in your image and just have blobs of color. At the smallest Stroke Sizes, you see no change. A Stroke Size of 12 is a good choice to keep image detail.

7. Set the Stroke Detail to 3.

   The Stroke Detail controls the shape of the paint strokes. The control ranges from 1 to 3. At a setting of 1, the colors are applied almost as if you were using the Crystallize filter. At a setting of 3, you see almost a dry brush effect, which is more attractive.

8. Finally, set the Softness to 0.

   The Softness setting controls the amount of anti-aliasing on the edges of the strokes. The setting ranges from 0-10, with 0 being aliased and 10 being very soft.

9. Click OK. Change the Blending mode to Hard Light with an Opacity of 90%. Figure 19 shows the result.

Figure 19

The Palette Knife filter applied over embossing.

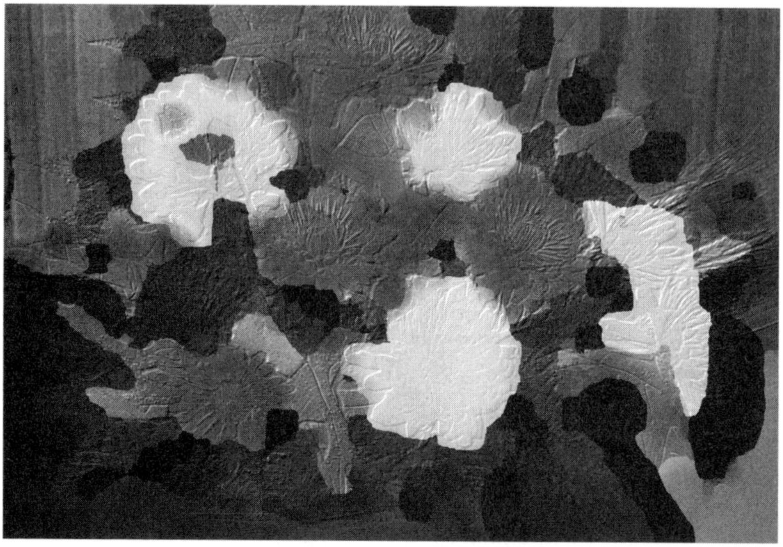

Filter type	Category	Supported Color Modes	Preview type	Data Dependent	Color Dependent
Parameter	Stylizing Filter	RGB, Grayscale	Small Filter Preview	Yes. A blank image produces a blank filtered image.	No. The Foreground/Background settings have no effect.

Plastic Wrap

4.0

Maxine Masterfield, in her book *Painting the Spirit of Nature* (Watson-Guptill, 1984), describes how she uses plastic wrap to create texture and shine in her abstract images. She often crumbles the plastic wrap into the wet paint and guides the paint into the paths that she wishes it to follow.

Unfortunately, you have no such control over the digital version. It follows the contours in your image rather than the reverse. However, it can still be used to give shine to portions of your image or to give you entire image an extremely dimensional look. The Plastic Wrap filter can also help to enhance a simple line art graphic. This filter looks good when used on text.

If you filter a solid-colored image at the highest settings, you get a star shape. Repeated filtering creates a very interesting plastic blob. If you take a portion of that blob and create a seamless pattern from it, you can get a bump map or a displacement map.

Try it:

1. Open the image "FallFlwr.Psd." Duplicate the image (Image➡Duplicate➡OK).
2. Open the Plastic Wrap dialog box shown in Figure 20 (Filter➡Artistic➡Plastic Wrap).

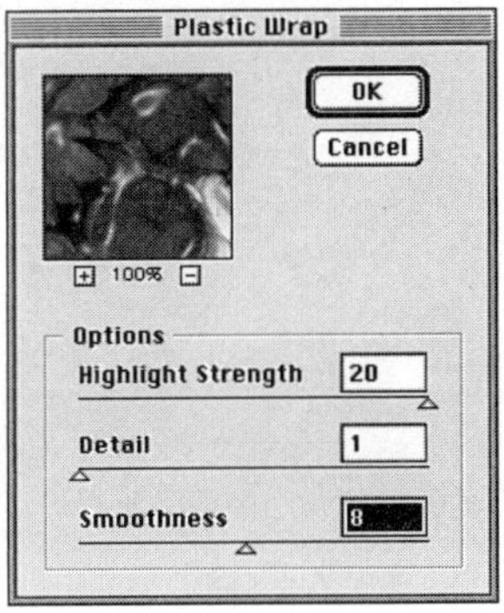

Figure 20

The Plastic Wrap dialog box.

3. Drag the Highlight Strength to 20.

   Highlight Strength, which goes from 0 to 20, must be greater than 0 in order to see some change in your image, regardless of the other settings. The highlight strength sets the amount of reflection that you get from the plastic wrap.
4. Set the Detail to 1.

   The Detail setting determines how closely the plastic wrap "clings" to the nooks and crannies in the image. A setting of 1 does not show much cling, whereas a setting of 15 (the maximum) follows every contour and causes many more (frequently too many) areas of reflectiveness.
5. Finally, set the Smoothness to 8.

The Smoothness setting seems to control the thickness of the film of plastic wrap. A setting of 1 gives only artifacting and is not useful at all. A setting of 15 buries the image in plastic.

6. Click OK. Figure 21 shows the result.

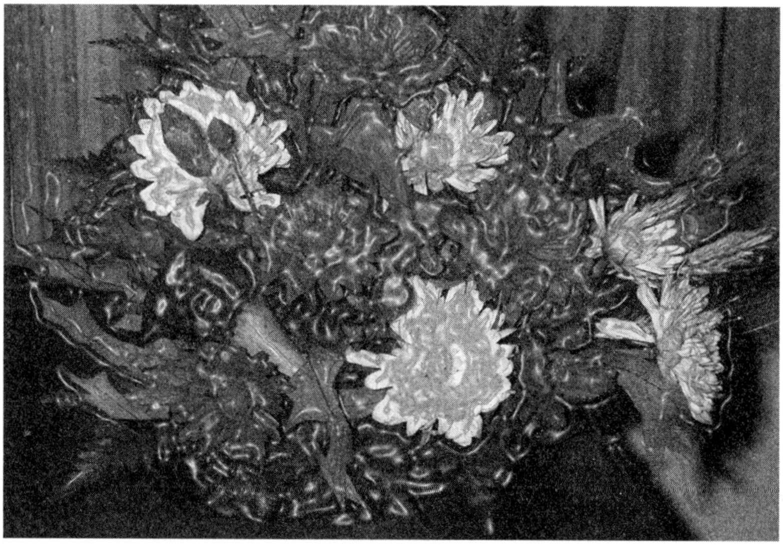

Figure 21

An example of the Plastic Wrap filter applied.

Filter type	Category	Supported Color Modes	Preview type	Data Dependent	Color Dependent
Parameter	Stylizing Filter	RGB, Grayscale	Small Filter Preview	No. A blank image produces a star shape.	No. The Foreground/Background settings have no effect.

Poster Edges

4.0

The Poster Edges filter posterizes the image in its own colors and adds black detail around the edges. All settings produce visible changes in the image. This can be good for a woodcut-type look. You can get similar results by using the High Pass filter at a setting of 1.6 and the Threshold command and placing this image over the original in Multiply mode.

Try it:

1. Open the image "FallFlwr.Psd." Duplicate the image (Image➡Duplicate➡OK).
2. Open the Poster Edges dialog box shown in Figure 22 (Filter➡Artistic➡Poster Edges).

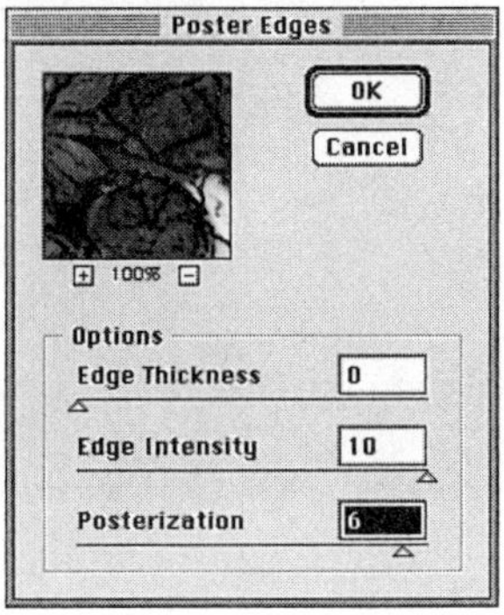

Figure 22

Poster Edges dialog box.

3. Drag the Edge Thickness to 0.

   The Edge Thickness controls how much black is placed around the edges of the image ("edges" here is used as in the Find Edges filter). The controls go from 0 to 10. A setting of 0 produces almost no edge.

4. Set the Edge Intensity to 10.

   The Edge Intensity controls the number of edges found. A setting of 0 finds only the major dark areas and shapes and intensifies the shadows around them. A setting of 10 finds many more edges—if the Edge Thickness is set low enough for the edges to be seen separately.

5. Finally, set the Posterization to 6.

   The Posterization setting works backwards. A setting of 0 produces the most posterization (as in dropping out the most colors), and a setting of 6 produces the least. Think of the Posterization setting as controlling the number of Levels in the Posterization, and it will work properly.

6. Click OK. Figure 23 shows the result.

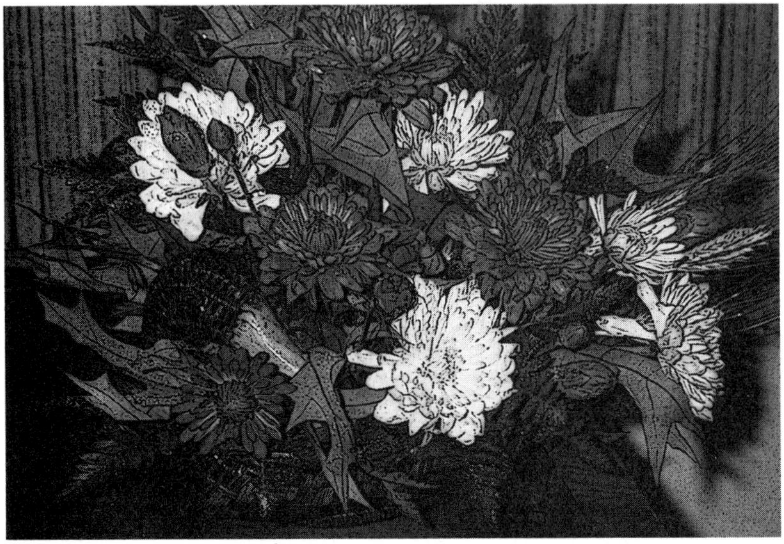

Figure 23

An example of the Poster Edges filter applied.

Filter type	Category	Supported Color Modes	Preview type	Data Dependent	Color Dependent
Parameter	Stylizing Filter	RGB, Grayscale	Small Filter Preview	Yes. A blank image produces a blank filtered image.	No. The Foreground/Background settings have no effect.

Rough Pastels

4.0

The Rough Pastels filter reacts to textures built-in to the filter, or it can use another file as a texture file. For a novel effect, apply any filter to a copy of your image. Use this filtered copy as the texture when you are asked to choose a texture for this filter. The pastels "rub-off" on the high parts of the texture (the darks). The Rough Pastels filter can help to enhance a simple line art graphic and looks good when used on text. The Rough Pastels filter is good for generating textures on a blank image filled with light to medium noise.

This is a very complex filter with a large number of parameters you can vary. The most critical parameter is the texture itself, which makes an enormous difference to the final result. The Rough Pastels filter looks much different with a brick texture than it does with a burlap texture. You can change the texture by inverting it or by changing the Scaling, the Amount of Relief, or the Light Direction.

Try it:

1. Open the image "FallFlwr.Psd." Duplicate the image (Image➡Duplicate➡OK).
2. Open the Rough Pastels dialog box shown in Figure 24 (Filter➡Artistic➡Rough Pastels).

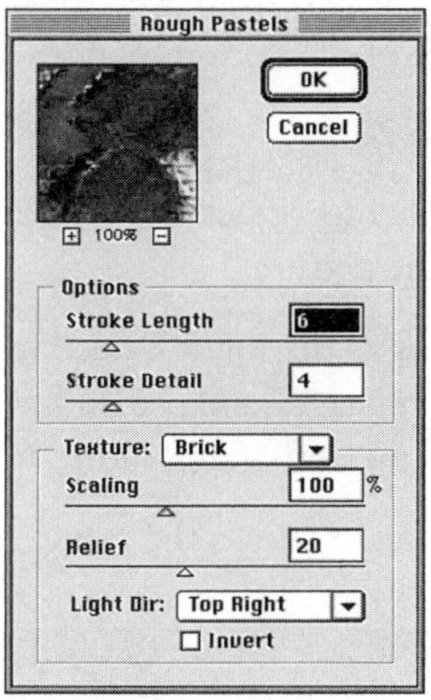

Figure 24

Rough Pastels filter dialog box.

3. Drag the Stroke Length to 24.

   The Stroke Length setting varies from 0-40. When the Stroke Length and Stroke Detail are set to their maximums (40 and 20, respectively), the image looks as if it were stroked back and forth diagonally across the canvas with multiple colors as the pastel was moved down diagonally. With the Stroke Length pulled back to 0, the long diagonal lines are broken, but the multiple colors remain.

4. Set the Stroke Detail to 15.

   The Stroke Detail can vary from 1-20 . When the Stroke Detail is reduced to 1, but the Stroke Length is left at 40, the pastels seem to be darker values of the colors in the image and move across the image horizontally in lines but on a diagonal as well. Making the Stroke Length shorter cuts the horizontal lines.

5. There are a number of settings that concern the texture to be applied. Set the Texture to Brick.

   The Textures included are Brick, Burlap, Canvas, and Sandstone, but you can load your own texture from a Photoshop file.

6. Set the Scaling to 100%.

   Textures can be scaled from 50-200%. At 100%, you are using the original size of the texture-pattern.

7. Set the Relief to 20.

   You can set Relief to values of 0-50. This sets the elevation or "3D-ness" of the texture.

8. Select Top Right as the Light Direction. You can select from any 45 degree angle. You may also invert the texture if you wish to reverse the embossing (don't for now).

9. Click OK. Figure 25 shows the result.

Figure 25

An example of the Rough Pastels filter applied.

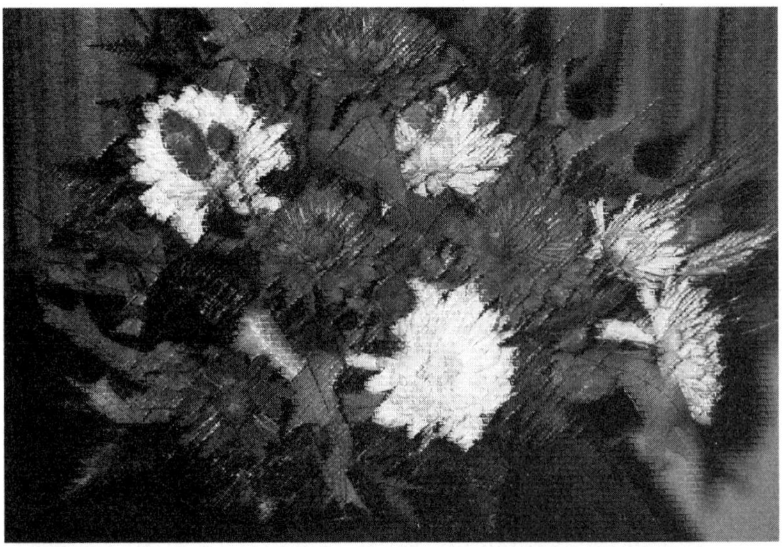

Filter type	Category	Supported Color Modes	Preview type	Data Dependent	Color Dependent
Parameter	Stylizing Filter	RGB, Grayscale	Small Filter Preview	No. A blank image still gets some texture but it can be very subtle.	No. The Foreground/Background settings have no effect.

Smudge Stick

The Smudge Stick filter looks as if you took a towel and smudged a chalk or pastel drawing. With all of the settings at their minimum values, the image looks gently smudged and muddied. The colors are muted and rubbed into one another. The Smudge Stick filter is another good texture-generating filter when used on a blank image that has had noise added.

Try it:

1. Open the image "FallFlwr.Psd." Duplicate the image (Image➡Duplicate➡OK).
2. Open the Smudge Stick dialog box shown in Figure 26 (Filter➡Artistic➡Smudge Stick).

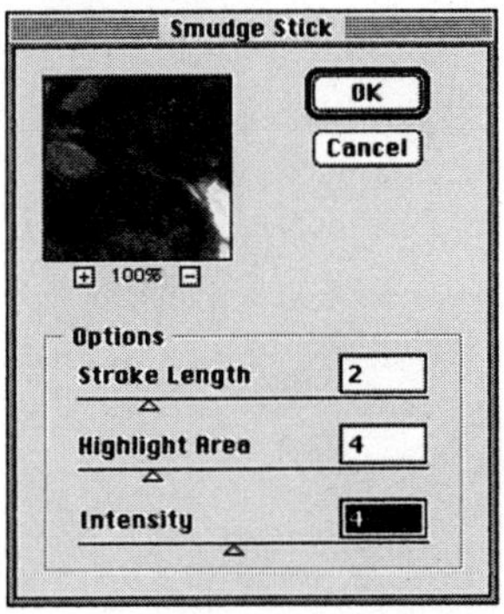

Figure 26

Smudge Stick dialog box.

3. Drag the Stroke Length to 2.

   The Stroke Length goes from 1-10 and determines how long you have "pushed the towel" before letting up on the pressure. A smaller Stroke Length seems to intensify the shadow areas of the image more.

4. Set the Highlight Area to 4.

   The Highlight Area can vary from 1-20 and is something that cannot be duplicated easily in the real world. This enables you to intensify the light areas in your image while muddying up the shadows.

5. Finally, set the Intensity to 4.

   The Intensity varies from 1-10, determining the degree to which the Highlight area is visible. A very high setting brightens the brights in the image, especially if a large Highlight Area setting is also selected. If a large Highlight Area is selected but the Intensity setting is low, you will not see it.

6. Click OK. Figure 27 shows the result.

Figure 27

An example of the Smudge Stick filter applied.

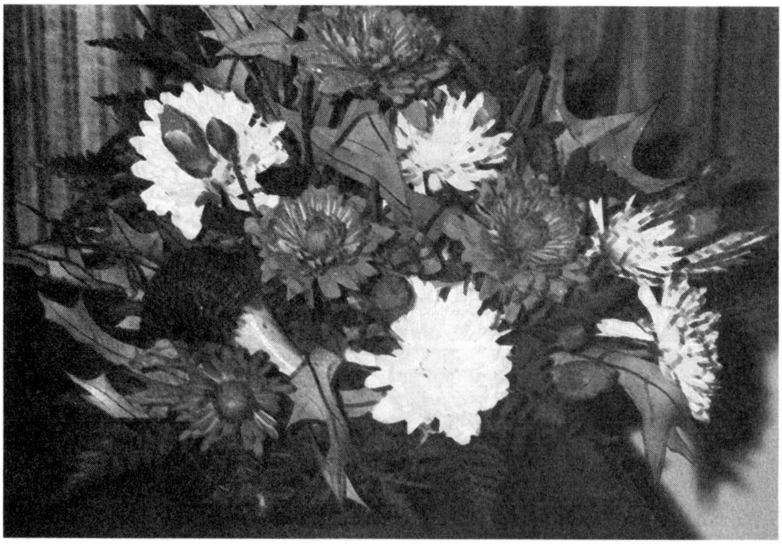

Filter type	Category	Supported Color Modes	Preview type	Data Dependent	Color Dependent
Parameter	Stylizing Filter	RGB, Grayscale	Small Filter Preview	Yes. A blank image produces a blank filtered image.	No. The Foreground/Background settings have no effect.

Sponge

The Sponge filter looks like someone is dabbing paint on the image. The amount of paint and the size of the sponge are controllable. This is one of the more successful stylizing filters.

The settings that use a small brush and a low Smoothness are very attractive—both with or without a high Definition. Larger brush sizes with high Smoothness settings look like the Median filter.

This makes a wonderful grained paper effect when applied repeatedly to a solid color image. Use the Sponge filter as is or make either a repeat texture or a texture in a channel to use as "paper," the way you would in Painter.

Try it:

1. Open the image "FallFlwr.Psd." Duplicate the image (Image➡Duplicate➡OK).
2. Open the Sponge dialog box shown in Figure 28 (Filter➡Artistic➡Sponge).
3. Drag the Brush Size to 0.

   The Brush Size setting varies from 1-10. The Brush Size controls the size of the sponge.
4. Set the Definition to 25.

   The Definition can vary from 1-25. The Definition controls the value difference of the sponge with the image behind it. A high definition causes the colors sponged on the image to take on a much darker value than the original.
5. Finally, set the Smoothness to 1.

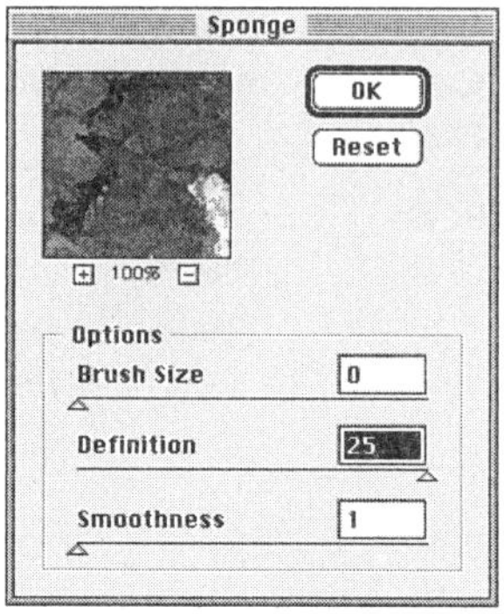

Figure 28

The Sponge dialog box.

The Smoothness varies from 1-15. The Smoothness setting determines the amount of aliasing at the edges of the sponge. A small setting causes a lot of aliasing; a large setting is anti-aliased.

6. Click OK. Figure 29 shows the result.

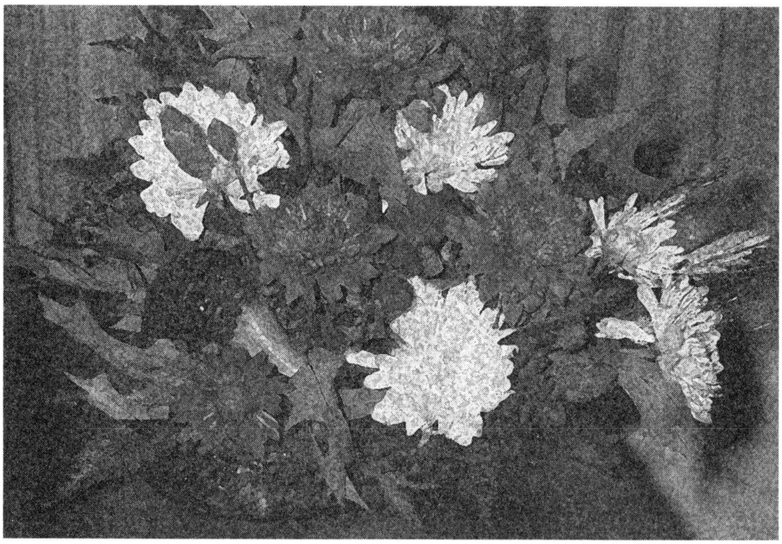

Figure 29

The Sponge filter applied to an image.

Filter type	Category	Supported Color Modes	Preview type	Data Dependent	Color Dependent
Parameter	Stylizing Filter	RGB, Grayscale	Small Filter Preview	No. A blank image can be textured.	No. The Foreground/Background settings have no effect.

Underpainting

It is almost uncanny how good the Underpainting filter is. Using the Canvas texture and a small brush with the highest Texture Coverage setting, you get an image so real that you'd think the paint was still wet. The image looks just the way it would if you had sketched in the details with thin oils on a canvas. It can also help to enhance a simple line art graphic.

You can use this exactly as you would traditional underpainting and add back in the detail from the original image. Here's how:

Try it:

1. Open the image "FallFlwr.Psd." Duplicate the image (Image➡Duplicate➡OK).
2. Open the Underpainting dialog box shown in Figure 30 (Filter➡Artistic➡Underpainting).

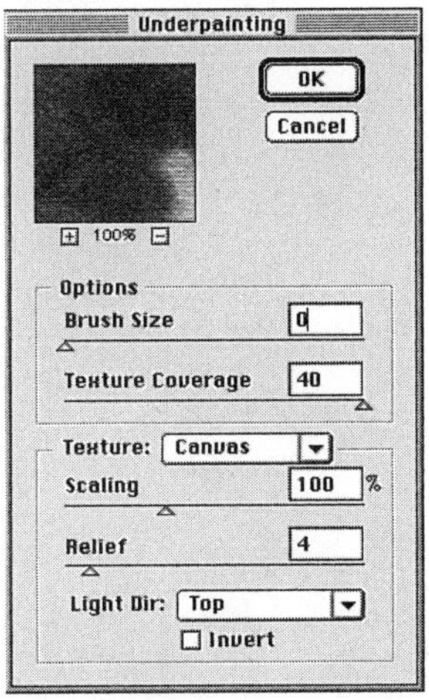

Figure 30

The Underpainting dialog box.

3. Drag the Brush Size to 0.

   The Brush Size setting varies from 0-40. If a large brush Size is used, the area covered by the brush does not show texture, so the coverage is very spotty.

4. Set the Texture Coverage to 40.

   The Texture Coverage can vary from 0-40. If both the Texture Coverage and the Brush Size settings are low, the texture appears chopped up.

5. A number of Texture settings exist. Set the Texture to Canvas.

   Textures included are Brick, Burlap, Canvas, and Sandstone, but you can load your own texture from a Photoshop file.

6. Set the Scaling to 100%.

   Textures can be scaled from 50-200%. At 100%, you are using the original size of the texture-pattern.

7. Set the Relief to 4.

   You can set Relief to values of 0-50.

8. Select Bottom as the Light Direction. You can select from any 45-degree angle. You may also invert the texture if you wish to reverse the embossing (don't for now). Click OK. Figure 31 shows the result.

Figure 31

The Underpainting filter applied to an image.

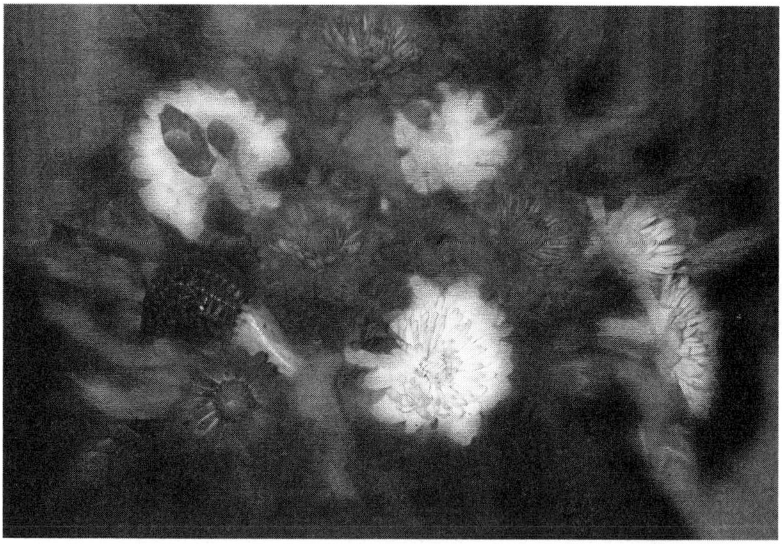

9. Press the Shift key (to make the images align) and with the Move tool, drag the original image on top of the filtered image as a new Layer.

10. Create a Layer Mask (Layer menu➥Add Layer Mask➥Hide All). This covers the entire original image so that none of it is visible.

11. Using white paint and a soft brush at low opacity, brush back in some of the original detail as desired. Figure 32 shows the result.

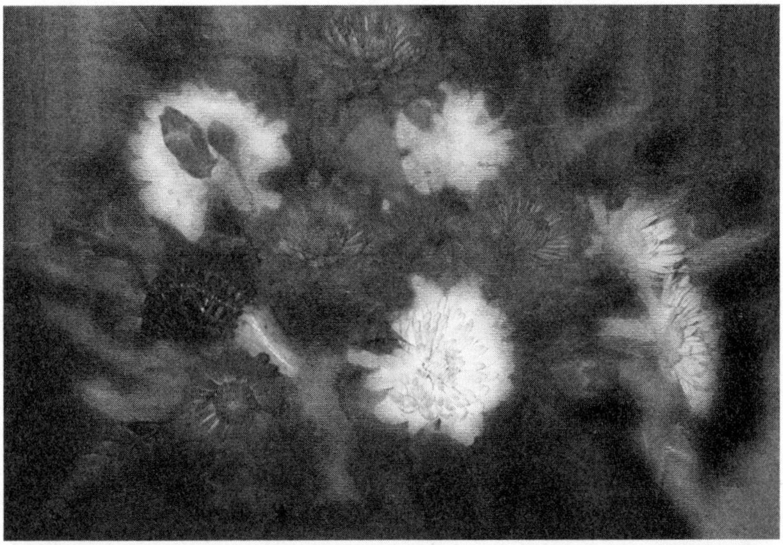

Figure 32

Here detail is added back to underpainting with the Underpainting filter.

Filter type	Category	Supported Color Modes	Preview type	Data Dependent	Color Dependent
Parameter	Stylizing Filter	RGB, Grayscale	Small Filter Preview	Yes. A blank image produces a blank filtered image.	No. The Foreground/Background settings have no effect.

Watercolor

The Watercolor filter is supposed to make an image look as if it was painted with watercolors. It doesn't. The Watercolor filter's results are very similar to the Fresco filter, but the Fresco filter adds more outlining around the edges of the shapes it identifies. The Watercolor filter does the "right" things in terms of finding shapes and simplifying colors. It produces a very good range of values and shapes in the process of simplifying the colors from "photographic" to "painted." The hallmark of a watercolor, however, is usually its light, airy feel, and this filter is very heavy. The Watercolor filter intensifies the dark areas in the image far too much, and the final colors are extremely strong. This filter is popular, however, as it provides the easiest way to "sort-of" get something to look like a watercolor in Photoshop—but if you paint with the Wet Edges option on in the Brush palette, you will get an image that is much closer to a watercolor.

An interesting variation on the Watercolor filter is to filter the image with a setting of 1 for the texture and then filter another copy of the original at a setting of 3. With the Move tool, drag one copy on top of the other and set the Blending mode to Difference. Duplicate the image (Image➡Duplicate) as Merged. At this point, you can:

- Select Image➡Adjust➡Auto Levels to apply the Auto Levels command.
- Invert the image and select New Adjustment Layer...from the Layers palette. Set the Type to Levels and the mode to Multiply. Click OK.
- Drag a Watercolor-filtered copy onto this image in Screen mode.
- Experiment with other Blending modes in a Levels Adjustment Layer.

Look at the file "WaterFX.Psd" on the CD-ROM to see how this is done. Figure 33 shows the effect in grayscale—much lighter and softer than the usual method.

Figure 33

The "Soft" Watercolor Effect is one of the variations you can create with the Watercolor filter.

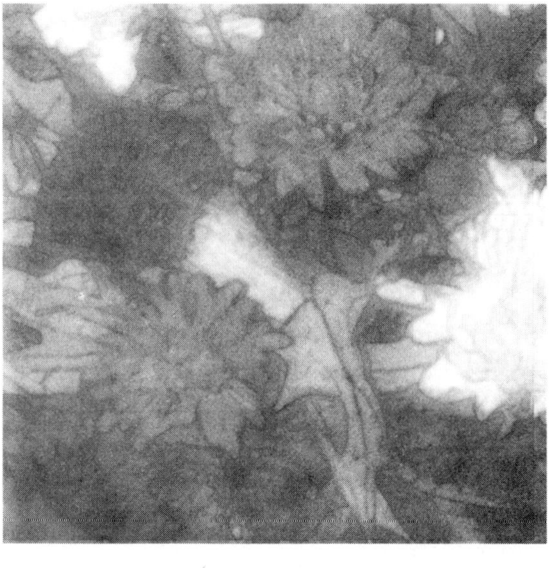

Try it the "normal" way:

1. Open the image "FallFlwr.Psd." Duplicate the image (Image➡Duplicate➡OK).
2. Open the Watercolor dialog box shown in Figure 34 (Filter➡Artistic➡Watercolor).

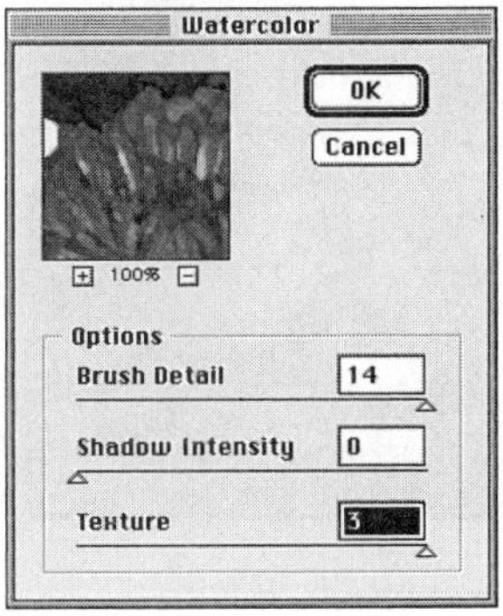

Figure 34

The Watercolor filter dialog box.

3. Drag the Brush Detail to

   The Brush Detail setting varies from 1-14, determining whether the filter tries to duplicate the original image or just picks up the general color and feel of the photograph. A setting of 14 keeps the detail, but even a setting of 1 produces a recognizable image if your original is large enough. This lightest setting produces an almost lacy effect as the "paint" is spattered about.

4. Set the Shadow Intensity to 10.

   The Shadow Intensity can vary from 1-10 but should be left to 1 unless you really like black watercolors. The image is too dark on the lowest setting and almost completely black at the higher settings.

5. Finally, set the Texture to 3.

   The Texture varies from 1-3. The Texture setting is very subtle. There is not a huge difference between using a setting of 1 or 3, but there is some. Actually many of the pixels change between the two settings, but unless you compare two versions using Difference, the changes may be hard to see.

6. Click OK. Figure 35 shows the result.

Figure 35

The Watercolor filter applied.

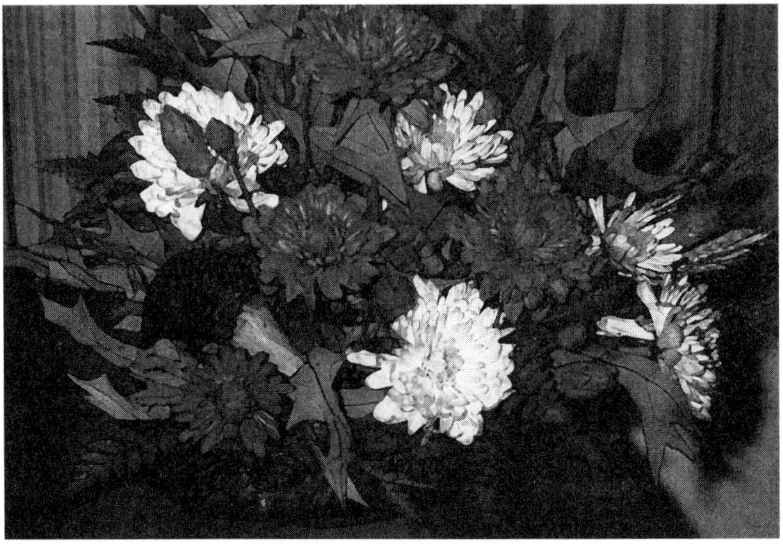

Filter type	Category	Supported Color Modes	Preview type	Data Dependent	Color Dependent
Parameter	Stylizing Filter	RGB, Grayscale	Small Filter Preview	Yes. A blank image produces a blank filtered image.	No. The Foreground/Background settings have no effect.

PHOTOSHOP'S NATIVE FILTERS—BLUR

The Blur filters are used to reduce the difference in color between nearby pixels. Depending upon the specific filter, you can select a pixel radius to blur. The Blur filters can all be used for production or for special effects, though some, such as the Radial Blur, tend to be more useful for special effects work.

Blur

The Blur filter applies a very tiny—almost unnoticeable—blur to an image or selection. It is not useful for major corrections, though it can be applied multiple times.

The Blur filter is used to "take the edge off" an image that is too sharp or to very gently soften it. Use the Gaussian Blur filter instead for more control.

Try it:

1. Open the image "Amanda.Psd." Duplicate the image (Image➡Duplicate➡OK).
2. Select the Blur filter (Filter➡Blur➡Blur). There is no image because the difference is not visible in the printed image.

Filter type	Category	Supported Color Modes	Preview type	Data Dependent	Color Dependent
One-Step	Production/ Focus	RGB, Grayscale CMYK, Lab	None	Yes. A blank image produces a blank filtered image.	No. The Foreground/Background settings have no effect.

Blur More

The Blur More filter applies a little more blurring than the Blur filter. Use this filter to give an image a tiny blur. Use the Gaussian Blur filter for more control.

Try it:

1. Open the image "Amanda.Psd." Duplicate the image (Image➡Duplicate➡OK).
2. Select the Blur More filter (Filter➡Blur➡Blur More). Once again, the results are not visible in print.

Filter type	Category	Supported Color Modes	Preview type	Data Dependent	Color Dependent
One-Step	Production/ Focus	RGB, Grayscale CMYK, Lab	None	Yes. A blank image produces a blank filtered image.	No. The Foreground/Background settings have no effect.

Gaussian Blur

The Gaussian Blur filter is one of the most useful and basic filters. It is the one critical filter used when making a drop shadow and is also useful when you need to anti-alias edges where they meet. The Gaussian Blur filter is used to soften the differences between nearby pixels and to help remove grain. It is also used to blur shadow areas for creating drop shadows.

You can use the Gaussian Blur filter after applying the Add Noise filter to soften an image's noise. You can also use it under a copy of an original image to get the effect of painting on ivory.

Let's create an "ivory painting" effect and then place text with a drop shadow on top of it.:

1. Open the image "Amanda.Psd." Duplicate the image (Image➡Duplicate➡OK).
2. Drag the icon for the Background layer to the New Layer icon (the center icon at the bottom of the Layers palette) to duplicate the Layer.
3. Change the Blending mode of the top Layer to Darken.
4. Make the Background Layer active by clicking it in the Layers palette.
5. Open the Gaussian Blur dialog box shown in Figure 36 (Filter➡Blur➡Gaussian Blur).

Figure 36

The Gaussian Blur filter dialog box.

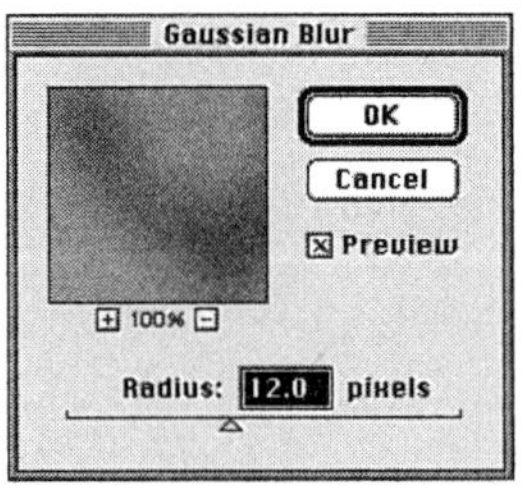

6. Drag the Radius to 12.

   The Radius setting, where you can specify the pixel-radius, varies from 0.1-250. This is the only control. A larger image needs more blurring to achieve the same results as a smaller image, so this filter is resolution dependent. The detail in the image will fade out a bit and the image will begin to glow. It will look as if it were drawn on ivory. Click OK.

7. Make a new layer (click the New Layer icon at the bottom of the Layers Palette).
8. Load Channel #4 (Option-Command-4)[Alt-Control-4].
9. Pick a color from the icing as your Foreground color and fill the selected area (Option-Delete)[Alt-Delete].
10. Drag the icon for the text layer to the New Layer icon (the center icon at the bottom of the Layers palette). Name this new Layer "Shadow" and drag it below the text in the Layers palette.
11. Click the Preserve Transparency button to turn it on.
12. Press D to set the colors back to the default of black and white.
13. Fill the area (Option-Delete)[Alt-Delete].

    Remove the Preserve Transparency button by clicking it.

15. Apply the Gaussian Blur filter to the Shadow channel with the same setting of 12 pixels.
16. Press the Modifier key (Command)[Control] and offset the shadow by moving it up and to the right.
17. Change the Layer opacity to 50%. Figure 37 shows the result.

Filter type	Category	Supported Color Modes	Preview type	Data Dependent	Color Dependent
Parameter	Production/ Focus/ Special Effects	RGB, Grayscale CMYK, Lab	Full Image	Yes. A blank image produces a blank filtered image.	No. The Foreground/Background settings have no effect.

Figure 37

Here the Gaussian Blur filter helps create a drop shadow.

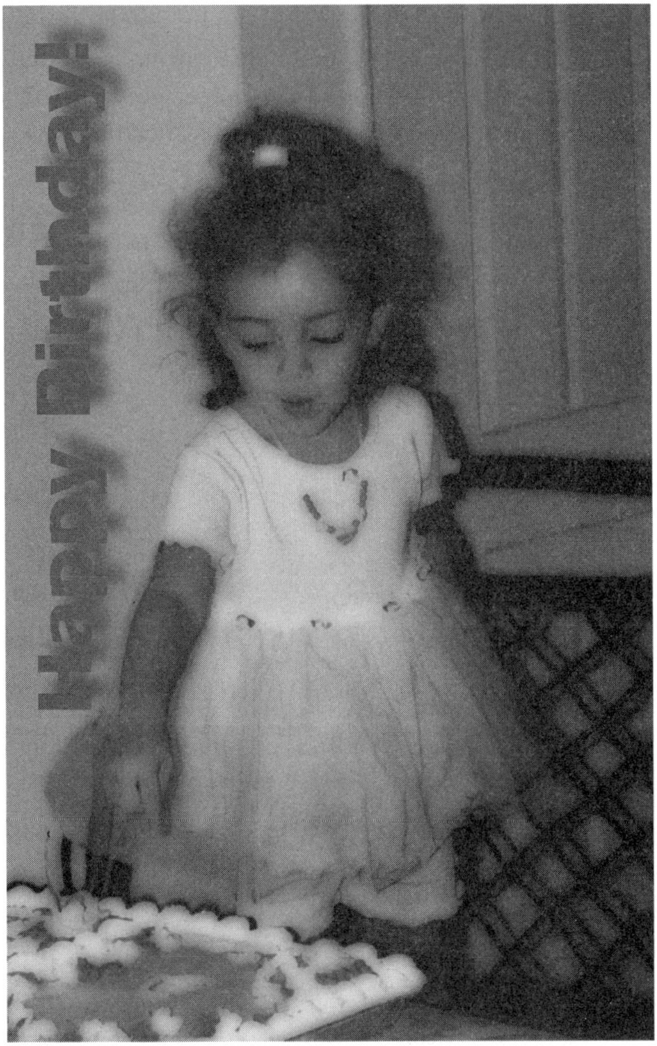

Motion Blur

The Motion Blur filter blurs your image so that it looks like either the camera or the subject moved as the picture was taken. It's interesting that we try to re-create digitally an image that we'd toss away if it came out of a camera!

The filter is used to add motion to an image. If you only want to add motion to part of the image or a portion of the main subject, control the Motion Blur filter using Layers.

Try it:

1. Open the image "Amanda.Psd." Duplicate the image (Image➡Duplicate➡OK).
2. Drag the icon for the Background layer to the New Layer icon (the center icon at the bottom of the Layers palette) to duplicate the Layer.
3. Open the Motion Blur dialog box shown in Figure 38 (Filter➡Blur➡Motion Blur).

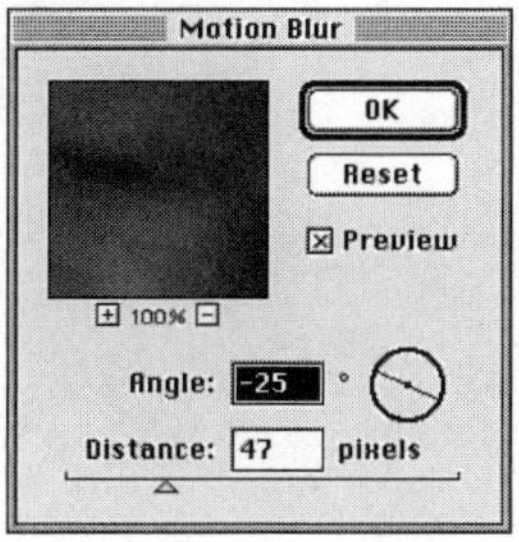

Figure 38

The Motion Blur dialog box.

4. Drag the Angle to -25.

   The Angle setting varies from 0-360 degrees (or in negative degrees if you drag backwards). The Angle setting is a dial you can set visually or numerically, determining the direction of the blur.

5. Set the Distance to 47.

   The Distance control, varying from 1-999, sets the distance for the blur and determines the length of the motion "trail" that is left.

6. Click OK. Figure 39 shows the result.

Figure 39

The Motion Blur filter applied.

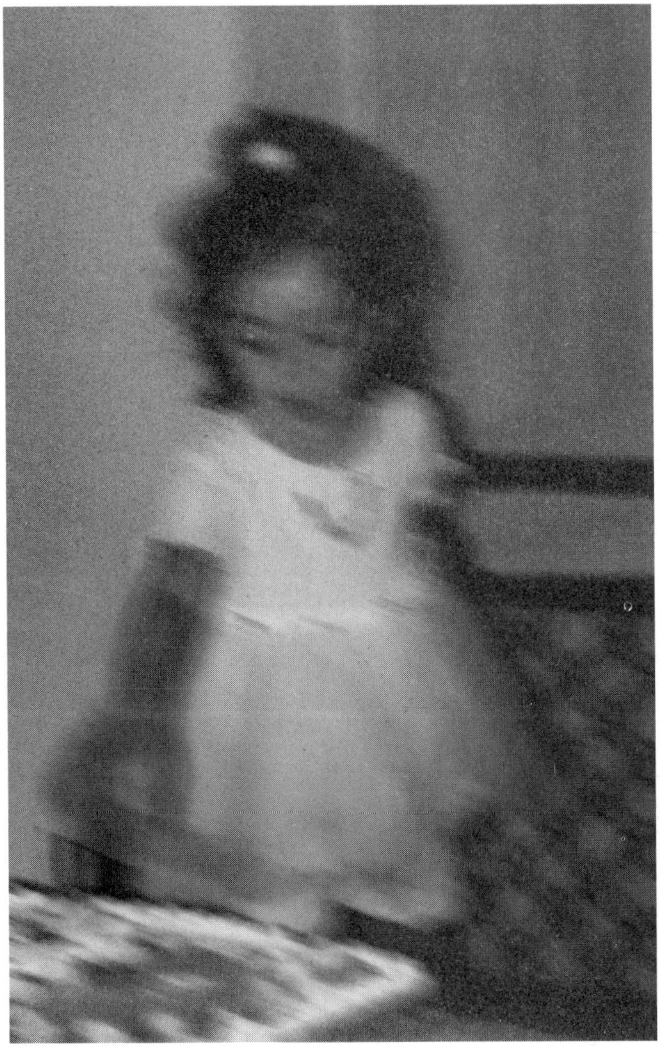

7. Add a Layer Mask (Layer➡Add Layer Mask➡Hide All). The "Hide All" setting makes the Layer mask remove the entire top Layer from view.
8. Using a soft brush and white "paint," paint back in the areas on the top Layer you wish to be blurred. Figure 40 shows the result.

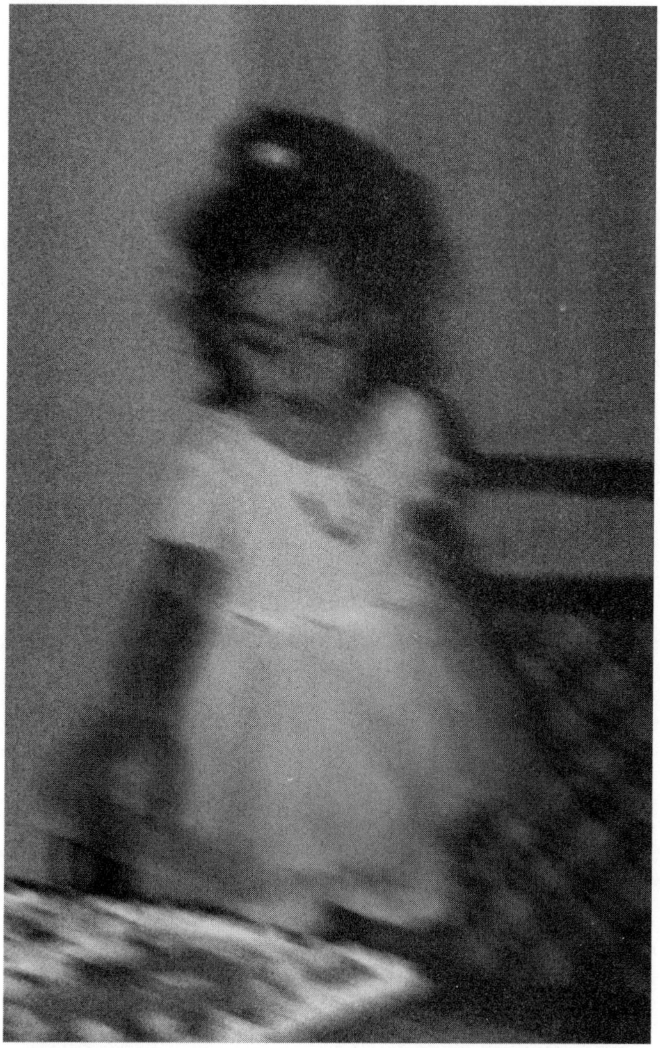

Figure 40

Here the Motion Blur filter is controlled.

This technique gives you the maximum amount of control, as you are not destroying any data and can change your mind as many times as you need to. If you do not like your results, paint over them with black to remove the editing.

The Motion Blur filter is also very good for creating textures. Here is one of my favorite texture "recipes."

1. Create a new image 400×400 pixels. Choose either White or Background Color as the Content because Transparent does not work with this "recipe."
2. Apply the Add Noise filter with Gaussian Noise of 200, not monochromatic.
3. Apply the Motion Blur filter with a Distance of 800 (twice the image width) and whatever angle you want (so long as it is not horizontal or vertical).
4. Drag the icon for the Background layer to the New Layer icon (the center icon at the bottom of the Layers palette) to duplicate it.
5. Change the Blending mode for the top Layer to Color Burn or Exclusion. Multiply, Screen, Overlay, Hard Light, or Soft Light also give you good results.

This technique makes a cross-hatching that is good for backgrounds. With some effort, it can also be changed into a seamless repeat.

Filter type	Category	Supported Color Modes	Preview type	Data Dependent	Color Dependent
Parameter	Focus/ Special Effects	RGB, Grayscale CMYK, Lab	Full Image	Yes. A blank image produces a blank filtered image.	No. The Foreground/Background settings have no effect.

Radial Blur

The Radial Blur filter causes the image to blur either by spinning it or by taking it up to warp speed as if you were making a space jump. This is clearly a Special Effects filter.

Simulating the effect of a space warp is probably the most consistent use *I* can find for this filter. You, however, can use it anywhere you want spinning or zooming blurs.

Try using the Radial Blur on the texture you created with the Motion Blur filter. If you select a Spin Blur with a fairly high Amount and place the center of the spin (by click-dragging in the Blur box) at the lower right of the image, you get a very subtle effect that also makes a good background. You may want to apply a Gaussian Blur to it to smooth it out a bit first.

Try it:

1. Open the image "Amanda.Psd." Duplicate the image (Image➡Duplicate➡OK).
2. Open the Radial Blur dialog box shown in Figure 41 (Filter➡Blur➡Radial Blur).

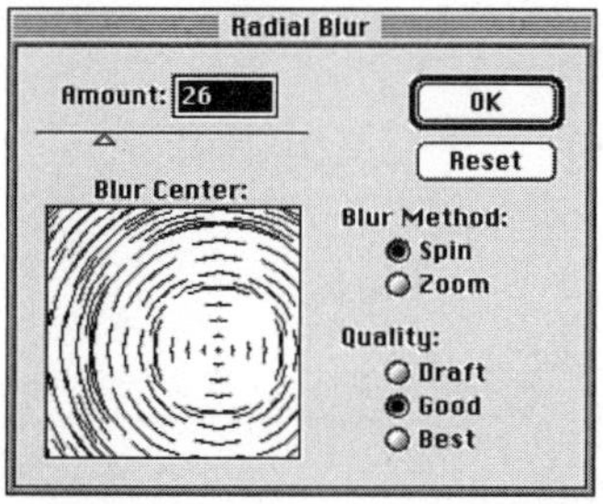

Figure 41

The Radial Blur dialog box.

3. Drag the Amount to 26.

   The Amount setting varies from 1-100. This parameter controls the intensity of the effect and specifies how much blurring occurs. The preview shows a motion trail of the settings that you select, but does not show any of your image (you have to guess what it will look like!).

4. Click the Spin button for Blur Method.

   The other option is Zoom.

5. Next, set the Blur Quality to Good. Draft or Good are usually sufficient; Best is exceptionally slow to compute.
6. Finally, drag the Blur center to the position shown in the dialog box (see Figure 41).
7. Click OK. Figure 42 shows the result.

Figure 42

An example of applying the Radial Blur filter.

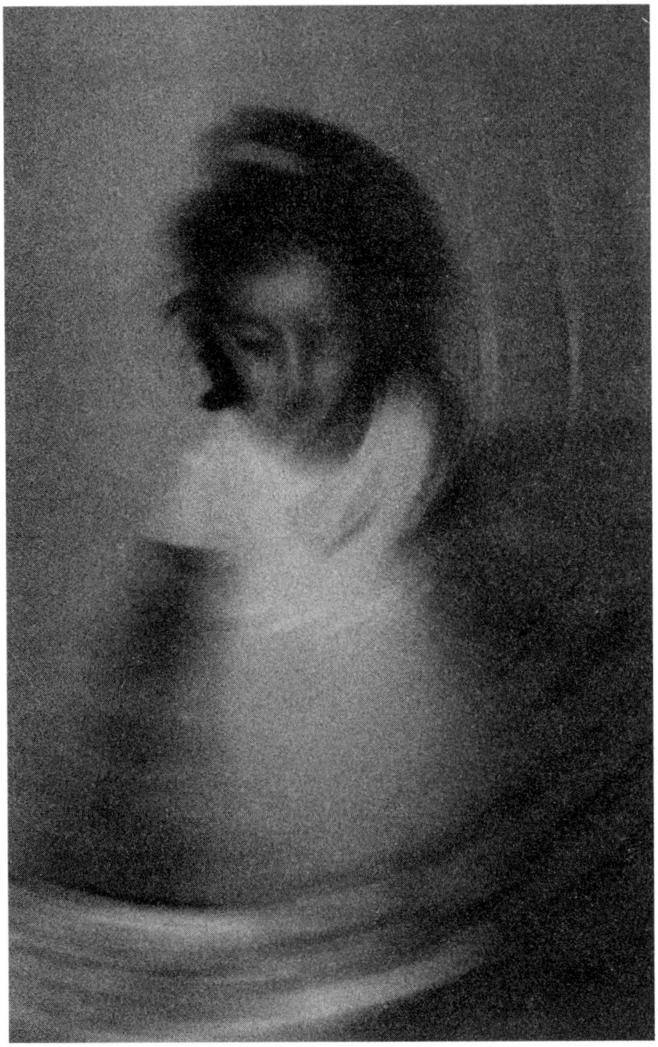

Filter type	Category	Supported Color Modes	Preview type	Data Dependent	Color Dependent
Parameter	Focus/ Special Effects	RGB, Grayscale CMYK, Lab	Wire Frame	Yes. A blank image produces a blank filtered image.	No. The Foreground/Background settings have no effect.

Smart Blur

The Smart Blur filter finds the edges in an image and blurs only within the area bordered by an "edge." The parameter settings determine where Photoshop "sees" the edge.

This is an excellent production filter to help you get rid of grain in fleshtones. Because the filter effects are localized, you don't get the muddying effects that you would from the Gaussian Blur filter. Keep the Threshold low and the Radius fairly low as well (though it can exceed the Threshold amount).

Mode options are Normal, Edge Only, and Overlay Edge. The Edge Only and Overlay Edge effects with high Thresholds will find only the major shapes in the image. This can be very helpful for turning your image into outlines or making masks. You can also get good Pencil sketches from this effect. In the Edge Only mode, The Smart Blur filter operates like an intelligent Find Edges filter.

Try it:

1. Open the image "Amanda.Psd." Duplicate the image (Image➥Duplicate➥OK).
2. Open the Smart Blur dialog box shown in Figure 43 (Filter➥Blur➥Smart Blur).

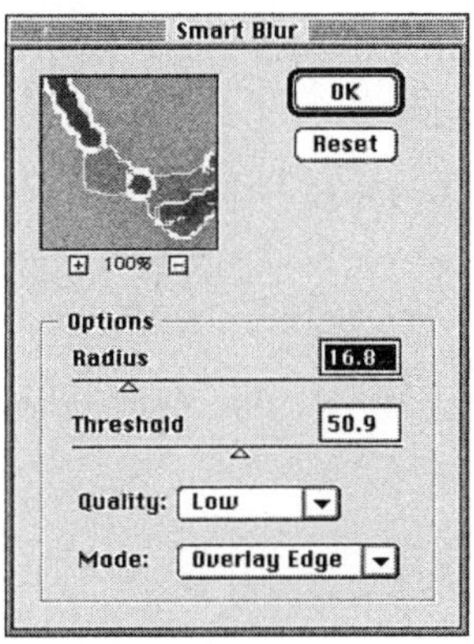

Figure 43

The Smart Blur dialog box.

3. Drag the Radius to 16.8.

The Radius setting varies from 0.1-100, determining how far from a given pixel the filter will blur the image. This setting works like the Radius in Pixels in the Gaussian Blur filter. However, the "edges" of the image become sharper and more pixelated as the radius amount increases.

4. Set the Threshold to 50.9.

   The Threshold can vary from .1-100. The Threshold setting seems to work the way the same setting does in Unsharp Mask—to determine how much the filter will affect the image—but it is actually the opposite. A low Threshold setting "sees" many edges, so the overall effect will be slight. A larger Threshold setting sees many fewer edges, so there will be a larger number of pixels in the area to be blurred.

5. Set the Quality setting to Low.

   The Quality setting determines the amount of processing needed to calculate the effect. Low or Medium are fine; High takes much longer—though not as long as the Best setting in the Motion Blur filter.

6. Select Overlay Edge as the Mode. The Mode is a very interesting setting as it totally changes the way in which the filter works and the results that the filter produces.

   - Normal blurs the areas between the edges, but does not show the edges.
   - Edge Only shows only the edges found by the filter (in white) on a black background. If you invert the image, you can almost see a Pencil sketch.
   - Overlay Edge shows the white edges on top of the blurred image.

7. Click OK. Figure 44 shows the result.

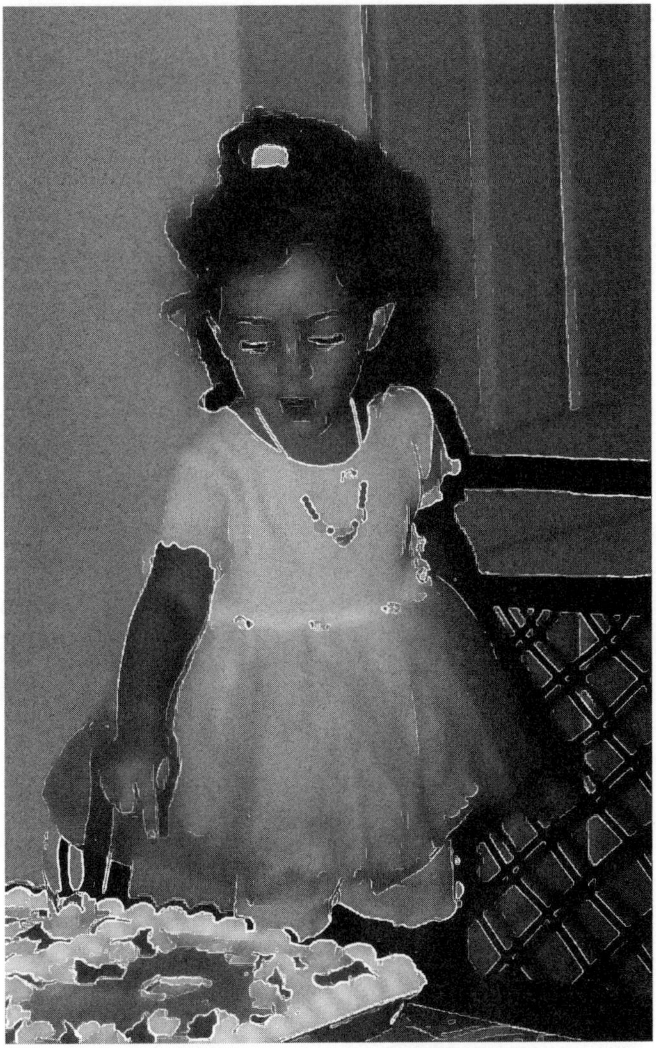

Figure 44

An example of the Smart Blur filter applied.

Filter type	Category	Supported Color Modes	Preview type	Data Dependent	Color Dependent
Parameter	Focus/ Special Effects/ Production	RGB only	Small Image Preview	Yes. A blank image produces a blank filtered image.	No. The Foreground/Background settings have no effect.

PHOTOSHOP'S NATIVE FILTERS—BRUSH STROKES

The Brush Strokes filters, new to Photoshop 4.0, are part of the Gallery Effects filter sets. None of them work in CMYK or Lab mode, and they all have small previews embedded in the filter dialog box. This class of filter is best used to stylize an image or to create texture. All of these filters work wonderfully on a blank image that has had the Add Noise filter run on it. Try this as the start of many exciting textures.

Accented Edges

4.0

The Accented Edges filter is another Edge filter that is similar to the Find Edges filter. But it can be used to give more texture to an image—hence it is in this Brush Strokes category. The Accented Edges filter looks best when the Edge Width is kept small—large edges destroy the image. With a tiny Edge Width and minimum Brightness and Smoothness, the image is dark but very textured, acquiring an almost woodcut look. At a small Edge Width, but maximum Brightness and Smoothness, you almost feel as if you are looking at liquid, colored chrome.

Try it:

1. Open the image "Deer.Psd." Duplicate the image (Image➡Duplicate➡OK).
2. Open the Accented Edges dialog box shown in Figure 45 (Filter➡Brush Strokes➡Accented Edges).

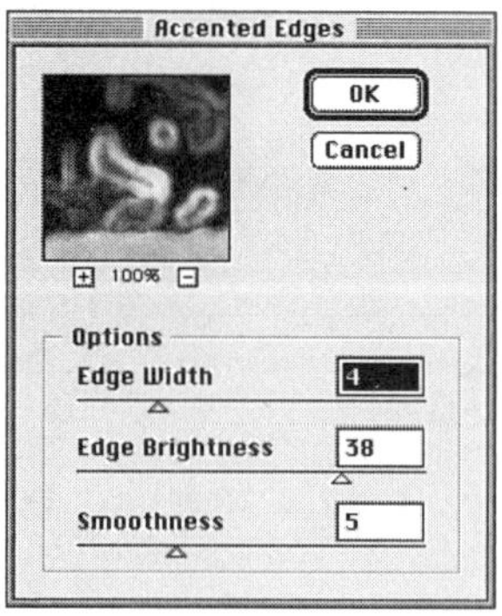

Figure 45

Accented Edges dialog box.

3. Drag the Edge Width to 4.

The Edge Width setting varies from 1-14, controlling the thickness of the edges that are found.

4. Set the Edge Brightness to 38.

   The Edge Brightness can vary from 0-50. This controls the intensity or glow of the edges. At 50, the edges are highly saturated.

5. Finally, set the Smoothness to 5.

   The Smoothness varies from 1-15, controlling the number of edges found and their Path. At 1, the filter will find many tiny edges. At 15, it finds fewer edges but they look longer and smoother.

6. Click OK. Figure 46 shows the result.

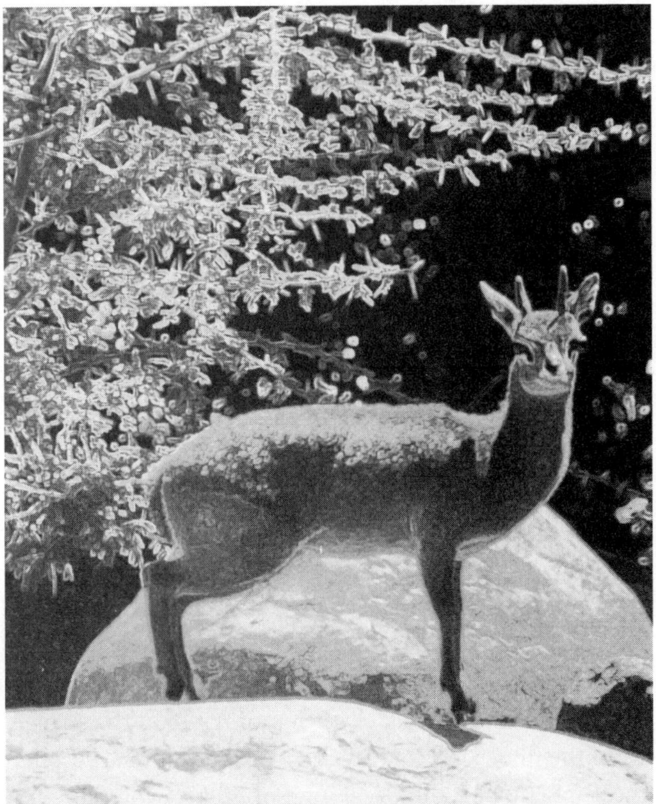

Figure 46

An example of the Accented Edges filter applied.

Filter type	Category	Supported Color Modes	Preview type	Data Dependent	Color Dependent
Parameter	Stylizing Filter	RGB, Grayscale	Small Filter Preview	Yes. A blank image produces a blank filtered image.	No. The Foreground/Background settings have no effect.

Angled Strokes

4.0

The Angled Strokes filter makes an image look as if diagonal brush strokes of oil paints have been applied to a canvas. The effect is really quite nice with a long, sharp stroke, though all settings in this filter produce results. This filter does a very good job of identifying main image areas.

Try it:

1. Open the image "Deer.Psd." Duplicate the image (Image➡Duplicate➡OK).
2. Open the Angled Strokes dialog box shown in Figure 47 (Filter➡Brush Strokes➡Angled Strokes).

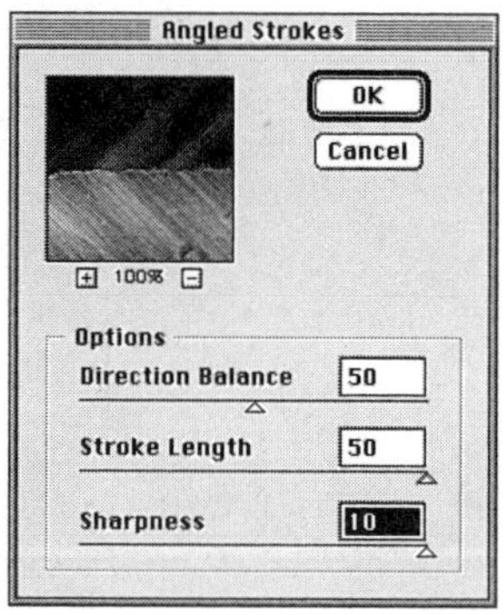

Figure 47

The Angled Strokes dialog box.

3. Drag the Direction Balance to 50.

   The Direction Balance setting varies from 0-100, controlling the direction of the strokes. A setting of 0 makes the strokes appear from the upper left to lower right. A setting of 100 puts them in the opposite direction. A setting of 50 gets you half-and-half.

4. Set the Stroke Length to 50.

   The Stroke Length can vary from 3-50. A stroke of 3 has a minimal result other than to make a gentle texture.

5. Finally, set the Sharpness to 10.

   The Sharpness varies from 0-10. A sharpness of 10 enables the "paint" to look as if you can see where each bristle on the brush went over the canvas. A setting of 0 blurs the stroke.

6. Click OK. Figure 48 shows the result.

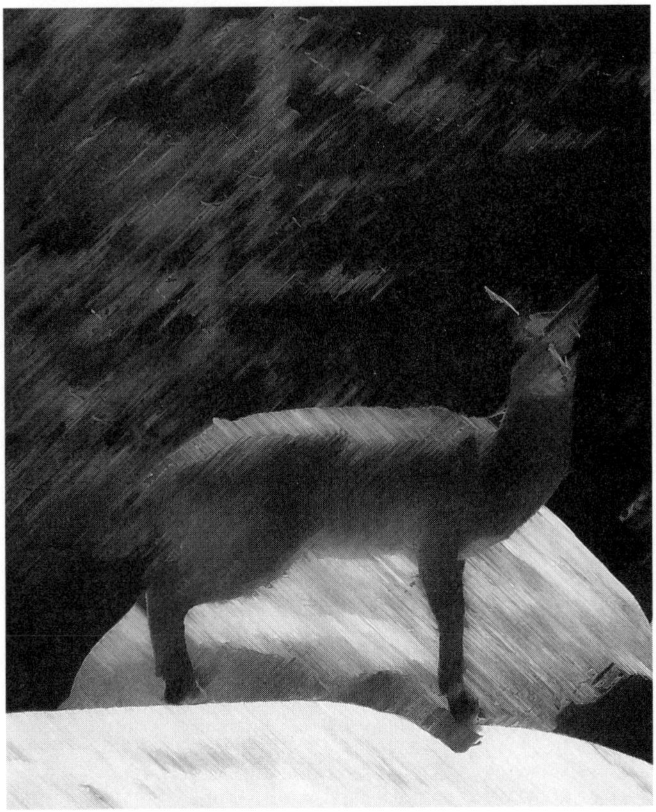

Figure 48

The Angled Strokes filter applied.

Filter type	Category	Supported Color Modes	Preview type	Data Dependent	Color Dependent
Parameter	Stylizing Filter	RGB, Grayscale	Small Filter Preview	Yes. A blank image produces a blank filtered image.	No. The Foreground/Background settings have no effect.

Crosshatch

4.0

The Crosshatch filter is one of my favorites. It can be attractive at most settings (especially the intermediate ones) and creates lovely textures. The Crosshatch filter can make an image look as if a brush were stroked at cross angles on a canvas. It can also give the impression of a random weave.

Try it:

1. Open the image “Deer.Psd.” Duplicate the image (Image➡Duplicate➡OK).
2. Open the Crosshatch dialog box shown in Figure 49 (Filter➡Brush Strokes➡Crosshatch).

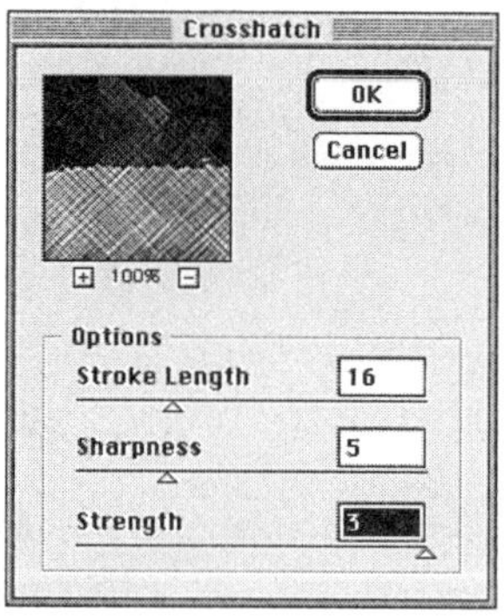

Figure 49

The Crosshatch dialog box.

3. Drag the Stroke Length to 16,

   The Stroke Length setting varies from 3-50, controlling the distance that the stroke travels. The stroke length should be above 6 for the characteristic “crosshatch” to appear. A setting of 3 with maximum sharpness and strength produces a wonderful “bramble and tangles” texture.

4. Set the Sharpness to 5.

   The Sharpness, varying from 0-20, controls the visibility of each stroke—how well you see it against all of the other strokes. At highest settings, this setting "fights" with the Strength control and adds spurious colors. It is best used high when Strength is low.

5. Finally, set the Strength to 3.

   The Strength varies from 1 to 3. This parameter controls the embossing that occurs on each stroke.

6. Click OK. Figure 50 shows the result.

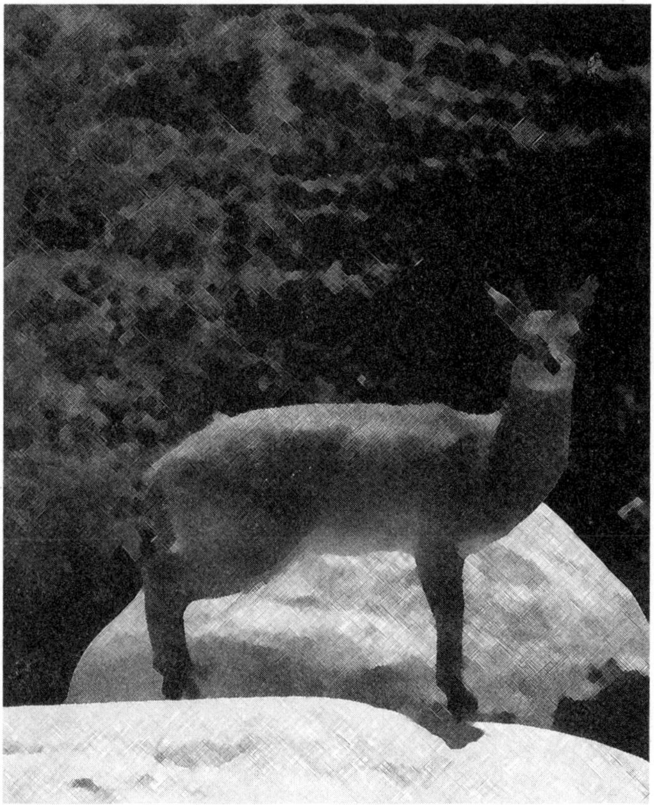

Figure 50

The Crosshatch filter applied.

Filter type	Category	Supported Color Modes	Preview type	Data Dependent	Color Dependent
Parameter	Stylizing/ Texture Filter	RGB, Grayscale	Small Filter Preview	Yes. A blank image produces a blank filtered image.	No. The Foreground/Background settings have no effect.

Dark Strokes

4.0

The Dark Strokes filter is similar to the Angled Strokes, but you cannot see the brush strokes clearly. The brush strokes are fairly soft and subtle (especially with a low White Intensity). The Dark Strokes filter gives more control over the colors in the finished effect. This is not one of my favorite filters as it is too similar to others in the set without adding any major benefit.

Try it:

1. Open the image "Deer.Psd." Duplicate the image (Image➥Duplicate➥OK).
2. Open the Dark Strokes dialog box shown in Figure 51 (Filter➥Brush Strokes➥Dark Strokes).

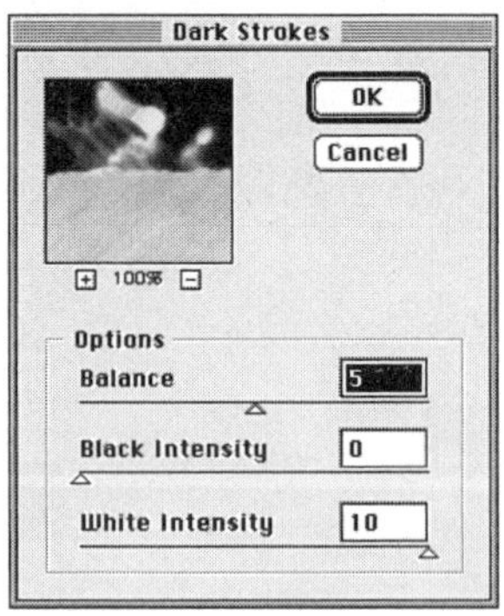

Figure 51

The Dark Strokes dialog box.

3. Drag the Balance to 5.

   The Balance setting varies from 0-10. This parameter controls the direction of the strokes. A setting of 0 makes all of the strokes appear from the upper left to lower right. A setting of 10 puts them in the opposite direction. A setting of 5 gets you half-and-half.

4. Set the Black Intensity to 0.

   The Black Intensity can vary from 0-10. When set higher than 0, it begins to remove all dark colors from the image and change them to black.

5. Finally, set the White Intensity to 10.

   The White Intensity varies from 0-10. A setting of 10 makes the light areas of the image bright and very saturated. A setting of 0 still shows up but it is, obviously, much darker.

6. Click OK. Figure 52 shows the result.

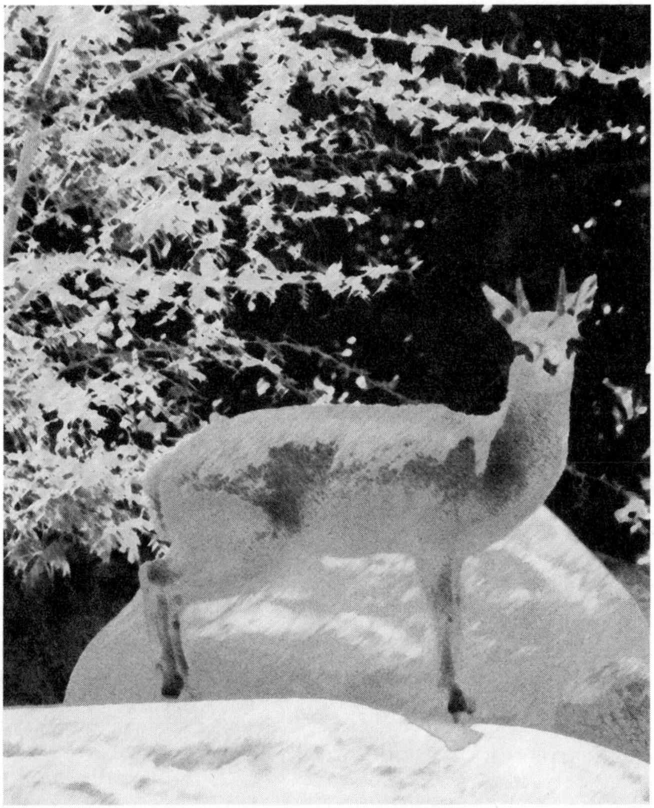

Figure 52

An example of the Dark Strokes filter applied to an image.

Filter type	Category	Supported Color Modes	Preview type	Data Dependent	Color Dependent
Parameter	Stylizing Filter	RGB, Grayscale	Small Filter Preview	Yes. A blank image produces a blank filtered image.	No. The Foreground/Background settings have no effect.

Ink Outlines

The Ink Outlines filter is very similar to the Dark Strokes filter, but it enables you to control the Stroke Length rather than the stroke direction. The Ink Outlines filter always strokes in a cross-hatched direction, but if the stroke length is short, that will not be apparent. It also performs a "sort-of" find edges that can be very attractive.

Try it:

1. Open the image "Deer.Psd." Duplicate the image (Image➡Duplicate➡OK).
2. Open the Ink Outlines dialog box shown in Figure 53 (Filter➡Brush Strokes➡Ink Outlines).

Figure 53

The Ink Outlines dialog box.

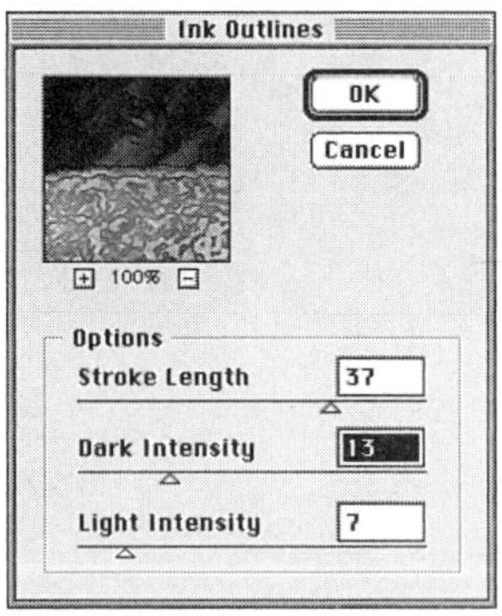

3. Drag the Stroke Length to 37.

   The Stroke Length setting varies from 1-50. This parameter controls the distance of the cross-hatch stroke. Both small and long strokes look good with this filter.

4. Set the Dark Intensity to 13.

The Dark Intensity can vary from 0-50. It looks best when kept low, so that it does not change all of the dark values to black.

5. Finally, set the Light Intensity to 7.

   The Light Intensity varies from 0-50. This parameter builds up quickly, so it looks best at low settings unless you want it to take over the image with super-saturated color.

6. Click OK. Figure 54 shows the result.

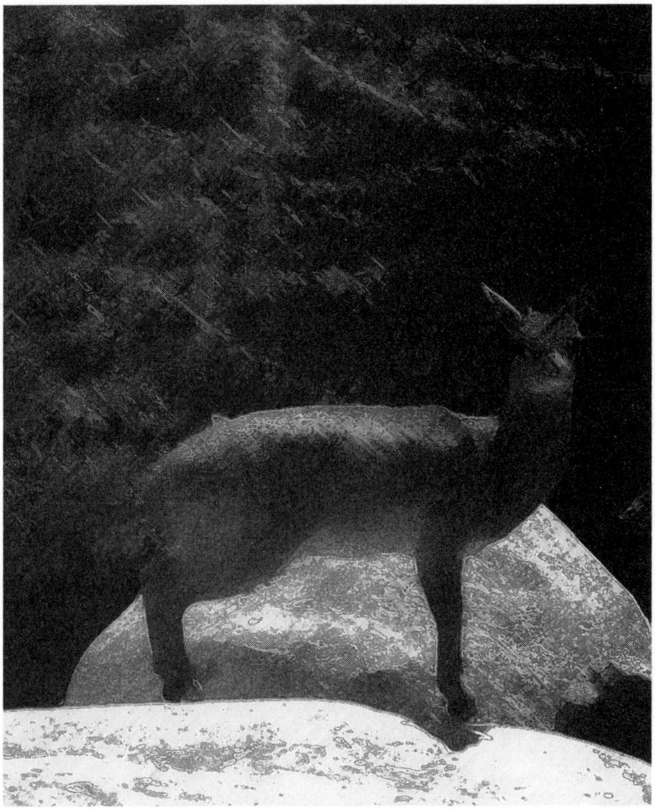

Figure 54

An example of the Ink Outlines filter applied.

Filter type	Category	Supported Color Modes	Preview type	Data Dependent	Color Dependent
Parameter	Stylizing Filter	RGB, Grayscale	Small Filter Preview	Yes. A blank image produces a blank filtered image.	No. The Foreground/Background settings have no effect.

Spatter

The Spatter filter can help to enhance a simple line art graphic. This filter looks good when used on text. At low Smoothness settings the Spatter filter looks as if someone forced the image through an airbrush and it came out in little dots of paint. At higher Smoothness settings, it would be very good for making reflections in water.

Try it:

1. Open the image "Deer.Psd." Duplicate the image (Image➥Duplicate➥OK).
2. Open the Spatter dialog box shown in Figure 55 (Filter➥Brush Strokes➥Spatter).

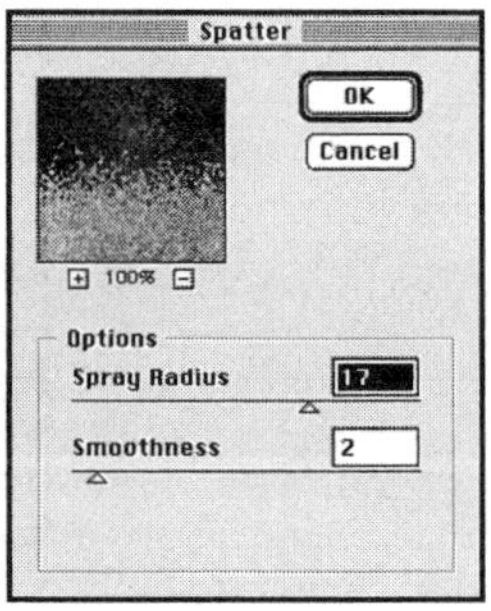

Figure 55

The Spatter dialog box.

3. Drag the Spray Radius to 17.

   The Spray Radius setting varies from 0-25. This parameter controls the size of the spray. As this parameter increases, more of the image becomes the spray. The lighter image areas are first affected and the radius continues to increase over more of the image as the setting increases.

4. Set the Smoothness to 2.

   The Smoothness can vary from 1-15. When the Smoothness is 1, the filter sprays fine dots. As the Smoothness increases, the effect becomes more painterly—as if paint were dribbled and smudged, but the Spray Radius needs to increase as well. A high Smoothness on a low Radius shows almost no effect, where as a setting of 3 and 3 looks very good.

5. Click OK. Figure 56 shows the result.

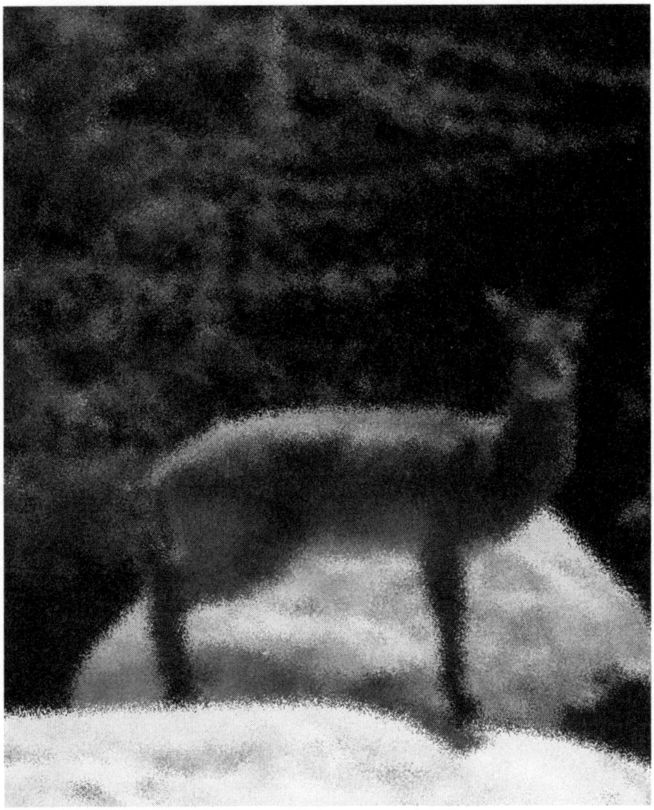

Figure 56

The Spatter filter applied.

Filter type	Category	Supported Color Modes	Preview type	Data Dependent	Color Dependent
Parameter	Stylizing Filter	RGB, Grayscale	Small Filter Preview	Yes. A blank image produces a blank filtered image.	No. The Foreground/Background settings have no effect.

Sprayed Strokes

The Sprayed Strokes filter can help to enhance a simple line art graphic. This is one of the few "stroke" filters that enables you to stroke an image horizontally or vertically. The Sprayed Strokes filter works well at most settings as long as the Stroke Radius is kept towards the lower end of the scale. It is similar to the Dark Strokes, Spatter, and Ink Outlines filters.

Try it:

1. Open the image "Deer.Psd." Duplicate the image (Image➡Duplicate➡OK).
2. Open the Sprayed Strokes dialog box shown in Figure 54 (Filter➡Brush Strokes➡Sprayed Strokes).

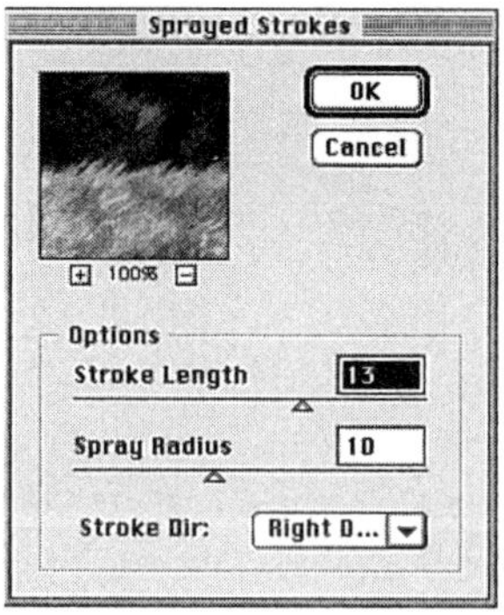

Figure 57

The Sprayed Strokes dialog box.

3. Drag the Stroke Length to 13.

   The Stroke Width setting varies from 0-20, controlling the linearity of the stroke. It is good at all settings, though it begins to show up at settings above 3.

4. Set the Spray Radius to 10.

   The Spray Radius can vary from 0-25. Keep this fairly low so that you see more of your image and fewer random sprays.

5. Finally, set the Direction to Right Diagonal.

   The Direction can also be Horizontal, Left Diagonal, or Vertical.

6. Click OK. Figure 58 shows the result.

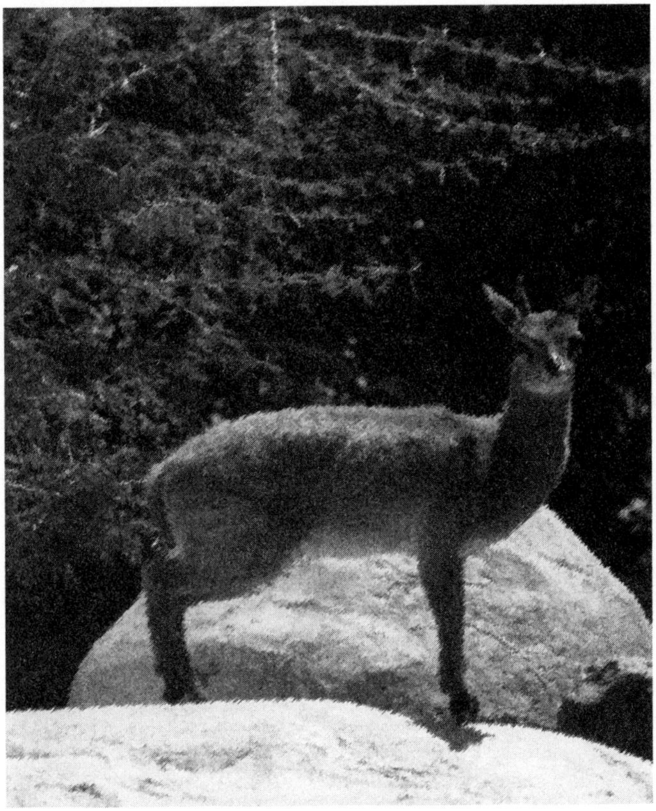

Figure 58

An example of the Sprayed Strokes filter applied to an image.

Filter type	Category	Supported Color Modes	Preview type	Data Dependent	Color Dependent
Parameter	Stylizing Filter	RGB, Grayscale	Small Filter Preview	Yes. A blank image produces a blank filtered image.	No. The Foreground/Background settings have no effect.

Sumi-e

4.0

The Sumi-e filter is a calligraphy filter that works very well in special effects and with text. The Stroke Pressure is the key control here. It makes the difference between the filter being unique and repeating much of what the other filters in the set do.

Try it:

1. Open the image "Deer.Psd." Duplicate the image (Image➡Duplicate➡OK).
2. Open the Sumi-e dialog box shown in Figure 59 (Filter➡Brush Strokes➡Sumi-e).

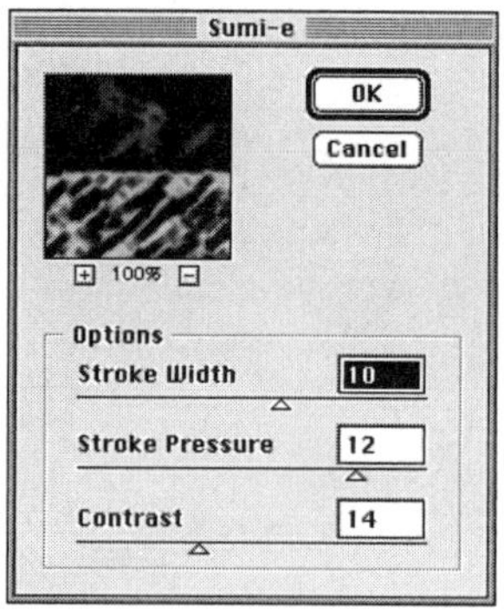

Figure 59

The Sumi-e dialog box.

3. Drag the Stroke Width to 10.

   The Stroke Width setting varies from 3-15. This parameter controls the width of the stroke (surprise!).

4. Set the Stroke Pressure to 12.

The Stroke Pressure can vary from 0-15, determining how much black appears carved out of the image. A high stroke pressure shows a lot of black, while a low stroke pressure results in a smooth appearance.

5. Finally, set the Contrast to

   The Contrast varies from 0-40. A low contrast maintains the original image lights and darks where as the higher settings intensify both the light and dark values. This parameter does better on the low side.

6. Click OK. Figure 60 shows the result.

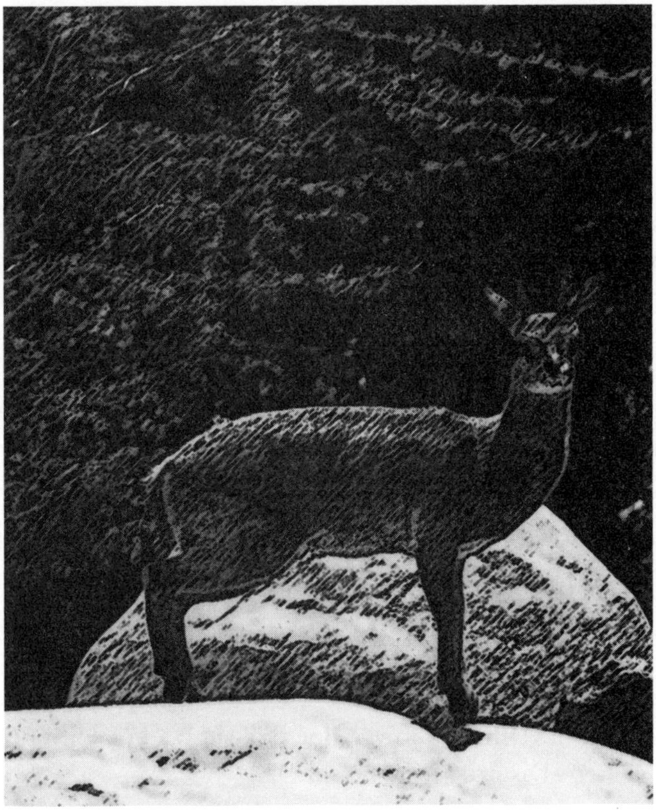

Figure 60

An example of the Sumi-e filter applied to an image.

Filter type	Category	Supported Color Modes	Preview type	Data Dependent	Color Dependent
Parameter	Stylizing Filter	RGB, Grayscale	Small Filter Preview	Yes. A blank image produces a blank filtered image.	No. The Foreground/Background settings have no effect.

PHOTOSHOP'S NATIVE FILTERS—DISTORT

The Distort category of filters includes a number of filters that turn your image into a tangle of pixels. They wave, ZigZag, spherize, ripple, displace, and generally mangle the contents of the image for special effects.

Diffuse Glow

The Diffuse Glow filter adds a subtle—or not-so-subtle—glow to the highlight areas of your image. I have no idea what it is doing in the "Distort" category of filters as it really does not change the geometry of the image as most of the Distort filters do. The Diffuse Glow filter is one of the original Gallery Effects filters. When you set all three controls to their lowest settings, you have no image—it replaces the entire image with your Background color. Setting all three controls to their highest point can still give you a usable image. The Diffuse Glow filter can be applied both to the entire image or to selected areas with good results. It also looks good when used on text.

Try it:

1. Open the image "Seal.Psd." Duplicate the image (Image➡Duplicate➡OK).
2. Set the background color to a soft yellow.
3. Open the Diffuse Glow dialog box shown in Figure 61 (Filter➡Distort➡Diffuse Glow).

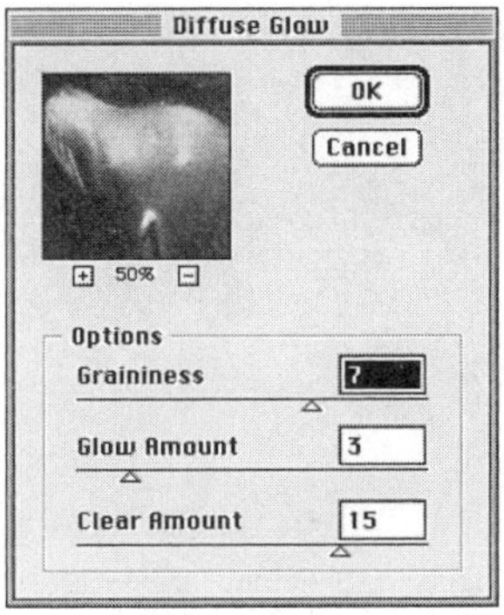

Figure 61

The Diffuse Glow dialog box.

4. Drag the Graininess slider to 7.

   The Graininess setting varies from 0-10. This parameter controls the amount of noise in the image. The noise is applied most heavily to the shadow areas in the image. If you move this control to 10 and set the other sliders to 0, you see the faint hint of your image in the pattern of graininess that emerges.

5. Set the Glow Amount to 3.

   The Glow Amount can vary from 0-20, controlling how much of the background color is visible in the image, but it is linked to the Clear Amount as well. A setting of 20 makes the glow overwhelm your image—regardless of the Clear Amount setting. But if you set the Clear Amount too low, all you see is the background color, even if the Glow amount is also set low. For most uses, you will probably want to keep the Glow Amount set below 10.

6. Finally, set the Clear Amount to 15.

   The Clear Amount varies from 0-20. The Clear Amount controls how much of the darker portions of the image are retained. At 0, none of the original image is seen. At 20, the amount of the visible image seen depends upon the Glow Amount setting. If the Glow Amount is also set to 20, only the deepest values in the original image appear.

7. Click OK. Figure 62 shows the result.

Figure 62

An example of the Diffuse Glow filter applied to an image.

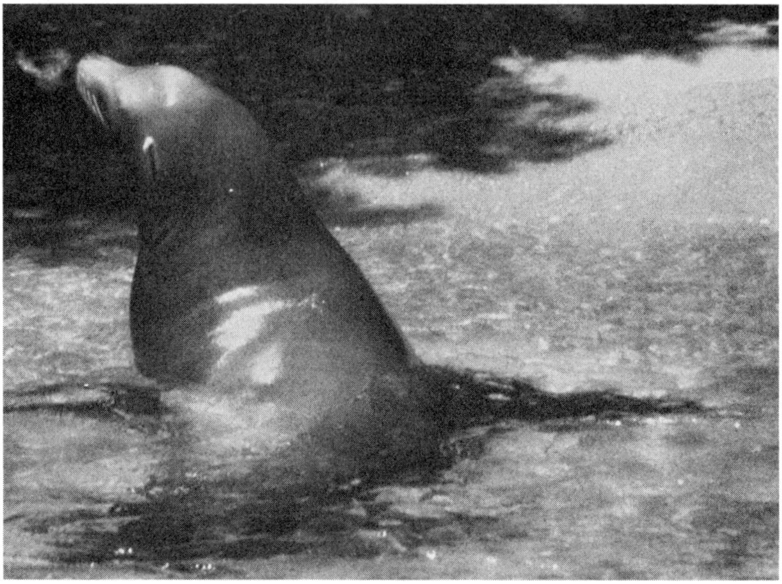

Filter type	Category	Supported Color Modes	Preview type	Data Dependent	Color Dependent
Parameter	Stylizing and Color Change	RGB, Grayscale	Small Filter Preview	Not exactly. A blank image can pick up the background color and noise.	Yes. The Background setting is the "glow" color.

Displace

The Displace filter is a very complex one. Briefly, it reads a second image (a Displacement map) and moves each pixel in the filtered image according to the values in the displacement map. White and black pixels in the displacement map have the most effect. They cause the pixels to be moved the maximum amount in opposite directions. A middle gray value (128) in the Displacement Map causes no movement.

The Displace filter is used for special effects. You can create realistic results that mimic looking at an image through a sheet of glass or through water. You can also create wild effects using one of the pre-created Displacement maps that are stored inside of the Plug-Ins/Filters folder. You can use any grayscale or color image as your displacement map so long as it is saved in Photoshop format. You should not, however, use a layered image as the Displacement map because you can get some unexpected results. You can get very interesting results by using the image as its own Displacement map or by using an otherwise-filtered version of the image as its Displacement map.

Try it:

1. Open the image "Seal.Psd." Duplicate the image (Image➥Duplicate➥OK).
2. Open the Displace dialog box shown in Figure 63 (Filter➥Distort➥Displace).

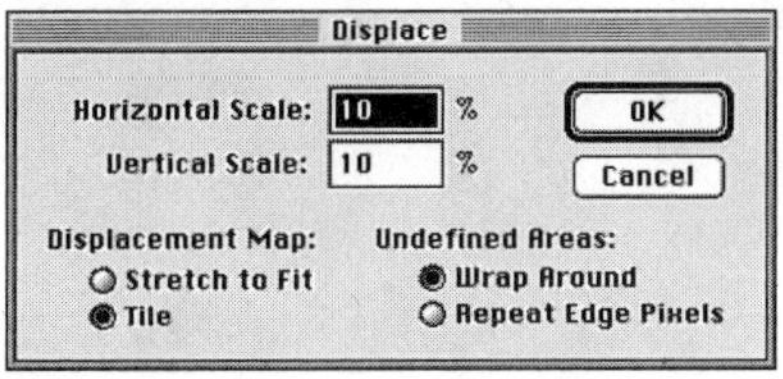

Figure 63

The Displace dialog box.

3. Set the Horizontal and Vertical scale boxes to 10%.

   The Horizontal and Vertical scale settings vary from -999 to 999. This parameter controls the direction and amount of the displacement. You may enter a different amount for each box.

4. Click the Tile button of the Displacement Map setting.

   You can elect to tile the Displacement map (use it as a repeat pattern if it is smaller than your original image) or have it Stretch to Fit (resized so that it is the same dimensions as your image).

5. Finally, set the Undefined Areas to Wrap Around.

The Undefined Areas are basically the outer the perimeters of your image (or the edges of the selection). These can wrap (the right edge moves to the left edge as it leaves the image) or the edges can repeat the pixels, which gives it almost the look of a motion blur.

6. Click OK. You will then see a standard "Open File" dialog box that asks you to select the Displacement map image. Select the Displace.Psd image (shown in Figure 64). Figure 65 shows the result.

Figure 64

The Dipslace.Psd Displacement Map.

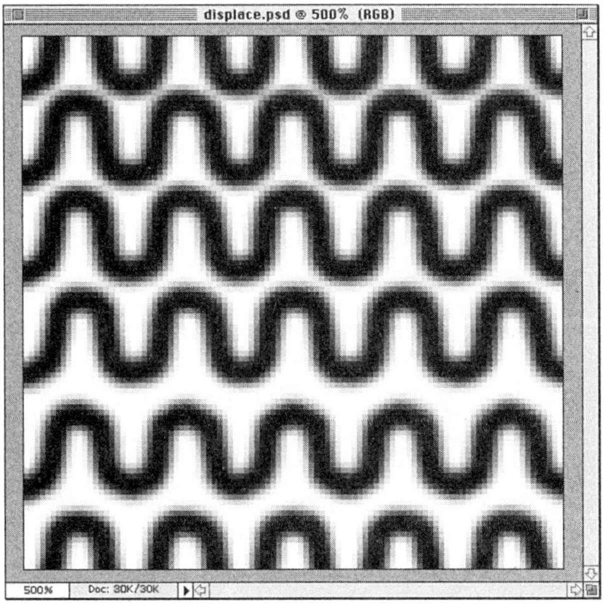

7. Either save this image and make another copy of the original or Undo the filter. See how much different a result you get by selecting Stretch to Fit. First, however, load Channel #4 (Option-Command-4)[Alt-Control-4]. This selects everything in the image *but* the seal.

8. Apply the filter again (Command-Option-F)[Alt-Control-F]. Click the Stretch to Fit button and click OK. Select the Displace.Psd image again. Figure 66 shows the result.

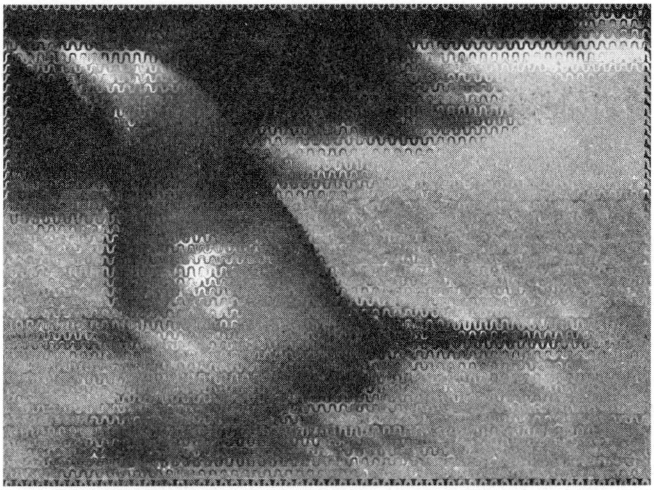

Figure 65

The Displace filter applied to an image.

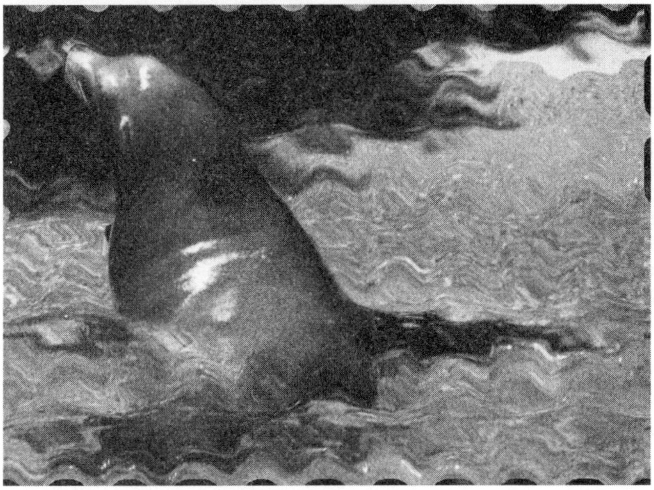

Figure 66

An example of the Displace filter applied with Stretch to Fit.

Filter type	Category	Supported Color Modes	Preview type	Data Dependent	Color Dependent
Parameter	Special Effects—Displacement Filter	RGB, Grayscale CMYK, Lab	No Preview	Yes. A blank image produces a blank filtered image.	No. The Foreground/Background settings have no effect.

Glass

Another one of the original Gallery Effects filters, the Glass filter is similar in concept to the Displace filter. It performs an action that is very close to a Displacement mapping. The Glass filter was designed, however, to simulate the effect of viewing your image through a pane of glass. It can be used to enhance a simple line art graphic, though you need to add some noise or shading to it first. The Glass filter also looks good when used on patterned text.

Try it:

1. Open the image "Seal.Psd." Duplicate the image (Image➡Duplicate➡OK).
2. Open the Glass dialog box shown in Figure 67 (Filter➡Distort➡Glass).

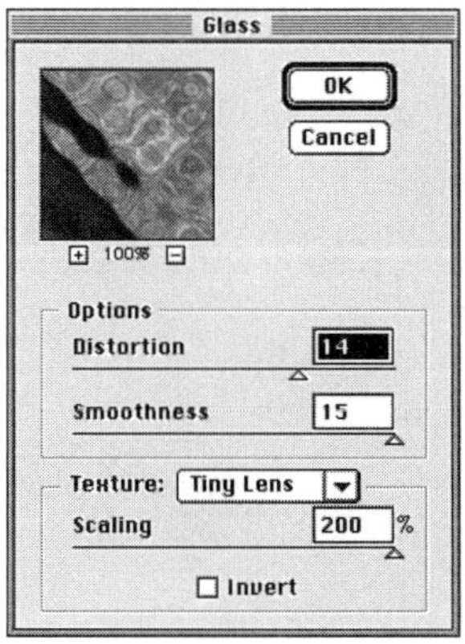

Figure 67

The Glass dialog box.

3. Drag the Distortion setting to 15.

   The Distortion setting varies from 0-20, controlling the amount of distortion applied. A setting of 0 produces almost no change. A setting of 20 represents a very thick pane of glass.

4. Set the Smoothness setting to 15.

   The Smoothness can vary from 1-15. A setting of 1 creates a distortion that is very noisy. As the smoothness increases, it is as if the waves in the pane of glass stretch and become more fluid.

5. Next, select the Texture.

   Choose the Tiny Lens texture from the list that includes Blocks, Canvas, Frosted, Tiny Lens, or a file that you have selected to use as a texture. You can use the Displacement maps very successfully as textures here. You can even try this with the Displace.Psd image on the CD-ROM.

6. You can Scale the texture from 50% to 200%.

   Select the 200% scaling. This makes the texture larger.

7. If you wish, you can Invert the texture. This makes the light areas of the texture pattern dark and vice versa, which inverts the filter effect. Do not select this option right now.

8. Click OK. Figure 68 shows the result.

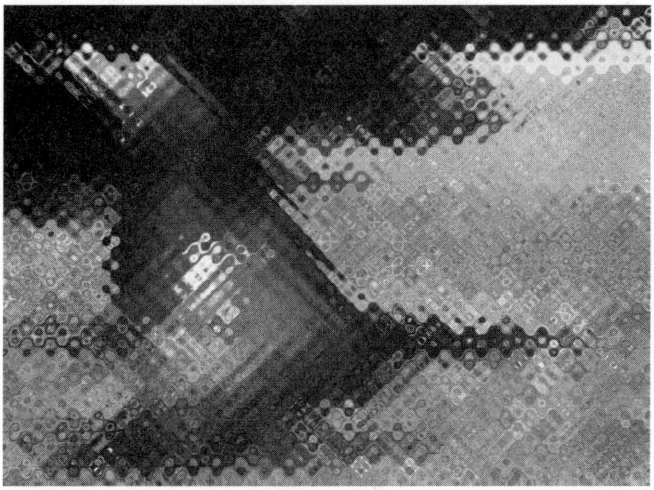

Figure 68

The Glass filter applied to an image.

Filter type	Category	Supported Color Modes	Preview type	Data Dependent	Color Dependent
Parameter	Special Effects—Displacement Filter	RGB, Grayscale	Small Filter Preview	Yes. A blank image produces a blank filtered image.	No. The Foreground/Background settings have no effect.

Ocean Ripple

4.0

The Ocean Ripple filter is another Gallery Effects that performs a displacement on the image. It is designed to make the image look as if it is under water. You can get much the same look with the Glass filter, but you have more control over the final Glass filter results. The Ocean Ripple filter is "hard-wired" and does not enable you to select the map used for the effect. It can help to enhance a simple line art graphic and looks good when used on text.

Try it:

1. Open the image "Seal.Psd." Duplicate the image (Image➡Duplicate➡OK).
2. Load Channel #4 (Option-Command-4)[Alt-Control-4]. This selects everything in the image *but* the seal.
3. Open the Ocean Ripple dialog box shown in Figure 69 (Filter➡Distort➡Ocean Ripples).

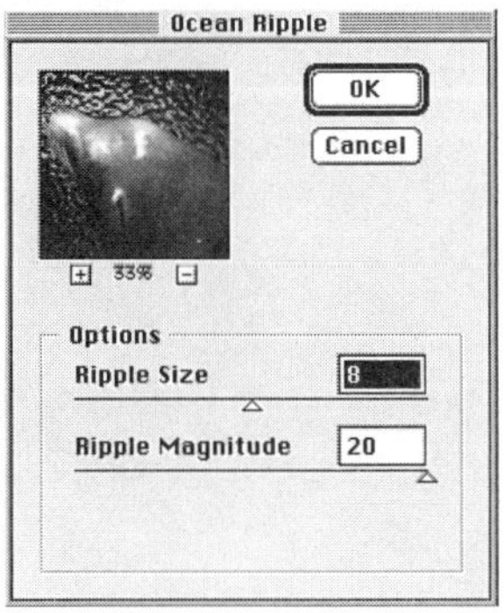

Figure 69

The Ocean Ripple dialog box.

4. Drag the Ripple Size to 8.

   The Ripple Size setting varies from 1-15, controlling the actual size of the wave that is used. A setting of 1 still produces a result.

5. Set the Ripple Magnitude to 15.

   The Ripple Magnitude can vary from 0-20. The Ripple Magnitude controls the pull the wave has on the image. A setting of 0 has no pull, therefore, no change occurs—regardless of the Ripple Size setting. By the time the setting is changed to 3, however, you can see an effect if you have a Ripple Size of more than 3. The setting of 15 gives a very noticeable effect—even if the Ripple Size is set to 1.

6. Click OK. Figure 70 shows the result.

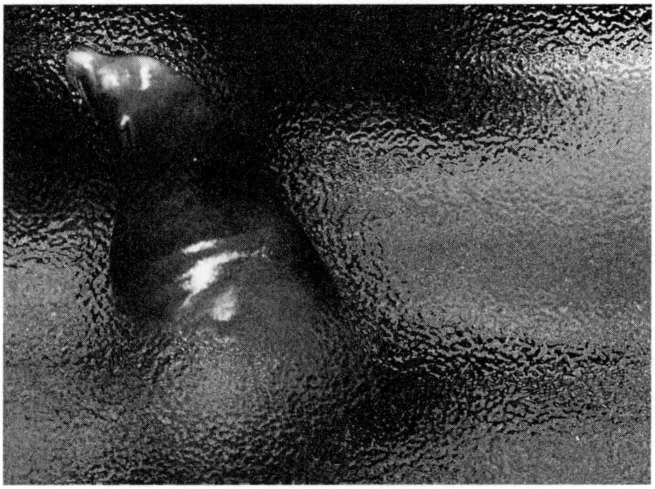

Figure 70

The Ocean Ripple filter applied.

Filter type	Category	Supported Color Modes	Preview type	Data Dependent	Color Dependent
Parameter	Special Effects—Displacement Filter	RGB, Grayscale	Small Filter Preview	Yes. A blank image produces a blank filtered image.	No. The Foreground/Background settings have no effect.

Pinch

A "bloat and pinch" filter, the Pinch filter can make the selected area smaller by squeezing in the center or can make it larger by inflating it through the center of the selection. This filter can be used for serious photo-correction if you have a careful hand and make a good selection. You can use the Pinch filter to reduce the size of a model's nose or lips, or to enhance the size of the model's eyes. It can also be used, of course, for special effects.

Try it:

1. Open the image "Seal.Psd." Duplicate the image (Image➡Duplicate➡OK).
2. Load Channel #4 (Option-Command-4)[Alt-Control-4}. Reverse the selection (Select➡Inverse). This selects only the seal.
3. Open the Pinch dialog box shown in Figure 71 (Filter➡Distort➡Pinch).

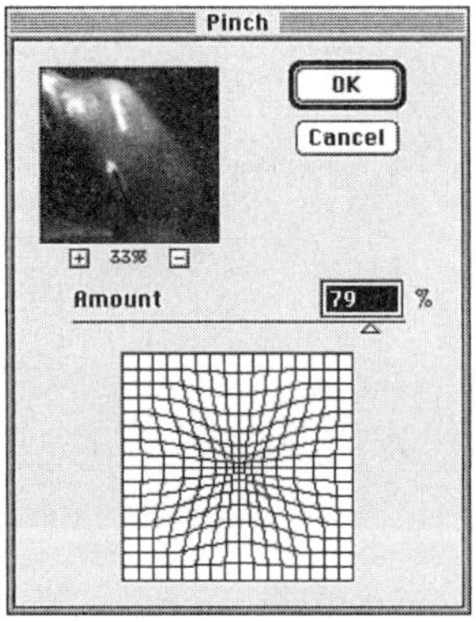

Figure 71

The Pinch dialog box.

4. Drag the Amount to 79%.

   The Amount setting varies from -100 to +100%. A negative amount bloats the selection, a positive amount pinches it.

5. Click OK. Figure 69 shows the result.

Filter type	Category	Supported Color Modes	Preview type	Data Dependent	Color Dependent
Parameter	Special Effects or Production Filter	RGB, Grayscale CMYK, Lab	Small Filter/ Wire Frame Preview	Yes. A blank image produces a blank filtered image.	No. The Foreground/Background settings have no effect.

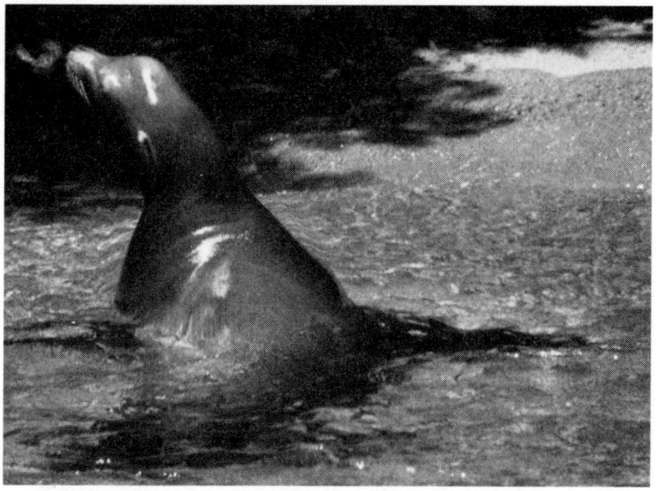

Figure 72

The Pinch filter applied to an image.

Polar Coordinates

The Polar Coordinates filter is a special effects filter that has a number of non-obvious uses. It remaps the pixels in an image is as they were going from Rectangular to Polar or Polar to Rectangular mapping (think of the difference between viewing the map of the world as a rectangle or as a flattened globe). You can use this filter to reshape images for wild special effects. You can also use it to create concentric circles from straight lines (Rectangular to Polar) or to make a pattern tile that is seamless on two sides (Polar to Rectangular). You can get very unique results if you work in one coordinate space, change the other, draw some more, and then change back.

Try it:

1. Open the image "Seal.Psd." Duplicate the image (Image➡Duplicate➡OK).
2. Make a new layer (press the modifier key (Option)[Alt] and click the New Layer icon at the bottom of the Layers Palette).
3. Press D to set the colors back to the default of black and white.

4. Select the Marquee tool (M) and choose the Elliptical shape. Draw a circle near the center of the new Layer (about 500 pixels in diameter). Press the Shift key to constrain the ellipse to a circle. Fill the circle with the foreground color, black.

5. Open the Polar Coordinates dialog box shown in Figure 73 (Filter➥Distort➥Polar Coordinates).

Figure 73

The Polar Coordinates dialog box.

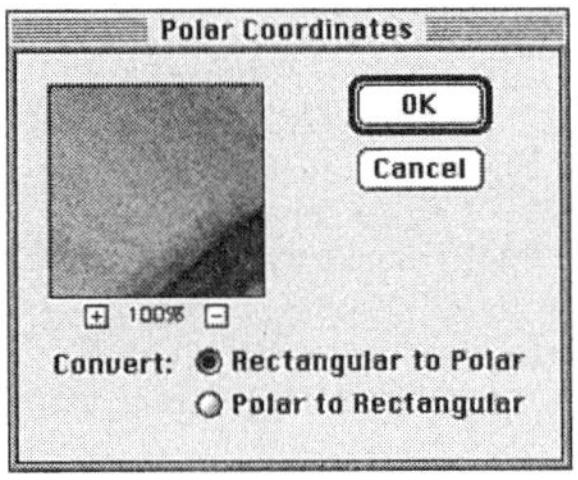

6. Select the Rectangular to Polar setting. Click OK.

7. Using the Line tool (L) set to draw 8-pixel lines, draw three diagonal lines across the circle in each direction.

8. Select the Polar Coordinates filter again (Command-Option-F) [Alt-Control-F]. Choose the Polar to Rectangular setting.

9. Click OK. Figure 74 shows the result.

Figure 74

An example of the Polar Coordinates filter applied.

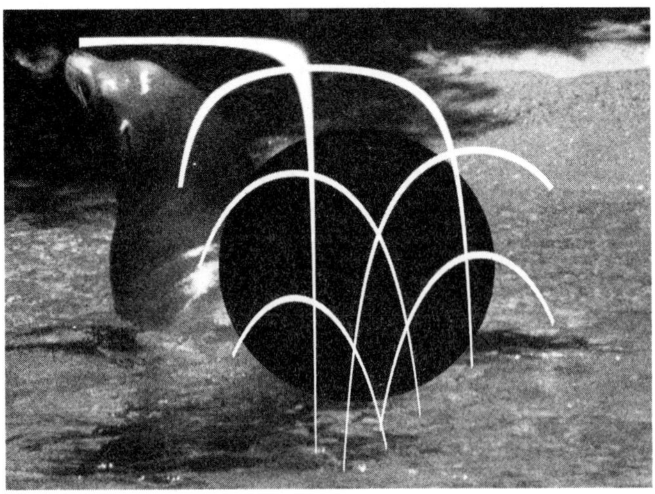

Filter type	Category	Supported Color Modes	Preview type	Data Dependent	Color Dependent
Parameter	Deformation Filter	RGB, Grayscale, CMYK, Lab	Small Filter Preview	Yes. A blank image produces a blank filtered image.	No. The Foreground/Background settings have no effect.

Ripple

The Ripple filter is very similar to the Ocean Ripple filter. It is, however, one of the original Photoshop filters, whereas the Ocean Ripple filter belonged to the Adobe Gallery Effects set. The uses are identical, but the results—though both wavy—are a bit different. The Ripple filter is good for simulating marbling.

Try it using a little different technique to localize the effect:

1. Open the image "Seal.Psd." Duplicate the image (Image➡Duplicate➡OK).
2. Drag the icon for the Background layer to the New Layer icon (the center icon at the bottom of the Layers palette).
3. Open the Ripple dialog box shown in Figure 75 (Filter➡Distort➡Ripple).

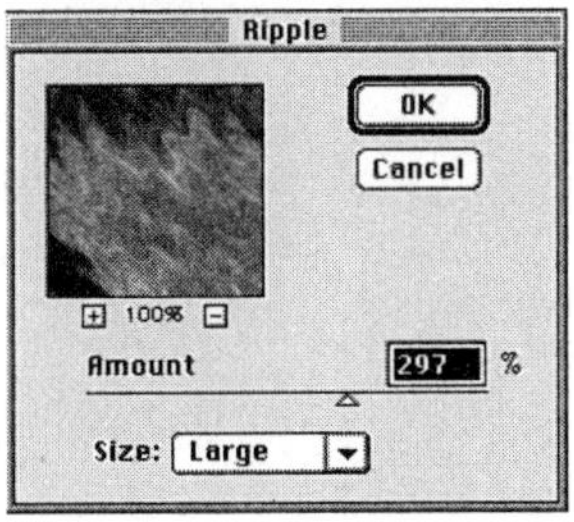

Figure 75

The Ripple dialog box.

4. Drag the Amount to 279.

   The Amount setting varies from -999 to 999. This parameter controls the height and direction of the wave. At the ends of the scale, the image begins to pixelate heavily. Your smoothest values are around the 100-300 (+ and -) settings.

5. Set the Size to Large.

   The Size is a drop-down menu of Small, Medium, or Large. The Small ripple is similar to a cross-hatching, the Medium to single waves, and the Large to a double wave.

6. Create a Layer Mask (click the Add Layer Mask icon—the left-most icon at the bottom of the Layers palette). Using black paint, paint over the details in the Seal's face and body until you have restored as much of the original image as you wish.

7. Click OK. Figure 76 shows the result.

Figure 76

The Ripple filter applied.

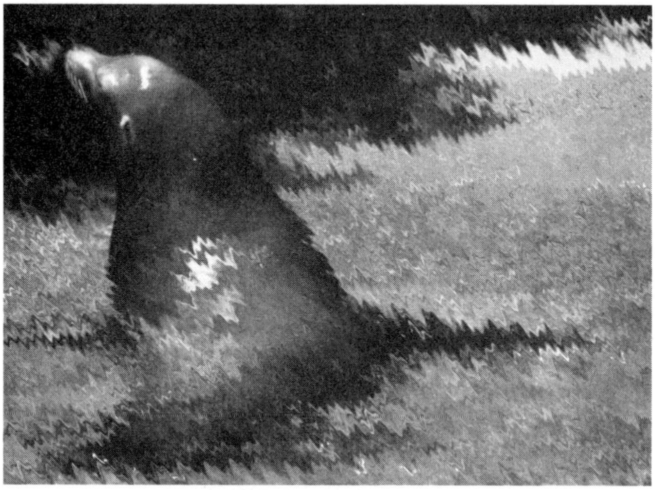

Filter type	Category	Supported Color Modes	Preview type	Data Dependent	Color Dependent
Parameter	Displacement/ Deformation Filter	RGB, Grayscale, CMYK, Lab	Small Filter Preview	Yes. A blank image produces a blank filtered image.	No. The Foreground/Background settings have no effect.

Shear

The Shear filter warps images vertically along a grid. The dialog box is a bit confusing, but you can create a variety of curves with it as well as creating straight line effects. The Shear filter is very useful for pattern work or for creating folds in garments. If you need to apply the filter horizontally, change the orientation of your image (Image➡Rotate Clockwise), apply the filter, then rotate back into its original position.

Try it by creating a pattern tile to composite with the main image:

1. Open the image "Seal.Psd." Duplicate the image twice (Image➡Duplicate➡OK).
2. Reduce one copy to 100 pixels wide (Image➡Image Size➡Pixel, Dimensions 100 pixels width, Constrain Proportions, Resample Image Bicubic).
3. Open the Shear dialog box shown in Figure 77 (Filter➡Distort➡Shear).

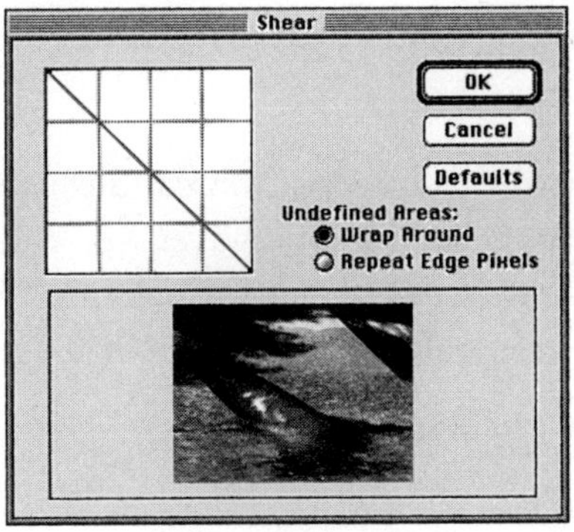

Figure 77

The Shear dialog box.

4. Drag the top point into the upper-left corner of the grid. Drag the bottom point into the lower-right corner of the grid.

   You can create additional points by clicking the black skew line to make a point and then moving the point somewhere along the grid. Leave the straight lines for this example. Click OK. Figure 78 shows the result.
5. Select the entire image (Command-A)[Control-A]. Define this as a pattern (Edit➡Define Pattern).
6. Click the other copy to make it active. Make a new layer (press the modifier key (Option)[Alt] and click on the New Layer icon at the bottom of the Layers Palette).

Figure 78

The Shear filter applied.

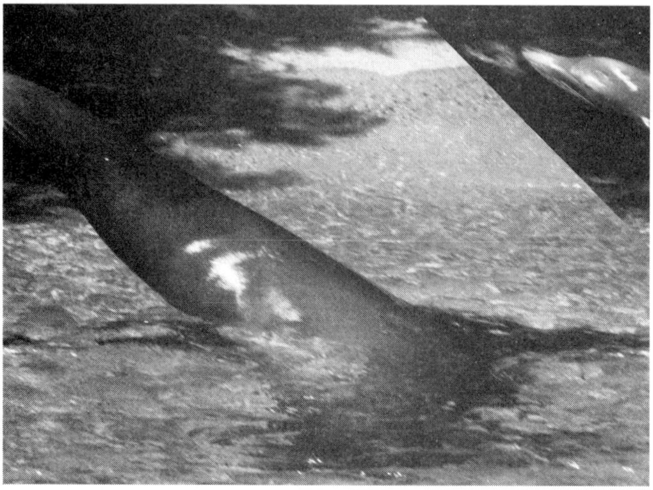

7. Fill the image with the pattern (Shift-Delete➡ Pattern, 100 percent opacity, Normal).
8. Load Channel #4 (Option-Command-4)[Alt-Control-4]. Create a Layer Mask (click the Add Layer Mask icon—the left-most icon at the bottom of the Layers palette). The seal is revealed and the pattern only shows up behind the seal.
9. Change the Blending mode to Screen. Figure 79 shows the result.

Figure 79

The Shear filter blended into an original image.

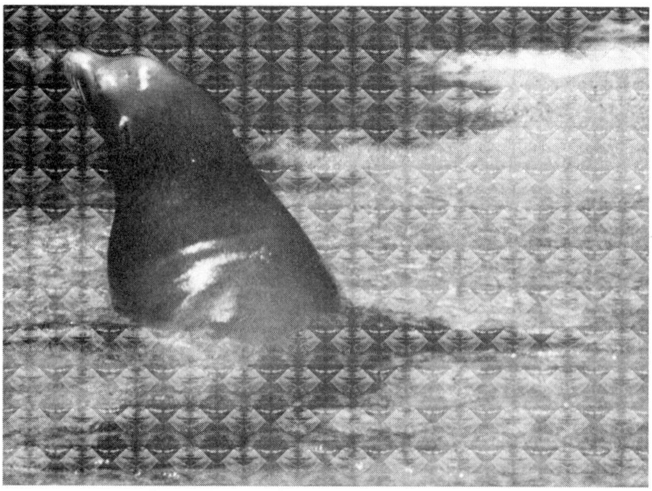

Filter type	Category	Supported Color Modes	Preview type	Data Dependent	Color Dependent
Parameter	Deformation Filter	RGB, Grayscale, CMYK, Lab	Small Filter Preview	Yes. A blank image produces a blank filtered image.	No. The Foreground/Background settings have no effect.

Spherize

The Spherize filter bloats a selection or creates a spherical form on an image. It works horizontally, vertically, or in both directions. The Spherize filter is only useful for special effects. It does not add lighting to the sphere as do the KPT Glass Lens filters. The Spherize filter is also useful for creating water drops.

Try this technique of filtering the image in only one channel:

1. Open the image "Seal.Psd." Duplicate the image (Image➡Duplicate➡OK).
2. In the Channels palette, click the Red channel so that it becomes the only one selected. Click the Eye next to the RGB channel to view the composite channel.
3. Open the Spherize dialog box shown in Figure 80 (Filter➡Distort➡Spherize).

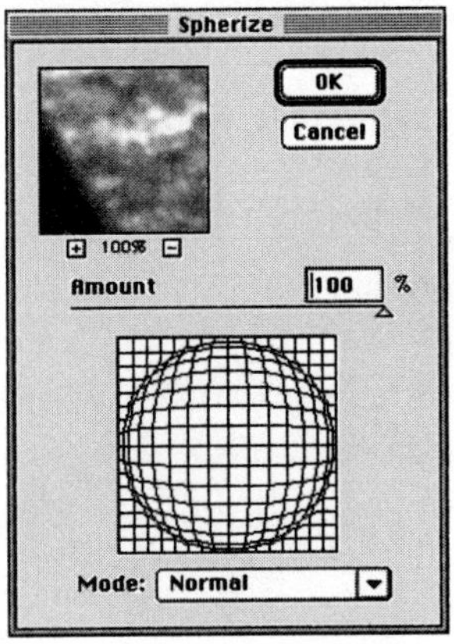

Figure 80

The Spherize dialog box.

4. Drag the Amount to 100%.

   The Amount varies from -100 to +100. The negative numbers squish the image.

5. Set the Mode to Normal.

   The Mode can be Normal, Horizontal Only, or Vertical Only.

6. Click OK. Figure 81 shows the result to the Red channel. This technique of spherizing in a channel creates a ghost image that shows up very well in color but does not reproduce in black and white.

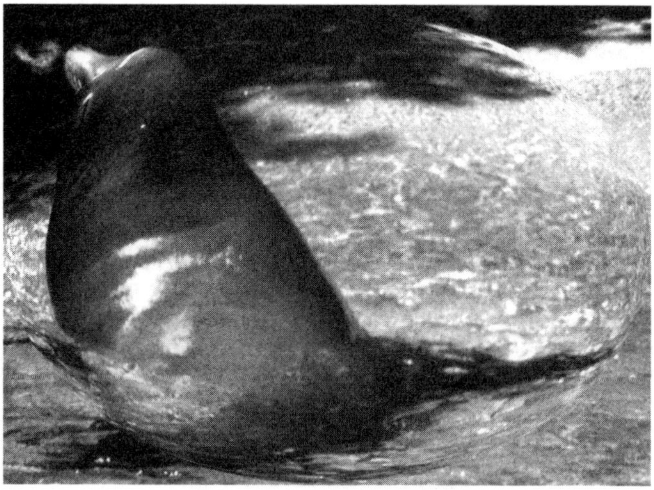

Figure 81

An example of the Spherize filter applied to the Red channel only.

Filter type	Category	Supported Color Modes	Preview type	Data Dependent	Color Dependent
Parameter	Deformation Filter	RGB, Grayscale, CMYK, Lab	Small Filter/ Wire Frame Preview	Yes. A blank image produces a blank filtered image.	No. The Foreground/Background settings have no effect.

Twirl

The Twirl filter can give an image a little twist, or it can place it in the center of a maelstrom. The Twirl filter takes the pixels in the image and stirs them as if they were liquid. The result, depending upon the settings selected, can look like you've just mixed chocolate into a bowl of vanilla cake batter by swirling it in a circular manner. This filter is very useful in creating seamless pattern effects when it is used to twirl the area where the tiles meet (you can see that technique in the Offset filter section).

Try it:

1. Open the image "Seal.Psd." Duplicate the image (Image➡Duplicate➡OK).
2. Load Channel #4 (Option-Command-4)[Alt-Control-4].
3. Open the Twirl dialog box shown in Figure 82 (Filter➡Distort➡Twirl).

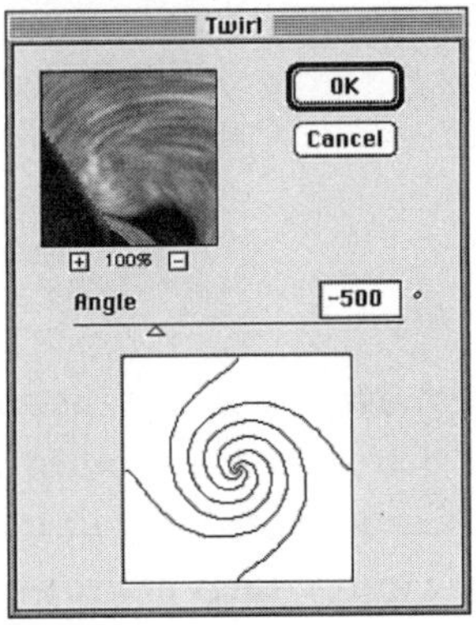

Figure 82

The Twirl dialog box.

4. Drag the Angle to -500.

   The Angle setting varies from -999 to +999, controlling the direction and angle of the twirl, which you can see in the wire frame preview. This setting rotates the center of the image more so than the outer edges, creating a twirl, or vortex, that is counter-clockwise (with negative settings) or clock-wise (with positive settings).

5. Click OK. Figure 83 shows the result.

Figure 83

The Twirl filter applied to an image.

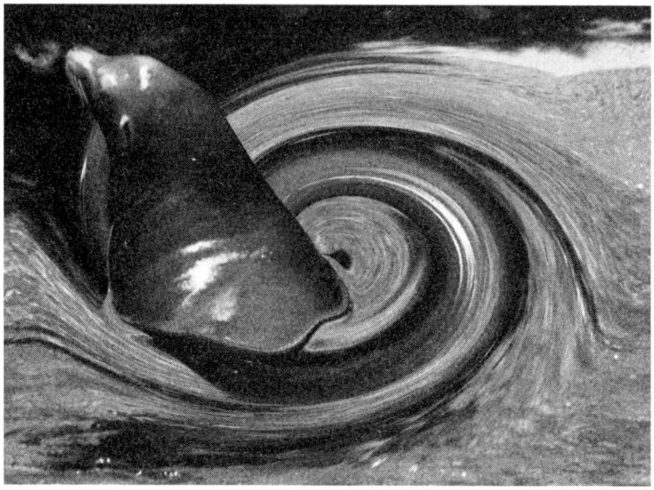

Filter type	Category	Supported Color Modes	Preview type	Data Dependent	Color Dependent
Parameter	Deformation Filter	RGB, Grayscale,	Small Filter/ Wire Frame Preview	Yes. A blank image produces a blank filtered image.	No. The Foreground/Background settings have no effect.

Wave

The Wave filter is the most complex of the native Photoshop filters. It has more parameters than almost any other filter. The Wave filter is a very useful filter for texture creation, but it can totally obliterate the content of the image. Most settings destroy the image completely. It is also used to simulate marbling. This filter's settings have no real "logic;" you need to fiddle with them until you see a preview you like. This is tacitly implied by the "randomize" button built into the filter.

Try the Wave filter at settings that do not quite remove the entire image:

1. Open the image "Seal.Psd." Duplicate the image (Image➡Duplicate➡OK).

2. Open the Wave dialog box shown in Figure 84 (Filter➡Distort➡Wave).

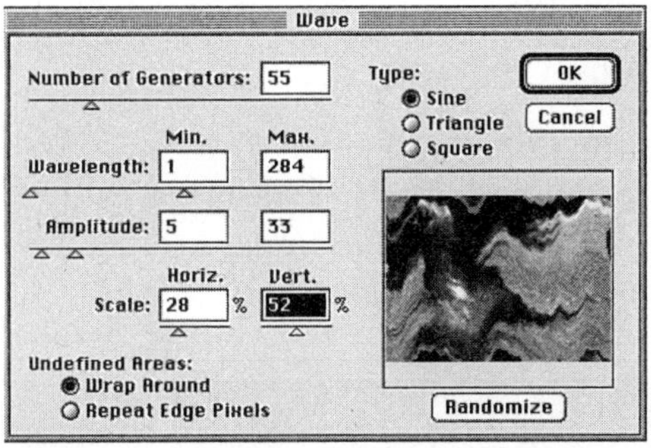

Figure 84

The Wave dialog box.

3. Drag the Number of Generators to 55.

   The Number of Generators setting varies from 1-999. This parameter controls the number of wave forms that the filter produces. The larger the number, the more complex the image. Good results, however, can be obtained with very few waves (3-5) as well.

4. Set the Wave Length minimum to 1 and the maximum to 284.

   The Wave Length, with settings ranging from 1-999, represents the distance horizontally between each up-and-down of the wave. A short wave length causes many more up-and-down spikes across the image, whereas the longest wave length is just a single curve.

5. Set the Wave Amplitude minimum to 5 and the maximum to 33.

   The Wave Amplitude varies from 1-999. It describes the height of the wave, with 1 being a shallow wave and 999 being very high.

6. Set the Horizontal Scale to 28% and the Vertical Scale to 52%.

   The Scale sets the size of the effect. At low numbers, depending upon the type of wave selected and the number of generators, you can create almost solid runs of colors. If both settings are 0, however, the filter shows no change.

7. Set the Undefined areas to Wrap Around.

   These are the areas where the wave leaves the canvas. You can set these to wrap or to repeat the edge pixels.

8. Set the Type to Sine.

   This specifies the shape of the wave: Sine, Triangle, or Square. The shape of the wave has a major impact on the filter results—even with all other settings held the same. Click OK. Figure 85 shows the result.

Figure 85

The Wave filter applied to an image.

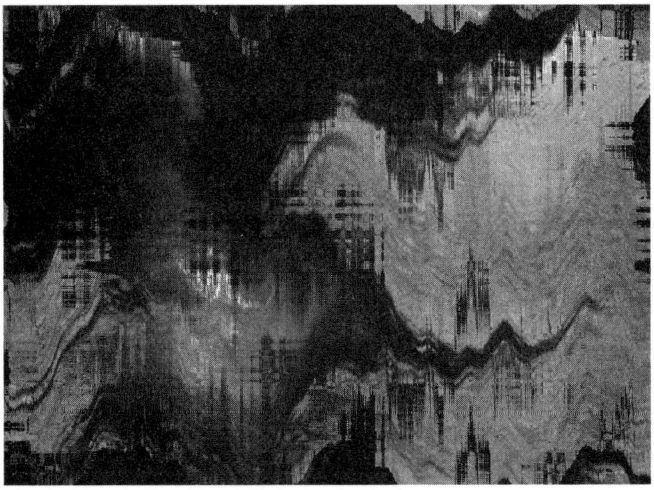

9. Drag the icon for the Background layer to the New Layer icon (the center icon at the bottom of the Layers palette). Re-open the filter dialog box (Command-Option-F)[Alt-Control-F].

10. Change the Type to Square. Leave all of the other settings alone. Click OK.

11. Change the Blending mode to Darken. Figure 86 shows the result.

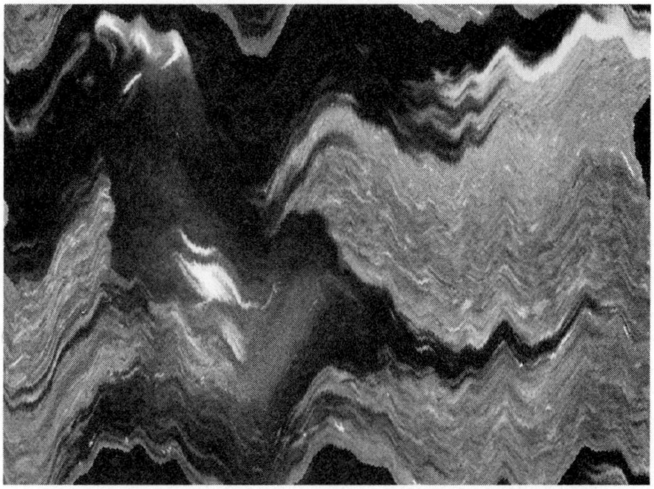

Figure 86

An example of the Square Wave filter applied with the Blending mode changed.

Filter type	Category	Supported Color Modes	Preview type	Data Dependent	Color Dependent
Parameter	Deformation Filter	RGB, Grayscale, CMYK, Lab	Small Filter Preview	Yes. A blank image produces a blank filtered image.	No. The Foreground/Background settings have no effect.

ZigZag

The ZigZag filter is another way to add ripples, ridges, or wavelets to your image. It is similar to the other wavelet filters (Ocean Ripple, Ripple, Twirl), but it works on concentric circles of sorts. The ZigZag filter is the best filter for producing the ripples of a stone cast into a river.

Try it:

1. Open the image "Seal.Psd." Duplicate the image (Image➥Duplicate➥OK).
2. Load Channel #4 (Option-Command-4)[Alt-Control-4].
3. Open the ZigZag dialog box shown in Figure 87 (Filter➥Distort➥ZigZag).

Figure 87

The ZigZag dialog box.

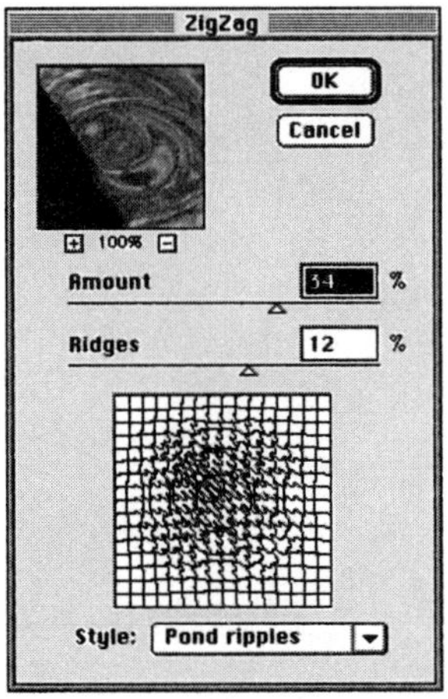

4. Drag the Amount to 34%.

   The Amount setting varies from -100 to +100%, controlling the direction and elevation of the ridge. A negative number ridges in where a positive setting ridges out.

5. Set the Ridges to 12%.

   The Ridges can vary from 1% to 20%. This controls the amount of rings in the final effect. The percent is not clear, but the effect docs work differently depending upon the size of the area being filtered. A set of numbers that looks wonderful on a tiny image looks lost on a larger one.

6. Finally, set the Style to Pond ripples.

   The other options are Around center, which looks like the Twirl filter with additional wavelets on each spoke, and Out from center, in which the pull of the effect is strongest along the four main "arms" right at the center of the filter.

7. Click OK. Figure 88 shows the result.

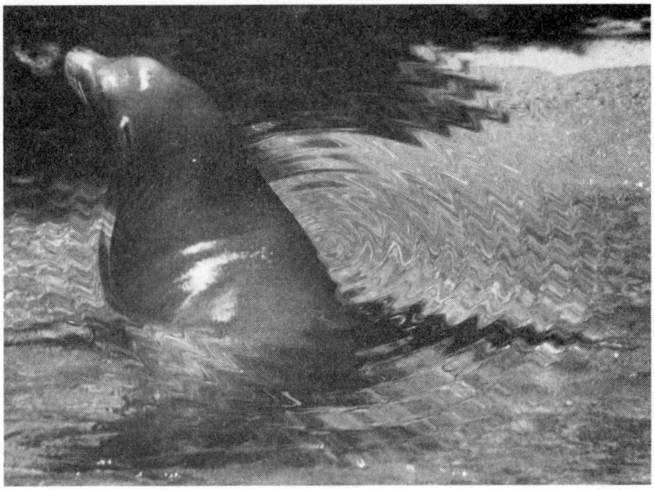

Figure 88

An example of the ZigZag filter applied.

Filter type	Category	Supported Color Modes	Preview type	Data Dependent	Color Dependent
Parameter	Deformation/ Displacement Filter	RGB, Grayscale, CMYK, Lab	Small Filter Preview	Yes. A blank image produces a blank filtered image.	No. The Foreground/Background settings have no effect.

PHOTOSHOP'S NATIVE FILTERS—NOISE

The Noise category of filters are used for pre-press as well as for special effects. They are among the most valuable and frequently used filters in Photoshop's native set. The filters both add and remove noise from images (Noise is defined as extraneous pixels that either are film grain or imperfections such as dust in the image).

Add Noise

The Add Noise filter is used to add some texture to an image by way of tiny pixel dustings. Add Noise is one of the only "something-for-nothing" filters. It gives you basically the same results regardless of the image content. The Add Noise filter and a blank image are frequently the starting ground for many interesting textures. Add Noise is used to conceal "touch-ups" of flat color on an image, on areas where an image needs to be re-grained, and, inside of individual channels to keep gradients from banding (by adding a tiny but different amount of noise to each channel).

Try it:

1. Open the image "Elf.Psd." Duplicate the image (Image➥Duplicate➥OK). This image is typical of a "bad-but-cute" photo that a photo lab might be asked to retouch. We need to remove the background and replace the door with a gradient.
2. Load Channel #4 (Option-Command-4)[Alt-Control-4].
3. Select the Gradient tool (G). In the Gradient Editor, select the NewBkg as the Gradient (Gradient Options➥Edit... button➥Load➥NewBkg). Drag the Gradient from the upper-left corner to the bottom-right corner. The Gradient is OK but too flat. It needs grain to match the image.
4. Open the Add Noise dialog box shown in Figure 89 (Filter➥Noise➥Add Noise).
5. Drag the Amount to 10.

   The Amount setting varies from 1-999, controlling the amount of noise added. A tiny bit of noise (10 and under) is all that is needed to match film grain. Amounts larger than that are for special effects or mezzotints and textures.
6. Set the Distribution to Gaussian.

   The Distribution can be Uniform or Gaussian. These are statistical concepts. A Uniform distribution has even coverage throughout, while a Gaussian distribution has some heavier clumps and some thinner spots (Have you ever noticed that a fast restaurant seems to be either very busy or empty? That people seem to enter a store in clumps rather than at a consistent rate? These are Gaussian distributions).

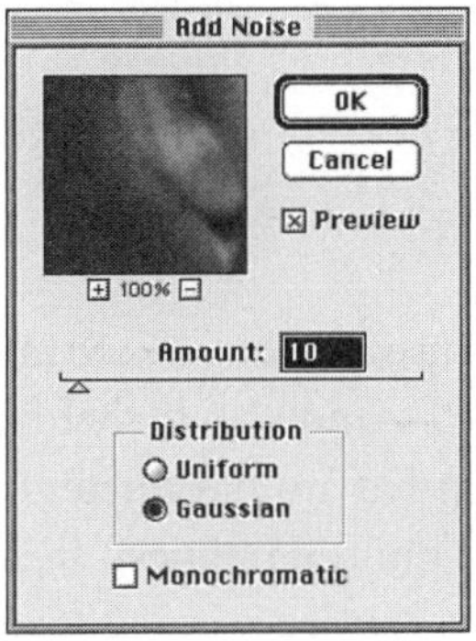

Figure 89

The Add Noise dialog box.

7. Finally, make sure Monochromatic is not checked.

   When it is set, the Noise that is added is only grayscale rather than RGB or CMYK.

8. Click OK. Figure 90 shows the result.

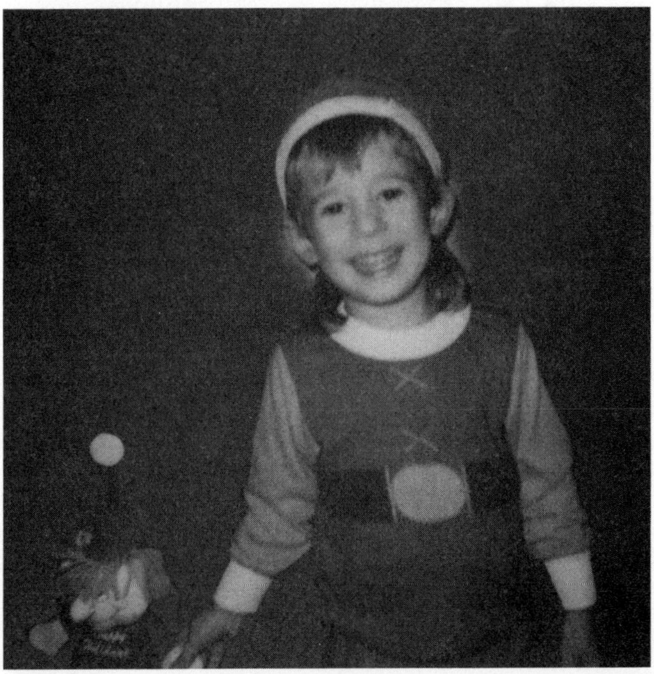

Figure 90

The Add Noise filter applied to an image.

Filter type	Category	Supported Color Modes	Preview type	Data Dependent	Color Dependent
Parameter	Production and Special Effects Filter	RGB, Grayscale, CMYK, Lab	Full Image Preview	No. This is a "something-for-nothing: filter.	No. The Fore-ground/Back-ground settings have no effect.

Despeckle

The Despeckle filter is used to remove extraneous bits of noise from an image after it is scanned—and usually before it is color-corrected. This is a one-step filter that has no parameters. The Despeckle filter can, however, be applied multiple times. It smoothes out a damaged histogram and helps to restore missing (gapped) values.

Try it:

1. Open the image "Elf.Psd." Duplicate the image (Image➡Duplicate➡OK).
2. Select the Despeckle filter (Filter➡Noise➡Despeckle). Before and After Levels histograms are shown in Figure 91 and 92. Notice the After is a bit more smooth and that some of the spikes on the histogram are less pronounced. There is no point in showing a filtered image however, as the difference is not apparent to the naked eye.

Figure 91

The Levels Histogram before the Despeckle filter is applied.

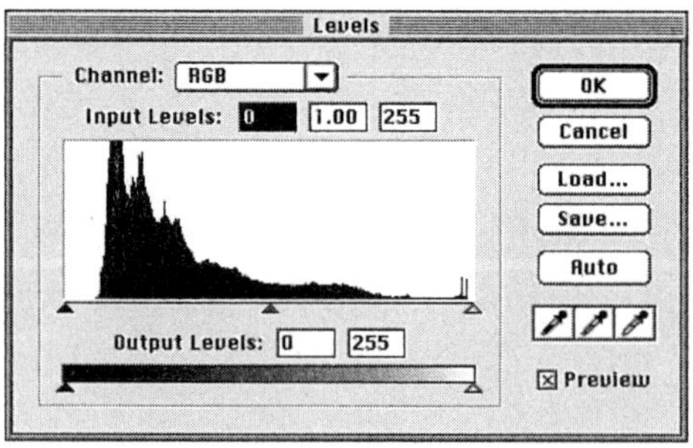

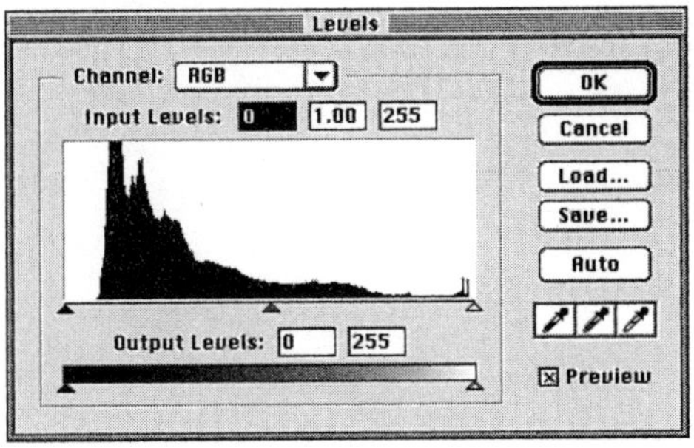

Figure 92

The Levels Histogram after the Despeckle filter is applied.

Filter type	Category	Supported Color Modes	Preview type	Data Dependent	Color Dependent
One-Step	PrePress Filter	RGB, Grayscale, CMYK, Lab	None	Yes. A blank image produces a blank filtered image.	No. The Foreground/Background settings have no effect.

Dust & Scratches

The Dust & Scratches filter helps remove imperfections from an image. It is best used in tiny selections, as it performs a blurring action within a selection and tries to make the colors in the selected area blend into one another. The Dust & Scratches filter can be used very successfully for special effects, however, by setting the Radius to 16 (the maximum) and the Threshold to 0 (the minimum). At these settings, the filter performs a full image blur that retains bright areas of the image without muddying them the way that the Gaussian Blur filter does. Figure 93 shows the dialog box and screen capture of the image with a tiny scratch selected.

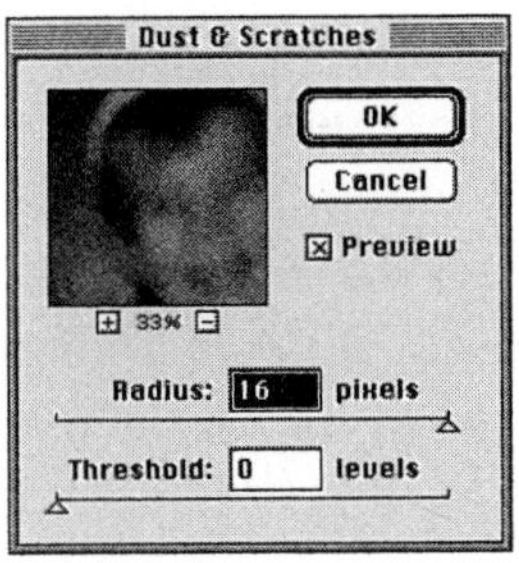

Figure 93

The Dust & Scratches dialog box with a scratch selected.

Try this example for special effects as a way to salvage this cute-but-low-quality photo:

1. Open the image "Elf.Psd." Duplicate the image (Image➡Duplicate➡OK).
2. Drag the icon for the Background layer to the New Layer icon (the center icon at the bottom of the Layers palette). Set the Blending mode to Darken.
3. Click the Background Layer name in the Layers palette to make the Background Layer the active one.
4. Open the Dust & Scratches dialog box shown in Figure 94 (Filter➡Noise➡Dust & Scratches).

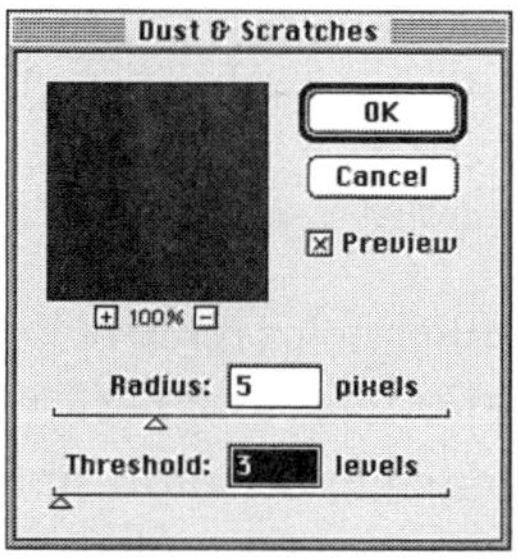

Figure 94

The Dust & Scratches dialog box.

5. Drag the Radius to 16.

   The Radius setting varies from 1-16. This parameter controls the distance from each pixel that the filter "looks" when calculating the result. A Radius of 16 blurs a very large area.

6. Set the Threshold to 0.

   The Threshold can vary from 0 to 255. This parameter controls how similar a value is needed before a pixel is considered in the calculation. A Threshold of 0 considers every pixel; as you increase the Threshold, you decrease the number of pixels to be filtered. By the time you reach a Threshold of 10, you have usually removed all of the nearby pixels and will see no change in your image.

7. Click OK. Figure 95 shows the result.

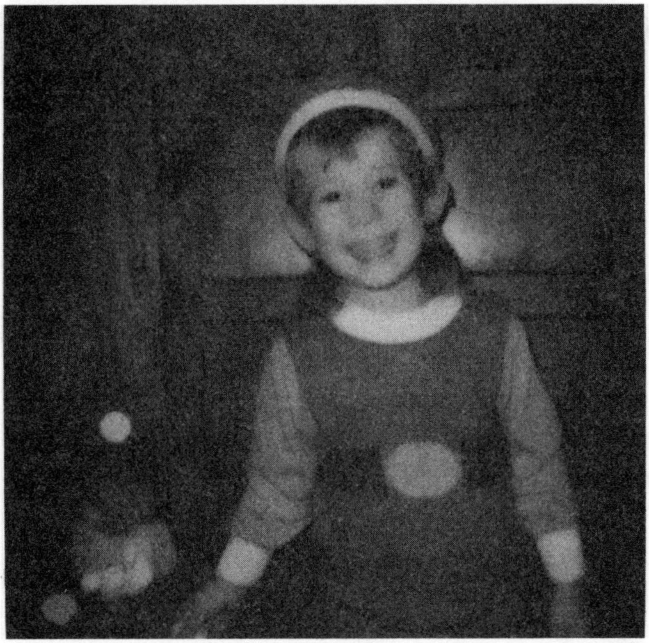

Figure 95

An example of the Dust & Scratches filter applied to a Background layer.

Filter type	Category	Supported Color Modes	Preview type	Data Dependent	Color Dependent
Parameter	PrePress and Special Effects/ Focus Filter	RGB, Grayscale, CMYK, Lab	Full Image Preview	Yes. A blank image produces a blank filtered image.	No. The Foreground/Background settings have no effect.

Median

One of the original Photoshop filters, the Median filter is the early prototype of the Watercolor filter. It selects the "average" or median color of a selection for the distance of the Radius. In that sense, the Median filter is very close to the Dust & Scratches filter (which made its debut in Photoshop 3.0), but it does not have as many controls, which is why Dust & Scratches is better for pre-press.

Try it:

1. Open the image "Elf.Psd." Duplicate the image (Image➡Duplicate➡OK).
2. Load Channel #5 (Option-Command-5)[Alt-Control-5]. This confines the filter to everywhere but the child's head.
3. Open the Median dialog box shown in Figure 96 (Filter➡Noise➡Median).

Figure 96

The Median dialog box.

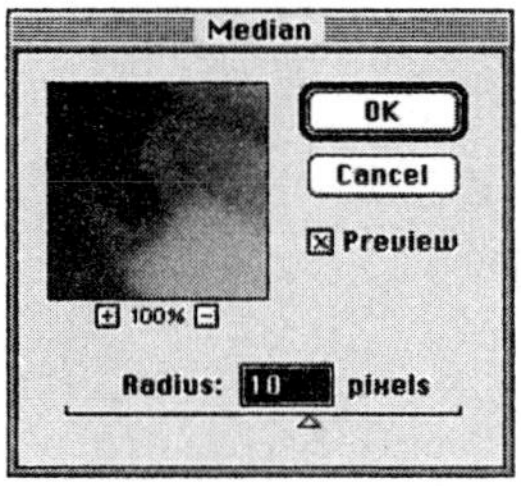

4. Drag the Radius to 10.

   The Radius setting varies from 1-16. This parameter controls the distance the filter looks from each pixel in order to calculate the result. A larger radius results in a blurrier image.

5. Click OK. Figure 97 shows the result.

Filter type	Category	Supported Color Modes	Preview type	Data Dependent	Color Dependent
Parameter	Special Effects/ Focus Filter	RGB, Grayscale CMYK, Lab	Full Image Preview	Yes. A blank image produces a blank filtered image.	No. The Foreground/Background settings have no effect.

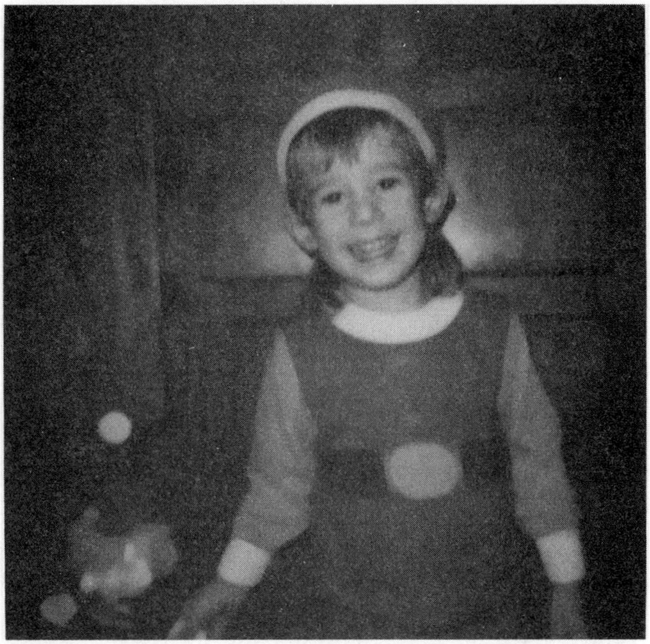

Figure 97

The Median filter applied to an image.

PHOTOSHOP'S NATIVE FILTERS—PIXELATE

The Pixelate filters work by breaking up the image into clumps of pixels—square blocks (Mosaic filter), irregular blocks (Crystallize), random dots (Mezzotint), and so on. They all stylize an image at low settings, and they can destroy the content of the image at higher settings.

Color Halftone

The Color Halftone filter changes your image into a poor quality newsprint color image. Why, you ask? This is basically a special effect. It has no value as a production tool. The Color Halftone filter makes images look like an old comic book strip, but you can select the size and angle of the halftone dots. My advice is to not change the default screen angles unless you really have a good reason to do so.

Try it:

1. Open the image "Cactus.Psd." Duplicate the image (Image➥Duplicate➥OK).
2. Open the Color Halftone dialog box shown in Figure 98 (Filter➥Pixilate➥Color Halftone).

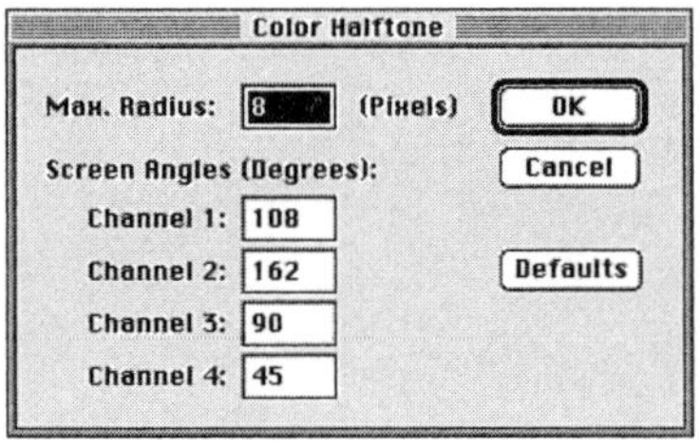

Figure 98

The Color Halftone dialog box.

3. Drag the Max Radius to 8.

   The Max Radius setting varies from 4-127. This parameter controls the size of the halftone dot. At 4, you get fine-grained poor quality newsprint; at 127, you obliterate your image totally.

4. Leave Channel #4's settings at their default. The values vary from 0 to 360 degrees. These represent the screen angles for each plate.
5. Click OK. Figure 99 shows the result.

Filter type	Category	Supported Color Modes	Preview type	Data Dependent	Color Dependent
Parameter	Sylizing/ special effects Filter	RGB, Grayscale CMYK, Lab	None	No. A blank image still produces a result.	No. The Fore-ground/Back-ground settings have no effect.

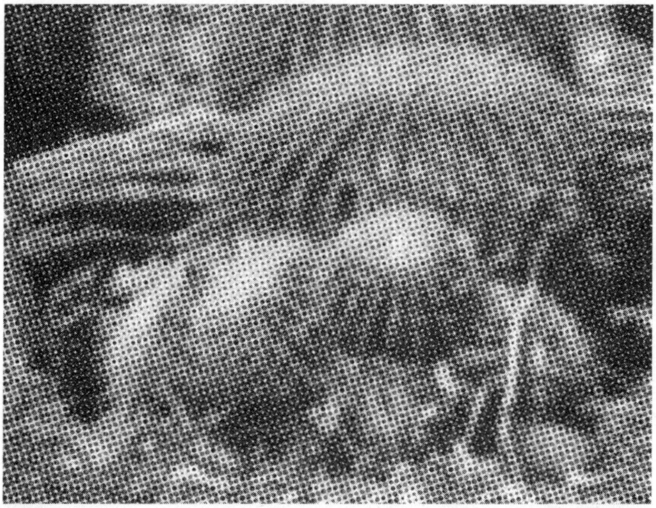

Figure 99

The Color Halftone filter applied.

Crystallize

The Crystallize filter changes your image into colored cells or honeycombs based on the image colors. This is a special effects filter that can leave your image looking very different. Crystallize is a very useful filter, however, for creating stylized versions of an image or for using in a channel and then using the channel as a mask for applying a different filter. The resulting shades of gray then vary the filter results in a seemingly random way.

Try it:

1. Open the image "Cactus.Psd." Duplicate the image (Image➡Duplicate➡OK).
2. Open the Crystallize dialog box shown in Figure 100 (Filter➡Pixilate➡Crystallize).
3. Drag the Cell Size to 40.

Figure 100

The Crystallize dialog box.

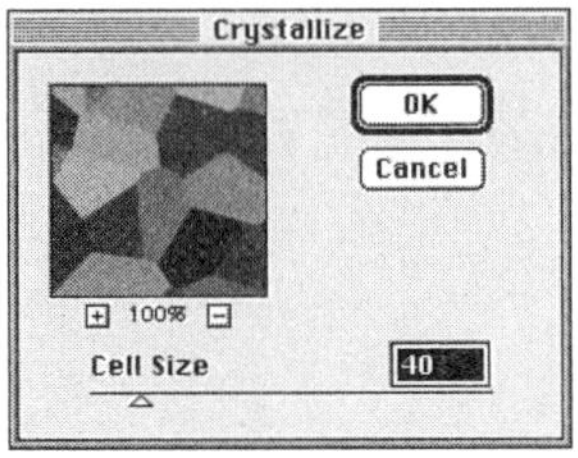

The Cell Size setting varies from 3-300, controlling the size of the crystal cells. If you want your image to be recognizable, you need to keep the size below about 10.

4. Click OK. Figure 101 shows the result.

Figure 101

An example of the Crystallize filter applied to an image.

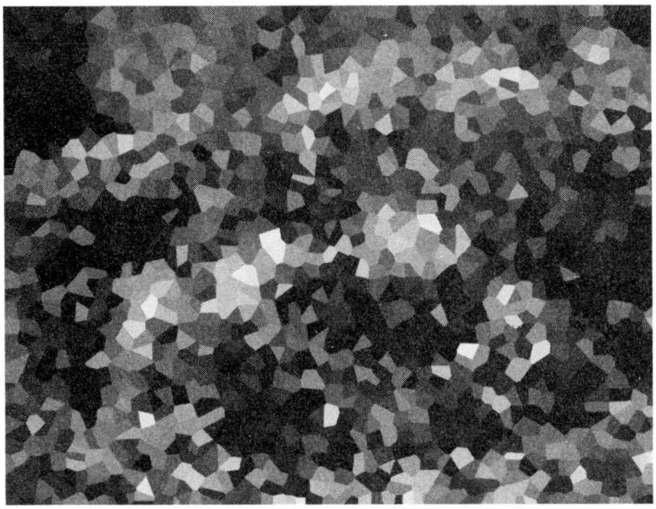

Filter type	Category	Supported Color Modes	Preview type	Data Dependent	Color Dependent
Parameter	Distressed Filter	RGB, Grayscale, CMYK, Lab	Small Filter Preview	Yes. A blank image produces a blank filtered image.	No. The Foreground/Background settings have no effect.

Facet

The Facet filter removes some of the anti-aliasing from the edges of an image. It is a One-Step filter that may need to be applied a number of times before you see a result. The Facet filter is a special effects filter.

Try it:

1. Open the image "Cactus.Psd." Duplicate the image (Image➡Duplicate➡OK).
2. Select the Facet filter (Filter➡Pixilate➡Facet). Figure 102 shows a close-up of the "before" image.

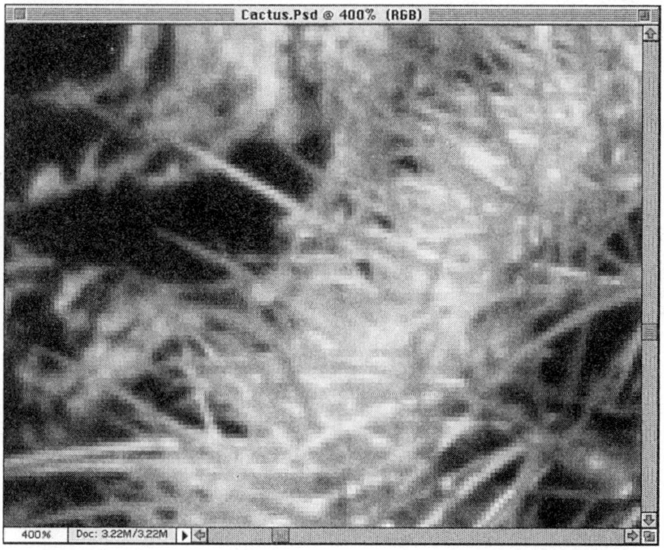

Figure 102

An image before the Facet filter is applied.

3. Figure 103 shows a close-up of the result.

Filter type	Category	Supported Color Modes	Preview type	Data Dependent	Color Dependent
One-Step	Stylizing Filter	RGB, Grayscale, CMYK, Lab	None	Yes. A blank image produces a blank filtered image.	No. The Foreground/Background settings have no effect.

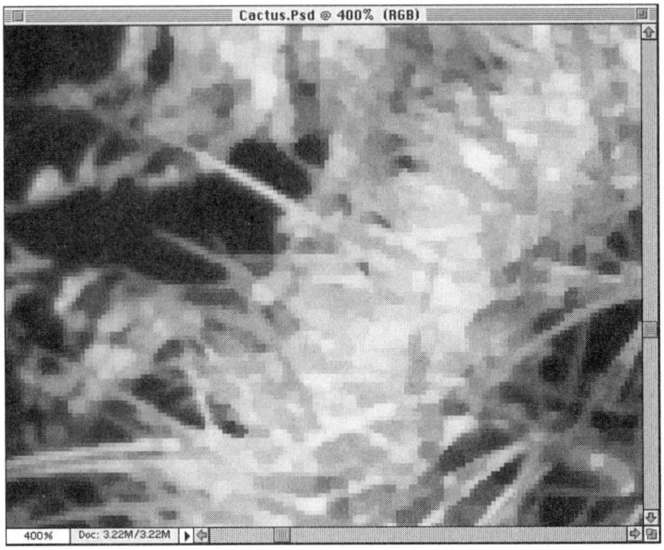

Figure 103

The image after the Facet filter is applied.

Fragment

The Fragment filter is a One-Step filter that makes your image look as if it has been in a 4.2 earthquake (just enough to look shaken, but not enough to get broken).

Try it:

1. Open the image "Cactus.Psd." Duplicate the image (Image➡Duplicate➡OK).
2. Select the Fragment filter (Filter➡Pixilate➡Fragment).
3. Click OK. Figure 104 shows the result.

Filter type	Category	Supported Color Modes	Preview type	Data Dependent	Color Dependent
One-Step	Stylizing Filter	RGB, Grayscale, CMYK, Lab	None	Yes. A blank image produces a blank filtered image.	No. The Foreground/Background settings have no effect.

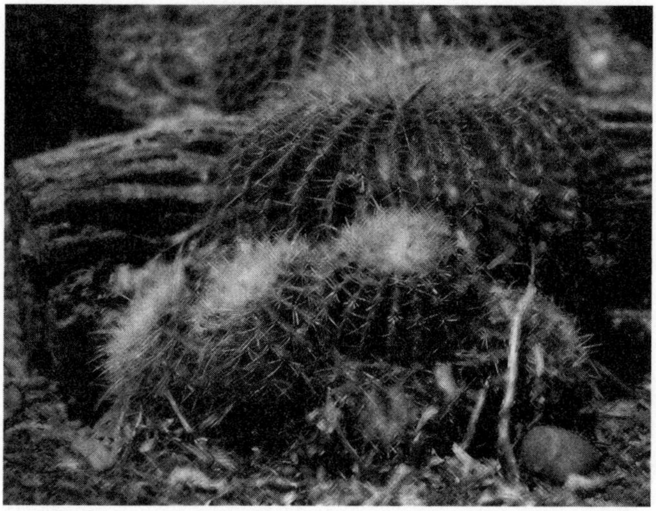

Figure 104

The Fragment filter applied.

Mezzotint

The Mezzotint filter is a very unsuccessful attempt to duplicate the traditional process of creating a mezzotint. I do not like this filter at any setting. It can be used for special effects work but produces much too coarse an image to use as a mezzotint. You get better results creating a grayscale mezzo by using the Diffusion Dither option on the Bitmap conversion. If you need a color mezzotint, break your file into the component channels (select Split Channels in the Channels palette—any layers will have to be merged or flattened first, if you wish to work with them). Change each channel to a bitmap and then back to grayscale mode, and re-combine them by selecting Merge Channels in the Channels palette.

Try it:

1. Open the image "Cactus.Psd." Duplicate the image (Image➡Duplicate➡OK).
2. Open the Mezzotint dialog box shown in Figure 105 (Filter➡Pixilate➡Mezzotint).

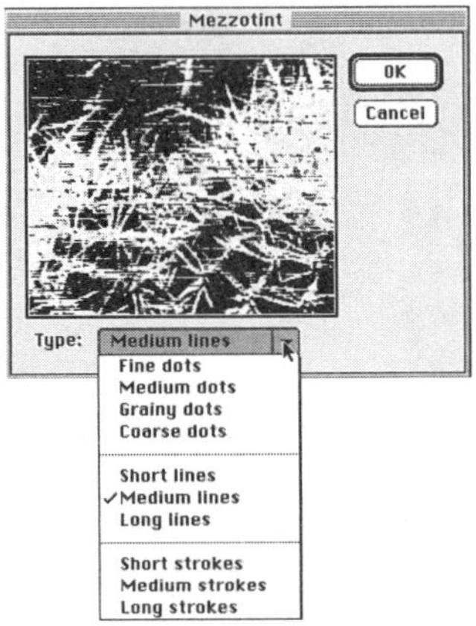

Figure 105

The Mezzotint dialog box.

3. Drag the pull-down menu to Medium Lines.

   This filter is really a One-Step filter with 10 filters combined. You can only control the method used. You can select from Dots: Fine, Medium, Grainy, or Coarse; Lines: Short, Medium, or Long; or Strokes: Short, Medium, or Long.

4. Click OK. Figure 106 shows the result.

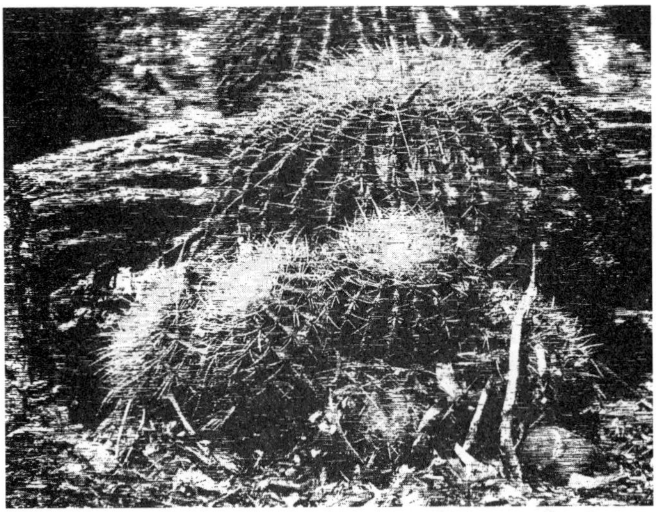

Figure 106

The Mezzotint filter applied.

Filter type	Category	Supported Color Modes	Preview type	Data Dependent	Color Dependent
Parameter	Stylizing/ Distressed Filter	RGB, Grayscale, CMYK, Lab	Small Filter Preview	No. A blank image produces an interesting texture.	No. The Foreground/Background settings have no effect.

Mosaic

The Mosaic filter changes your image into large pixels—solid blocks of color. It finds the average color in the size block that you select and uses that to create the blocks. The Mosaic filter produces a result that is an abstraction of the image. It is similar in action to the Crystallize filter, but it makes square blocks rather than polygonal cells. The Mosaic filter is very useful for simplifying an image or background.

Try it:

1. Open the image "Cactus.Psd." Duplicate the image (Image➡Duplicate➡OK).
2. Open the Mosaic dialog box shown in Figure 107 (Filter➡Pixilate➡Mosaic).

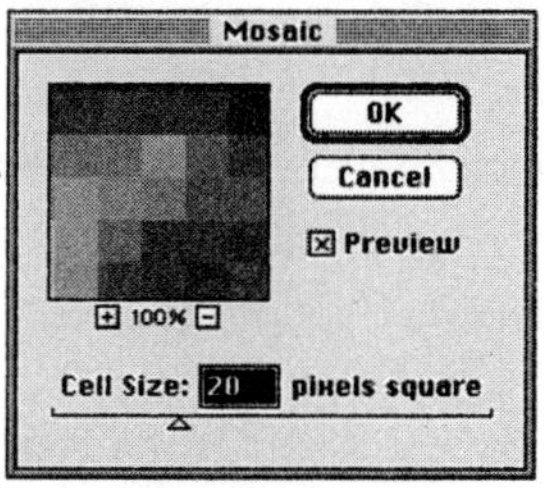

Figure 107

The Mosaic dialog box.

3. Drag the Cell Size to 24.

   The Cell Size setting varies from 2-64. This parameter controls the size of the blocks created.

4. Click OK. Figure 108 shows the result.

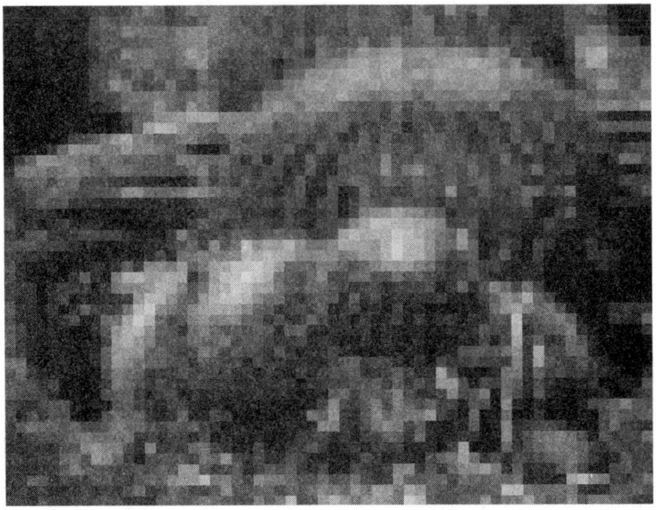

Figure 108

An example of the Mosaic filter applied.

Filter type	Category	Supported Color Modes	Preview type	Data Dependent	Color Dependent
Parameter	Stylizing/ Distressed Filter	RGB, Grayscale, CMYK, Lab	Full Image Preview	Yes. A blank image produces a blank filtered image.	No. The Foreground/Background settings have no effect.

Pointillize

The Pointillize filter changes your image into tiny dots—like a pointillist painting by Georges Seurat. This can create a lovely stylized effect. The Pointillize filter is a special effects filter, and can also be used for texture creation.

Try it:

1. Open the image "Cactus.Psd." Duplicate the image (Image➡Duplicate➡OK).

2. Select a brownish tone from the image as your background color. This is the color that will appear between the dots as the background.

3. Open the Pointillize dialog box shown in Figure 109 (Filter➡Pixilate➡Pointillize).

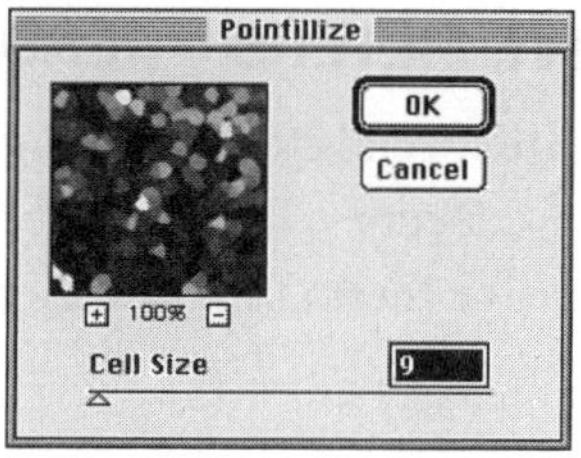

Figure 109

The Pointillize dialog box.

4. Drag the Cell Size to 9.

   The Cell Size setting varies from 3-300, controlling the size of the dots created. Sizes over about 15 (depending upon your original image size) make the original unrecognizable.

5. Click OK. Figure 110 shows the result.

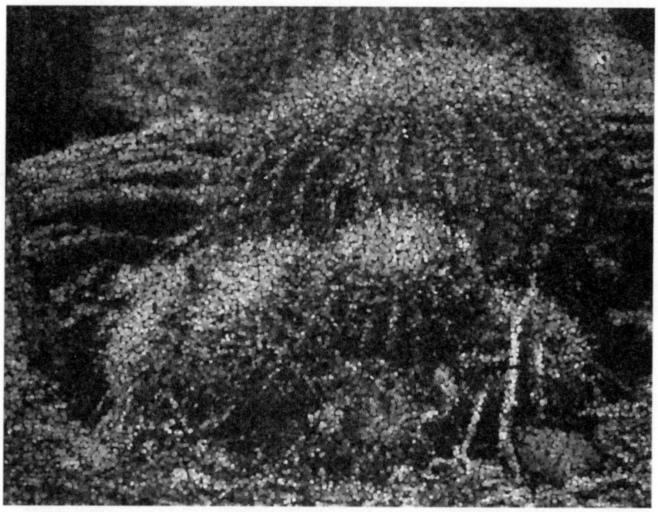

Figure 110

The Pointillize filter applied to an image.

Filter type	Category	Supported Color Modes	Preview type	Data Dependent	Color Dependent
Parameter	Stylizing/ Distressed Filter	RGB, Grayscale, CMYK, Lab	Full Image Preview	No. A blank image produces a very pretty dot pattern.	Yes. The Background color setting becomes the background color.

PHOTOSHOP'S NATIVE FILTERS—RENDER

The Render filters create special effects with light. They add clouds, lens flares, and lighting effects. The Render filters are the most computationally intensive filters in Photoshop.

Clouds

The Clouds filter is the only filter that works in a totally transparent, empty Layer. The filter replaces any image data that is present and does not take the image data into its calculations at all. You can use this filter to create cloudy environments such as skies, smoke, and haze. Your best technique is to apply the Clouds filter to an empty Layer and then composite it into the image.

Try it:

1. Open the image "Tulips.Psd." Duplicate the image (Image➡Duplicate➡OK).
2. Make a new layer (press the modifier key (Option)[Alt] and click the New Layer icon at the bottom of the Layers Palette).
3. Select white as your foreground color and pick a brown from the image as your background color.
4. Apply the Clouds filter (Filter➡Render➡Clouds).
5. Change the Blending mode to Darken. Figure 111 shows the result.

Figure 111

The Clouds filter applied.

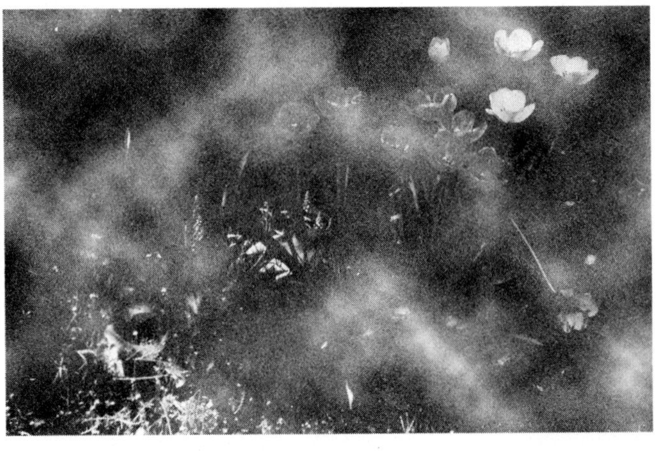

Filter type	Category	Supported Color Modes	Preview type	Data Dependent	Color Dependent
One-Step	Destuctive Filter	RGB, Grayscale	None	No. You can use an empty layer.	Yes. The Foreground/Background settings become the cloud colors.

Difference Clouds

The Difference Clouds filter takes the Clouds filter and uses the foreground and background colors to apply a Difference calculation to the existing image. As the filter creates the clouds, instead of seeing their color, you see the difference between the cloud color and pixel in the image. This can produce startlingly beautiful results, but the Difference Clouds filter is only a special effects filter.

Note

This filter does not work with Lab mode images.

Try it:

1. Open the image "Tulips.Psd." Duplicate the image (Image➥Duplicate➥OK).
2. Pick a yellow and purple from the image as your foreground and background colors.
3. Apply the Difference Clouds filter (Filter➥Render➥Difference Clouds). Figure 112 shows the result.

Filter type	Category	Supported Color Modes	Preview type	Data Dependent	Color Dependent
One-Step	Stylizing/ Special Effects Filter	RGB, Grayscale, CMYK	None	No. A Blank image still let the Difference calculations appear.	Yes. The Foreground/Background settings have a major effect.

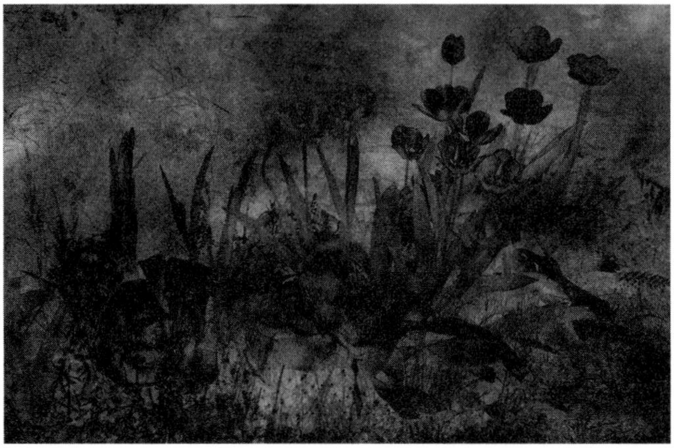

Figure 112

The Difference Clouds filter applied.

Lens Flare

The Lens Flare filter simulates the effect of the sun hitting a camera lens as the picture is taken. It is the kind of "real effect" that you'd probably toss out a negative for, but in the digital world, you actually create it deliberately. Truthfully, the Lens Flare filter is a neat effect. You can keep the effect fluid by applying in a Layer that is filled only with neutral gray and a Blending mode of Overlay, or Soft or Hard Light. That way you can control how it composites with the rest of your image.

Try it:

1. Open the image "Tulips.Psd." Duplicate the image (Image➡Duplicate➡OK).
2. Make a new layer: press the modifier key (Option)[Alt] and click the New Layer icon at the bottom of the Layers Palette. In the Options dialog box, select Hard Light mode and Fill with Hard Light—Neutral Color (50% Gray).
3. Open the Lens Flare dialog box shown in Figure 113 (Filter➡Render➡Lens Flare).
4. Drag the Brightness to 1

   The Brightness setting varies from 0-300%. This parameter controls the intensity of the effect. If the setting gets too high, all you see is a flash of white light.

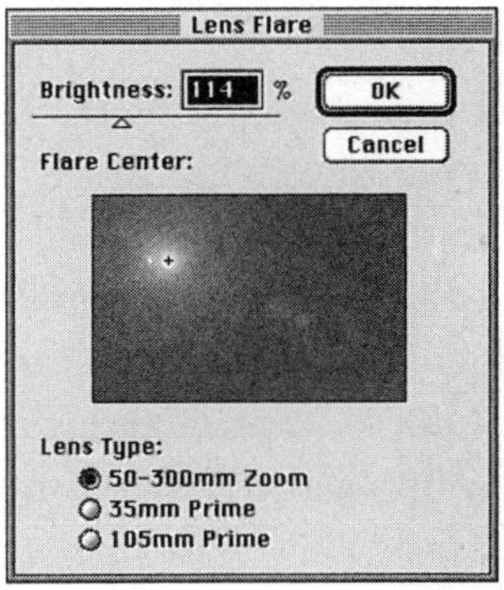

Figure 113

The Lens Flare dialog box.

5. Set the Style to 50-300mm Zoom.

   Your other choices are 35mm Prime and 105mm Prime.

6. Click OK. Figure 114 shows the result.

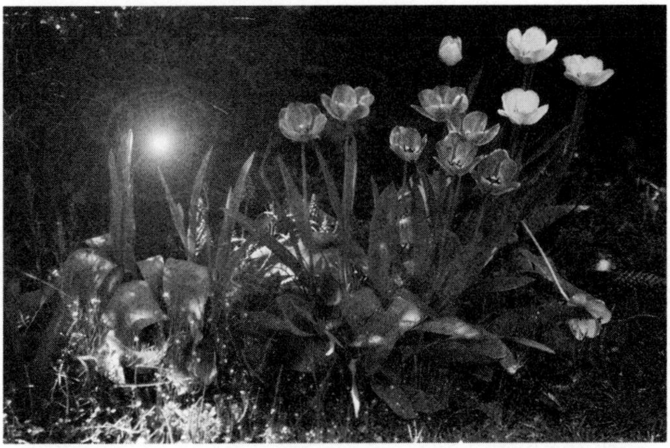

Figure 114

The Lens Flare filter applied to an image.

Filter type	Category	Supported Color Modes	Preview type	Data Dependent	Color Dependent
Parameter	Special Effects Filter	RGB only	Small Filter Preview	No	No. The Foreground/Background settings have no effect.

Lighting Effects

The Lighting Effects filter is, along with the Wave filter, the most complicated filter in Photoshop's native set. This filter enables you to change the lighting in the image and to add texture and embossing effects. The Lighting Effects filter can simulate the effects of a light source or multiple light sources on the colors in your image. It can be used as a production filter to correct lighting or to correct images being composed so that they fit together better. You can also use this filter to emboss text into your image. Of course, it is also useful for wild special effects. Photoshop comes with a large number of lighting styles built-in, and you can save and load your own as well. This is the closest native filter to a mini-application within the program.

Try it:

1. Open the image "Tulips.Psd." Duplicate the image (Image➡Duplicate➡OK).
2. Open the Lighting Effects dialog box shown in Figure 115 (Filter➡Render➡Lighting Effects).

Figure 115

The Lighting Effects dialog box.

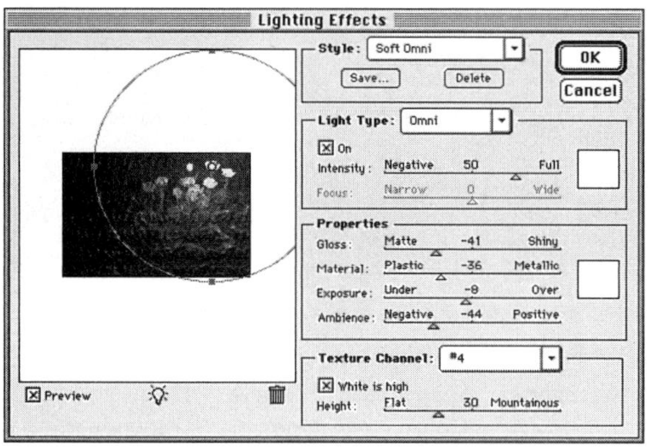

3. Set the Style to Soft Omni.

   There are many styles from which to choose. Preview a few before selecting the Soft Omni style.

4. Move the Omni light on the preview box so that the center of the light is on top of the middle yellow tulip in the top right.

You can move the light by clicking its center and dragging it. Stretch the light by clicking and dragging the small box on top of it until it touches the top of the preview area.

5. Finally, Select Channel #4 as your texture channel and check the "White is High" box. Move the Height slider to 30.

   By checking "White is High," you tell the Lighting Effects filter to use the lightest values in Channel #4 as a bump map to give the image the optical illusion of height or embossing. The darkest areas of the channel become the "low points" in the filtered image.

6. Click OK. Figure 116 shows the result. Notice how the text was embossed into the image.

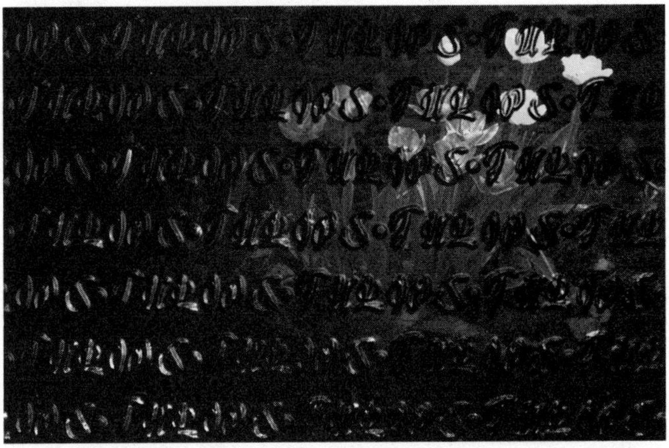

Figure 116

An example of the Lighting Effects filter applied.

Filter type	Category	Supported Color Modes	Preview type	Data Dependent	Color Dependent
Mini-app	Color Change/ 3D Filter	RGB only	Small Filter Preview	No. A blank image can still be lit.	No. The Fore-ground/Back-ground settings have no effect.

Texture Fill

The Texture Fill filter is a "helper" filter for the Lighting Effects filter. It opens a grayscale image (and *only* grayscale) saved in Photoshop format, uses that file as a pattern, and fills your image with it. The Texture Fill filter is designed to be used on a channel, which then becomes a texture channel for the Lighting Effects filter.

Try it:

1. Open the image "Tulips.Psd." Duplicate the image (Image➡Duplicate➡OK).
2. Click the New Channel icon in the center of the Channels palette to create a new channel (Channel #5).
3. Select the Texture Fill filter (Filter➡Render➡Texture Fill) and choose the image Texure.Psd as the fill pattern. Figure 117 shows this image.

Figure 117

The Texture Fill "source" pattern.

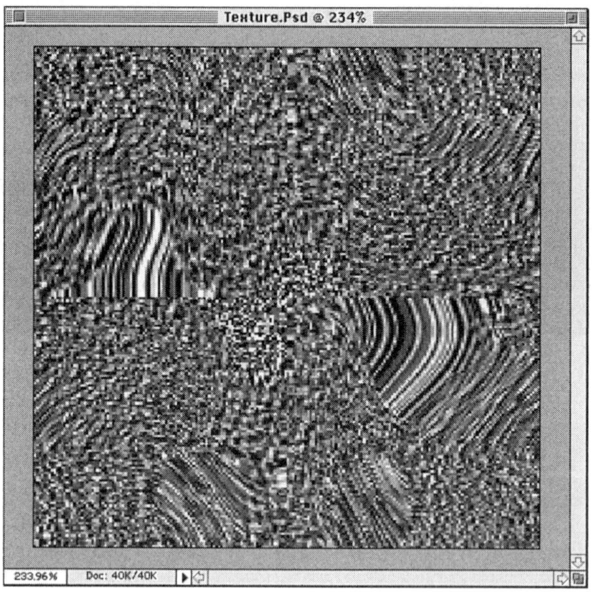

4. Apply the Lighting Effects filter to the RGB channel (Filter➡Render➡Lighting Effects). Select the Five Lights Down style.
5. Click OK. Figure 118 shows the result.

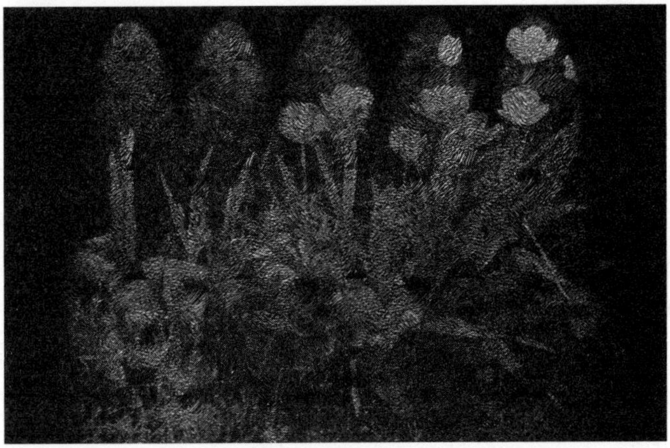

Figure 118

The Texture Fill filter applied.

Filter type	Category	Supported Color Modes	Preview type	Data Dependent	Color Dependent
Parameter	Destructive Filter	RGB, Grayscale, CMYK, Lab	None	No	No. The Fore-ground/Back-ground settings have no effect.

PHOTOSHOP'S NATIVE FILTERS—SHARPEN

The Sharpen filters are production-oriented filters that help enhance the focus of the image to improve its quality and to help prepare it for the slight loss of focus (softening) that occurs when it is half-toned prior to printing. The only filter you really need to use is the Unsharp Mask filter, however.

Sharpen

The Sharpen filter is a One-Step filter that applies a tiny bit of sharpening. The amount is so slight that it is not always visible to the eye.

Try it:

1. Open the image "Tulip.Psd." Duplicate the image (Image➡Duplicate➡OK).
2. Apply the Sharpen filter. (Filter➡Sharpen➡Sharpen).

Filter type	Category	Supported Color Modes	Preview type	Data Dependent	Color Dependent
One-Step	Focus	RGB, Grayscale, CMYK, Lab	None	Yes. A blank image produces a blank filtered image.	No. The Foreground/Background settings have no effect.

Sharpen More

The Sharpen More filter is a little bit stronger than the Sharpen filter—but not much.

Try it:

1. Open the image "Tulip.Psd." Duplicate the image (Image➥Duplicate➥OK).
2. Apply the Sharpen More filter (Filter➥Sharpen➥Sharpen More).

Filter type	Category	Supported Color Modes	Preview type	Data Dependent	Color Dependent
One-Step	Focus Filter	RGB, Grayscale, CMYK, Lab	None	Yes. A blank image produces a blank filtered image.	No. The Foreground/Background settings have no effect.

Sharpen Edges

The Sharpen Edges filter is another basically useless filter in the Sharpen category. It, too, is a One-Step filter and is also almost invisible unless you home in on the individual pixels.

Try it:

1. Open the image "Tulip.Psd." Duplicate the image (Image➥Duplicate➥OK).
2. Apply the Sharpen Edges filter (Filter➥Sharpen➥Sharpen Edges).

Filter type	Category	Supported Color Modes	Preview type	Data Dependent	Color Dependent
One-Step	Focus Filter	RGB, Grayscale, CMYK, Lab	None	Yes. A blank image produces a blank filtered image.	No. The Foreground/Background settings have no effect.

Unsharp Mask

The Unsharp Mask filter is the most significant pre-press filter in the native filter set. This production filter is used to replace the focus that an image has lost when it is scanned and to sharpen the image prior to half-toning. Most images require two "rounds" of sharpening. One, just after the image is scanned (or during the scanning process) to restore lost focus, and the other, as the last step in the color-correction process prior to conversion to CMYK mode. The amount applied in this last sharpening step depends upon the final image use. An image that is going to be halftoned can stand significantly more sharpening than an image that is destined for a film recorder. Because blurring is *not* the inverse of sharpening, it is important not to over-sharpen an image because you cannot get it back to where it was. The correct use of the Unsharp Mask filter could almost occupy an entire chapter on its own. I will give you only some general guidelines here.

Try it:

1. Open the image "Tulip.Psd." Duplicate the image (Image➥Duplicate➥OK).
2. Open the Unsharp Mask dialog box shown in Figure 119 (Filter➥Sharpen➥Unsharp Mask).
3. Drag the Amount to 136.

   The Amount setting varies from 1-500. This parameter controls how much sharpening is applied. The Rule of thumb is to drag this parameter up to 500 and then cut back (generally a lot!). When you see a sharp halo on the screen, you are probably over-sharpening the image.

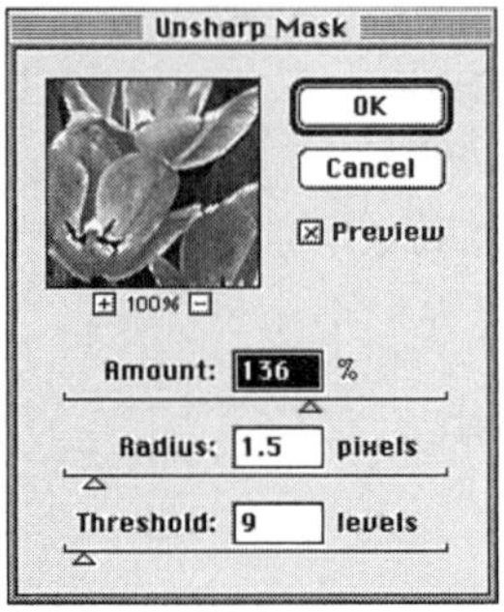

Figure 119

The Unsharp Mask dialog box.

4. Set the Radius to 1.5.

   The Radius can vary from .1 to 250. A good starting value is to divide your resolution by 200 (300 dpi /200 = 1.5). The Radius and Amount are seesaw controls: you can vary them, but to keep the same general degree of sharpening, as one goes up, you need to bring the other down. The Radius determine how far from each pixel the effect is applied.

5. Finally, set the Threshold to 9.

   The Threshold varies from 0-255, working with levels (values) of the pixels. Threshold determines how different a pixel can be from the pixel being filtered, in order to include it in the filtering process. At a Threshold of 0, everything is included. As the Threshold increases, a pixel has to be very similar in value in order to be sharpened. Because the sharpening works by emphasizing the *edges* found in an image (an edge is an area where the colors change) and making more of a color difference at those edges, you will see much less sharpening on an image with a high Threshold. You should, generally, set the Threshold to at least 5 or so to keep from sharpening noise in the image.

6. Click OK. Figure 120 shows the result.

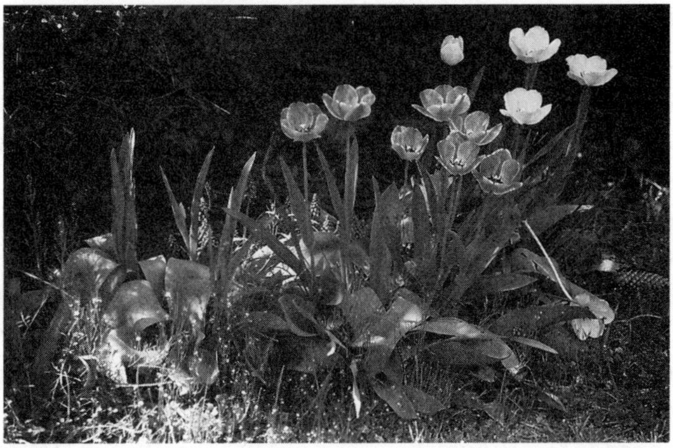

Figure 120

The Unsharp Mask filter applied.

Filter type	Category	Supported Color Modes	Preview type	Data Dependent	Color Dependent
Parameter	Production Filter	RGB, Grayscale, CMYK, Lab	Full Image Preview	Yes. A blank image has nothing to sharpen.	No. The Foreground/Background settings have no effect.

PHOTOSHOP'S NATIVE FILTERS—SKETCH

The Sketch filters are all taken from the Adobe Gallery Effects set of filters. They represent a variety of artistic styles resembling hand-drawing an image using limited color palettes. In most cases, the foreground and background colors you set in the Toolbox become the main colors in the image. These filters tend to simplify the shapes in the image, and, as such, are helpful in constructing gross masks for your image. The Sketch filters typically use the logic of either the Find Edges or the Threshold commands in order to work. They only are applicable to RGB or grayscale images.

Bas Relief

The Bas Relief filter helps simplify complex images and helps enhance a simple line art graphic. This filter looks good when used on text and is a lovely filter if you select the right colors for the image. The Bas Relief filter creates a relief of the image—almost as if it is embossing the shapes within it. It uses the Foreground color for the highlights and the Background color for the shadows. So picking colors too strong or of unnatural values for the lights and darks results in a confusing image. The Bas Relief filter can produce good results at either end of the scale, but the settings that I really like use the lowest values of smoothness. The settings in the example create an image that looks like it has been cast in sand. You should, however, also try changing the Detail control to the lowest value instead of the highest. There is a lot of artifacting, but the effect is wonderful.

Try it:

1. Open the image "Clown.Psd." Duplicate the image (Image➡Duplicate➡OK).
2. Pick a yellow from the image as a foreground color and red from the image as a background color.
3. Open the Bas Relief dialog box shown in Figure 121 (Filter➡Sketch➡Bas Relief).

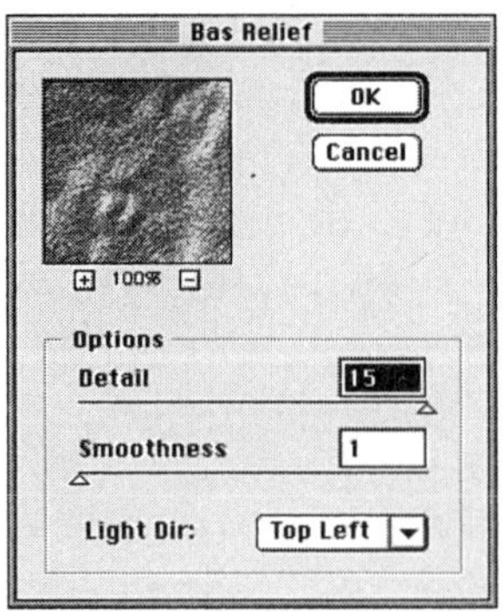

Figure 121

The Bas Relief dialog box.

4. Drag the Detail to 15.

The Detail setting varies from 1-15. This parameter controls the amount of detail and works at just about any setting—especially at either end of the scale.

5. Set the Smoothness to 1.

   The Smoothness can vary from 1-15. This setting looks best towards the lower end as it begins to remove too much detail—regardless of detail setting as it becomes very smooth.

6. Finally, set the Light Direction to Top Left.

   The Light Direction can be set from the Bottom, Bottom Left, Left, Top Left, Top, Top Right, Right, or Bottom Right.

7. Click OK. Figure 122 shows the result.

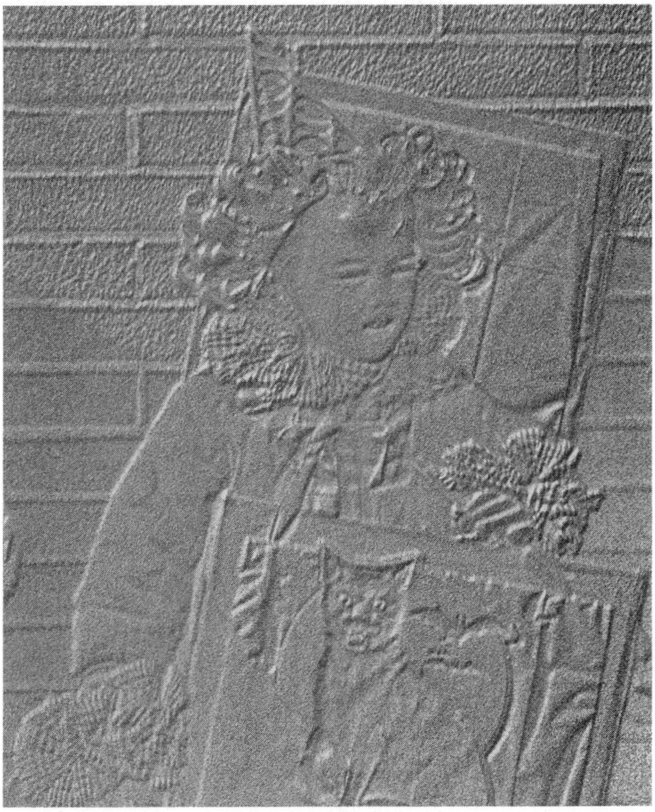

Figure 122

An example of the Bas Relief filter applied.

Filter type	Category	Supported Color Modes	Preview type	Data Dependent	Color Dependent
Parameter	Texture/ 3D Filter	RGB, Grayscale	Small Filter Preview	No. A blank image produces a gradient.	Yes. The Fore-ground/Back-ground are the only colors used.

Charcoal

4.0

The Charcoal filter simulates the look of charcoal on paper. Using black and white, you can get a very convincing sketch at the right settings. This filter can help simplify complex images. It renders the areas of greatest contrast—unlike the "edge finding" filters in the Brush Strokes category. The Charcoal filter is one of the best of the stylizing/sketching filters.

Try it:

1. Open the image "Clown.Psd." Duplicate the image (Image➡Duplicate➡OK).
2. Press D to set the colors back to the default of black and white.
3. Open the Charcoal dialog box shown in Figure 123 (Filter➡Sketch➡Charcoal).

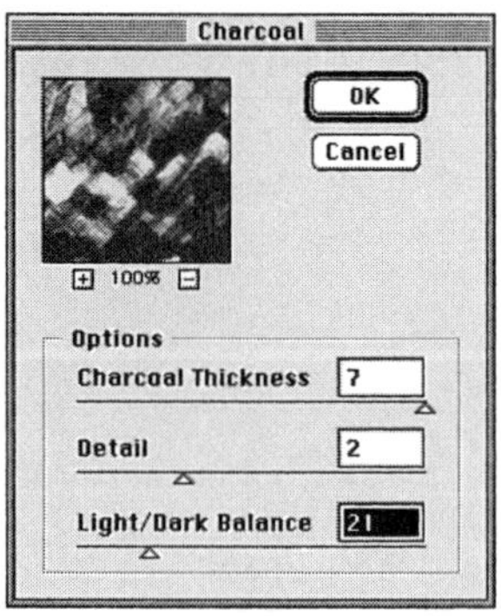

Figure 123

The Charcoal dialog box.

4. Set the Charcoal Thickness to 7.

The Charcoal Thickness can vary from 1-7. This setting works at all values along the scale. It varies from a light look at 1 to a bold statement at 7.

5. Set the Detail to 2.

   The Detail varies from 0-5. A Detail of 0 is attractive with a Charcoal Thickness of 7, but if all three settings are dragged to the left, you get a solid background-colored image. Detail usually looks good at the higher settings.

6. Drag the Light/Dark Balance to 21.

   The Light/Dark Balance setting varies from 0-100. This parameter controls the proportion of foreground to background color.

7. Click OK. Figure 124 shows the result.

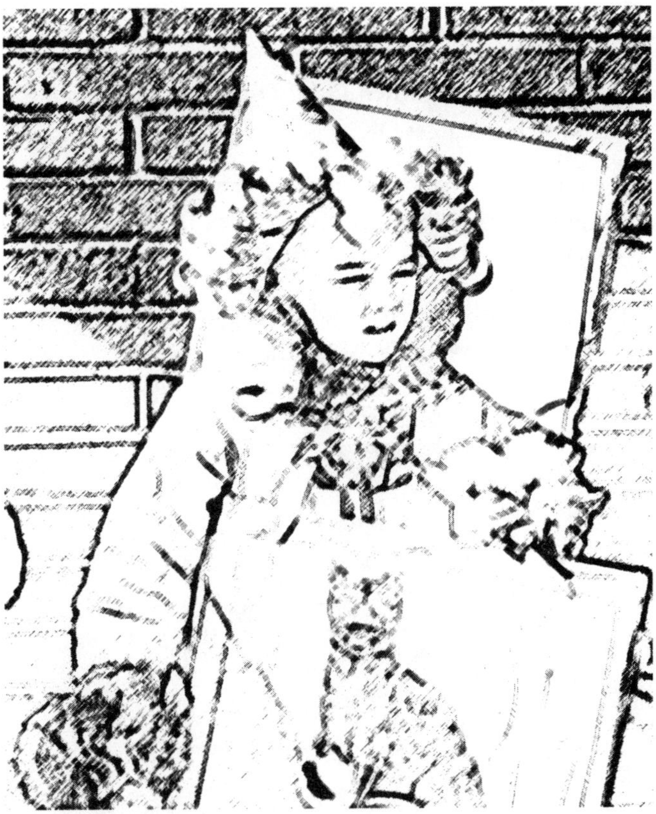

Figure 124

The Charcoal filter applied to an image.

Filter type	Category	Supported Color Modes	Preview type	Data Dependent	Color Dependent
Parameter	Stylizing Filter	RGB, Grayscale	Small Filter Preview	Yes. A blank image produces a background-colored image.	Yes. The Foreground/Background settings are the only colors in the effect.

Chalk & Charcoal

The Chalk & Charcoal filter shows the effect of drawing with both chalk and charcoal. The Chalk uses the background color and the Charcoal uses the foreground color. This filter looks for areas of contrast in the image. You can set the chalk and the charcoal intensities separately. Once again, the choice of colors helps the success of the Chalk & Charcoal filter, black and white being two of the better colors.

Try it:

1. Open the image "Clown.Psd." Duplicate the image (Image➡Duplicate➡OK).
2. Select a Yellow for the Foreground color and a Red for the background (or whichever two colors from the image you prefer).
3. Open the Chalk & Charcoal dialog box shown in Figure 125 (Filter➡Sketch➡Chalk & Charcoal).

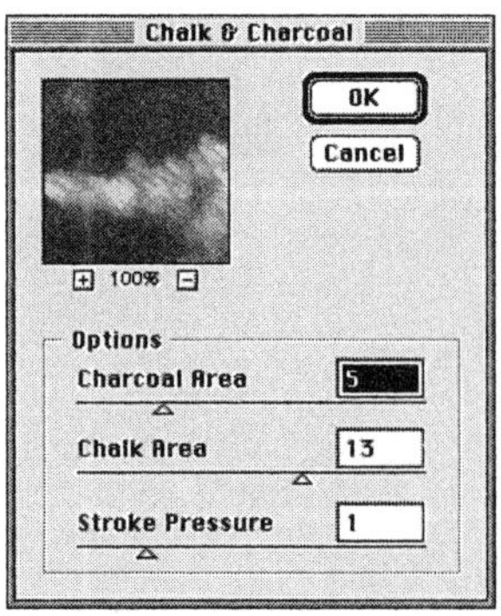

Figure 125

The Chalk & Charcoal dialog box.

4. Drag the Charcoal Area to 5.

   The Charcoal Area setting varies from 0-20. This parameter controls the darkness of the chalk setting. Areas not colored appear in gray.

5. Set the Chalk Area to 13.

   The Chalk Area can vary from 0-20, controlling the darkness of the chalk setting. Areas not colored appear in gray. Even at the lowest settings, you see some chalk and charcoal.

6. Finally, set the Stroke Pressure to 1.

   The Stroke Pressure varies from 0-5. The intensity builds up very fast in this filter. You may find that settings above 1 produce a solid color.

7. Click OK. Figure 126 shows the result.

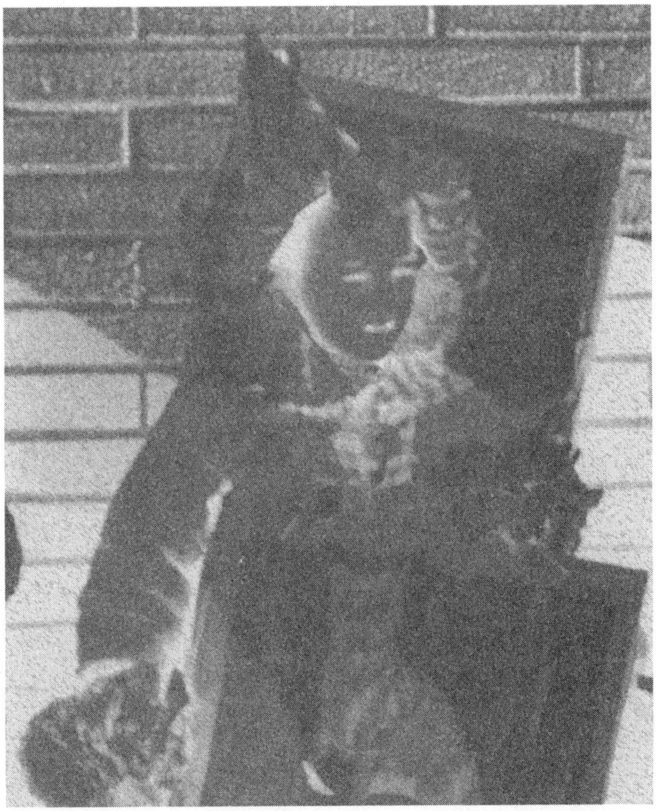

Figure 126

The Chalk & Charcoal filter applied to an image.

Filter type	Category	Supported Color Modes	Preview type	Data Dependent	Color Dependent
Parameter	Stylizing Filter	RGB, Grayscale,	Small Filter Preview	Yes. A blank image produces a gray filtered image.	Yes. The Foreground/Background settings produce the effect.

Chrome

4.0

The Chrome filter can help enhance a simple line art graphic and looks good when used on text. It changes the image into a grayscale image that looks as if it is reflecting light—as chrome does. The image, however, becomes almost unrecognizable at any setting. The best way to control this filter is to use it under an image (the original or another reflected image) that is placed in Color mode.

Try it:

1. Open the image "Clown.Psd." Duplicate the image (Image➡Duplicate➡OK).
2. Drag the icon for the Background layer to the New Layer icon (the center icon at the bottom of the Layers palette).
3. Turn the Eye icon off for Layer 1 and click the Background name in the Layers palette to select it.
4. Open the Chrome dialog box shown in Figure 127 (Filter➡Sketch➡Chrome).

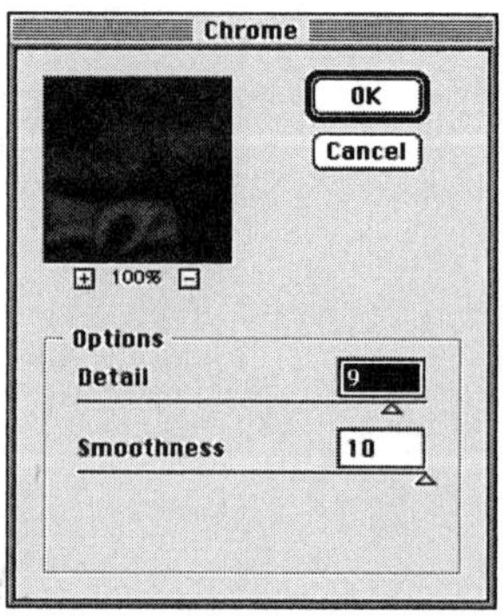

Figure 127

The Chrome dialog box.

5. Drag the Detail to 9.

   The Detail setting varies from 0-10, controlling the number of reflective edges found.

6. Set the Smoothness to 10.

   The Smoothness can vary from 0-10. This controls the smoothness of the edges—a higher smoothness setting also sees fewer edges. Click OK.

7. Select Layer 1 in the Layers palette and change its Blending mode to Color. Drag the Opacity setting to around 80%. Figure 128 shows the result.

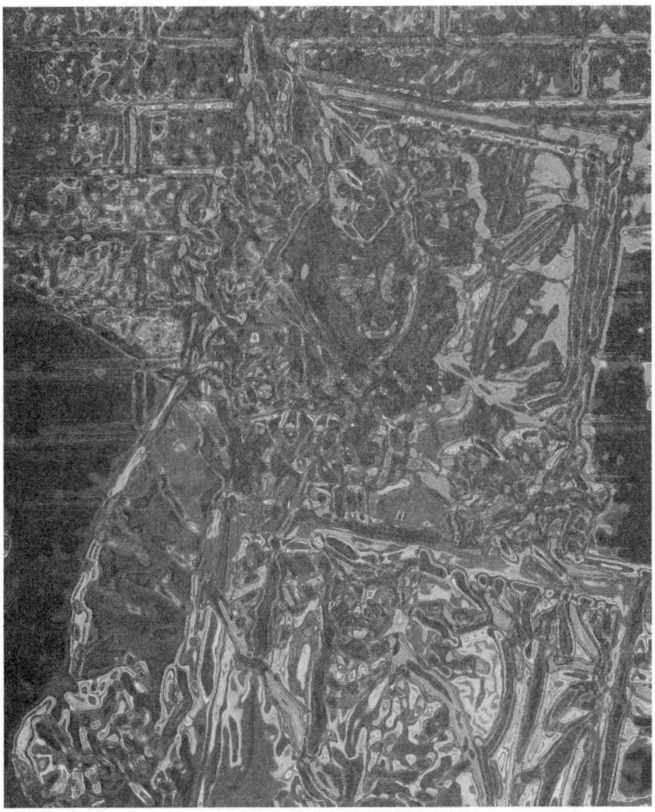

Figure 128

The Chrome filter applied.

Filter type	Category	Supported Color Modes	Preview type	Data Dependent	Color Dependent
Parameter	3D/ Distressed Filter	RGB, Grayscale,	Small Filter Preview	Yes. A blank image is changed to a solid gray.	No. The Foreground/Background settings have no effect.

Conté Crayon

The Conté Crayon filter can help simplify complex images when it is run with no texture. It looks best when done in black and white or with tones of gray because it always uses a mid-gray for the mixture of colors—regardless of the other two colors you select. In black and white, this is a very attractive filter. The Conté Crayon filter is a good choice for Web graphics as well, as the image easily reduces to about six colors. This filter works best on images that have areas of contrast—definite lights and darks. On a muddy image, it cannot locate enough "different" areas to give interest to the image.

Try it:

1. Open the image "Clown.Psd." Duplicate the image (Image➡Duplicate➡OK). Press D to set the colors back to the default of black and white.
2. Open the Conté Crayon dialog box shown in Figure 129 (Filter➡Sketch➡Conté Crayon).
3. Drag the Foreground Level to 8.

   The Foreground Level setting varies from 1-15. This parameter controls the intensity of the foreground color in the image. At low settings, you see gray and a fair amount of whatever texture you have selected. At the higher settings, you see almost no texture in the foreground color, but very little gray as well.
4. Set the Background Level to 8.

   The Background Level can vary from 1-15. The low setting produces a background-colored area with very little texture and a mixture of gray. At the highest setting, you see mostly background color with a lot of texture if the foreground setting is also high. You see somewhat less texture if the Foreground Level is set low.

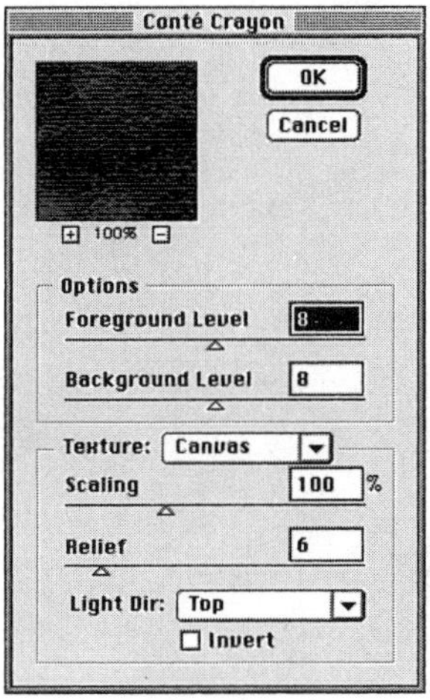

Figure 129

The Conté Crayon dialog box.

5. There are a number of settings that concern the texture to be applied. Set the Texture to Canvas.

   The Textures included are Brick, Burlap, Canvas, and Sandstone, but you can load your own texture from a Photoshop file.

6. Set the Scaling to 100%.

   Textures can be scaled from 50-200%.

7. Set the Relief to 6.

   You can set Relief to values of 0-50. At settings well past 10, all you see is the texture—you have wiped away the image detail.

8. Click OK. Figure 130 shows the result.

Figure 130

An example of the Conté Crayon filter applied to an image.

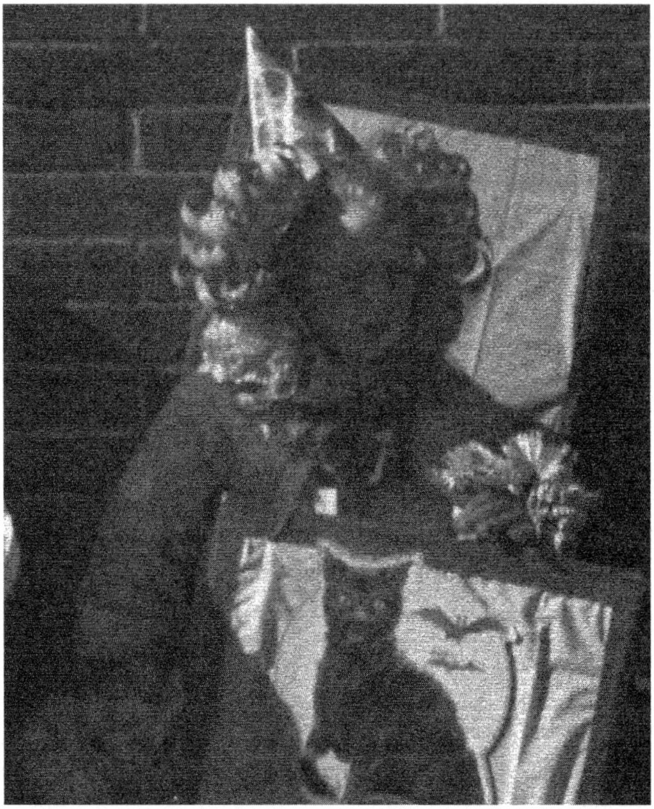

Filter type	Category	Supported Color Modes	Preview type	Data Dependent	Color Dependent
Parameter	Stylizing/ Texture Filter	RGB, Grayscale	Small Filter Preview	No. This filter adds texture to a blank image.	Yes. The Fore-ground/Back-ground settings are the colors used for this effect.

Graphic Pen

4.0

The Graphic Pen filter can help simplify complex images. This filter looks good when used on text. It does its best on an image that has a good range of lights and darks and is large enough to tolerate being "scratched over." The Graphic Pen filter renders a photograph as if it were a sketch drawn with ink in long strokes (or short dots, depending upon the setting). The filter uses only two colors with no in-between shades generated. If you like the look of Conté crayon but want to use colors other than black and white, this filter may be better for you than the Conté Crayon filter. It is not as suitable, however, for Web work, even though it uses fewer colors: unless your image is very simple and very contrasty, at small sizes, the filter loses all detail. On a large image destined for 150 lpi printing, the Graphic Pen filter is wonderful. The optical illusion of the lines will show up as a marvelous black and white bitmap. It does a very good job of preparing an image for bitmapped printing as either a type of mezzotint or as an alternative method of screening.

Try it:

1. Open the image "Clown.Psd." Duplicate the image (Image➡Duplicate➡OK).
2. Open the Graphic Pen dialog box shown in Figure 131 (Filter➡Sketch➡Graphic Pen).

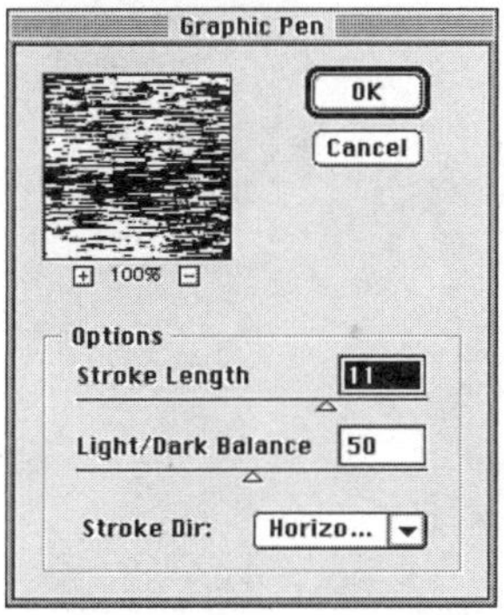

Figure 131

The Graphic Pen dialog box.

3. Drag the Stroke Length to 11.

   The Stroke Length setting varies from 1-15, controlling the length of the stroke. At tiny sizes, you see dots instead of lines.

4. Set the Light/Dark Balance to 50.

   The Light/Dark Balance can vary from 0-100. At either end of the scale, you get a blank image in either the foreground or background color—not very useful. Keep the balance towards the mid-range. At 50%, you get the best all-over detail.

5. Finally, set the Stroke Direction to Horizontal.

   The Stroke Direction can be Right Diagonal, Horizontal, Left Diagonal, or Vertical. This is one of the few filters that lets you stroke horizontally or vertically.

6. Click OK. Figure 132 shows the result.

Figure 132

The Graphic Pen filter applied to an image.

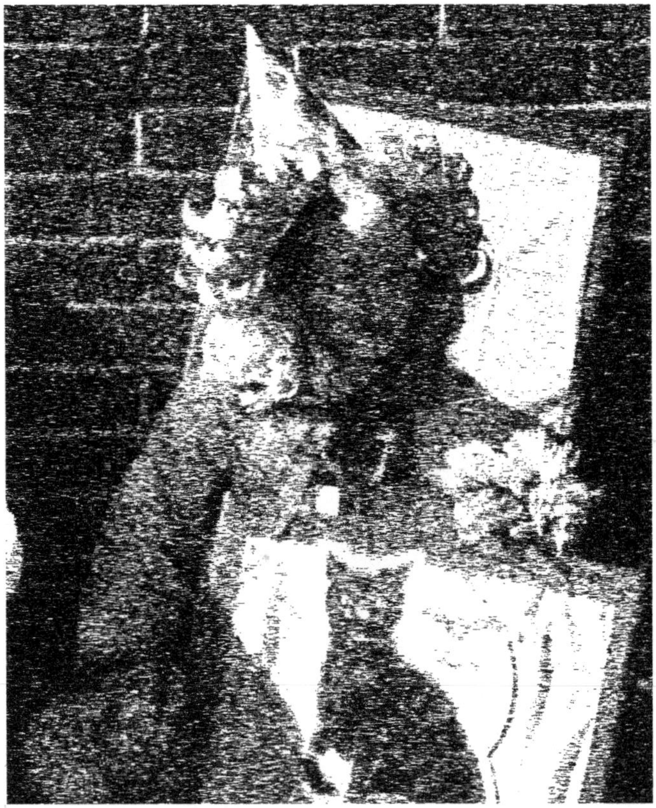

Filter type	Category	Supported Color Modes	Preview type	Data Dependent	Color Dependent
Parameter	Stylizing Filter	RGB, Grayscale	Small Filter Preview	No. This filter adds texture to a blank image.	No. The Foreground/Background settings are the effect colors.

Halftone Pattern

The Halftone Pattern filter is a wonderful use of halftoning that offers significant differences from the standard bitmap conversion halftoning. You can apply a halftone pattern *over* an image—without converting the image to bitmap. This lets you retain areas of gray and still get a definite pattern. The Circle Pattern type is completely different for other halftoning algorithms as it halftones by drawing a concentric circle over the image. At large pattern sizes, this filter makes a major graphic statement. It can tolerate being viewed at a distance (or at high resolution) where the optical illusion gets full room to be appreciated. The Halftone Pattern filter really does create a bi-level image if the contrast is set at the maximum. If you select colors other than black and white, make the darker color your foreground color unless you wish the halftone to look like a negative.

Try it:

1. Open the image "Clown.Psd." Duplicate the image (Image➡Duplicate➡OK).
2. Open the Halftone Pattern dialog box shown in Figure 133 (Filter➡Sketch➡Halftone Pattern).

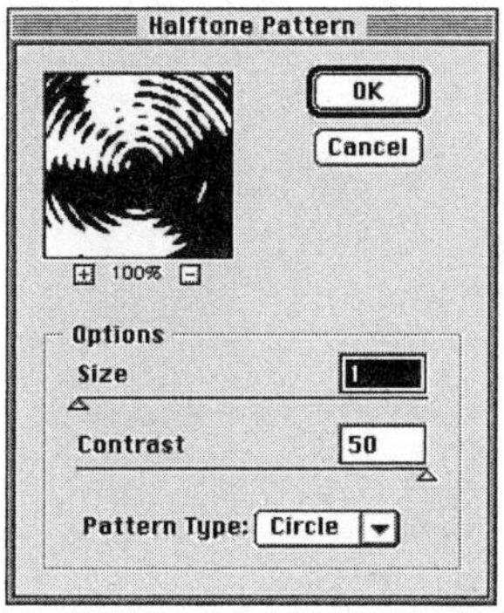

Figure 133

The Halftone Pattern dialog box.

3. Drag the Size to 1.

The Size setting varies from 1-12, controlling the size of the halftone pattern. You can get good results at all sizes, but the larger the size you select, the more graphic and abstract the results will be. Also, an image with many pixels can tolerate a higher setting without losing all detail.

4. Set the Contrast to 50.

   The Contrast can vary from 0-50. At low settings, you get a pattern superimposed over a grayscale (or duotone) image. As you move the slider towards the higher contrast, however, you begin to lose the intermediate values. As you increase the contrast, you need to think about how the image will look when it is printed—when it needs to be halftoned again if it still contains gray values. You might want to skip directly to the highest contrast setting once you are in the top quarter of the range.

5. Finally, set the Type to Dot.

   The Type can be a Circle, Dot, or Line. All effects look good, though the dot is the most traditional of them.

6. Click OK. Figure 134 shows the result.

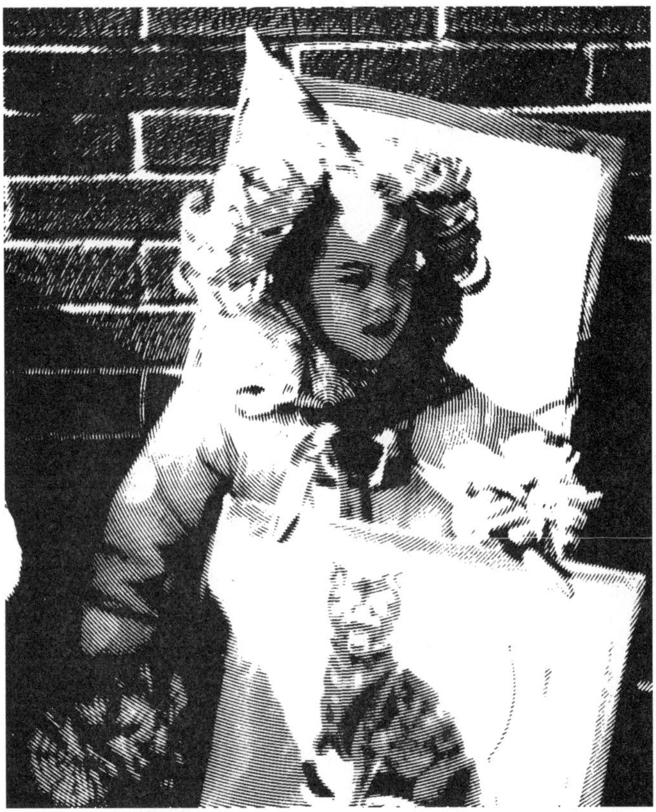

Figure 134

The Halftone Pattern filter applied to an image.

Filter type	Category	Supported Color Modes	Preview type	Data Dependent	Color Dependent
Parameter	Stylizing Filter	RGB, Grayscale	Small Filter Preview	No. This filter adds texture to a blank image.	Yes. The Foreground/Background settings are the effect colors.

Note Paper

The Note Paper filter can help simplify complex images and can also help to enhance a simple line art graphic. This filter looks good when used on text.

Try it:

1. Open the image "Clown.Psd." Duplicate the image (Image➥Duplicate➥OK).
2. Open the Note Paper dialog box shown in Figure 135 (Filter➥Sketch➥Notepaper).

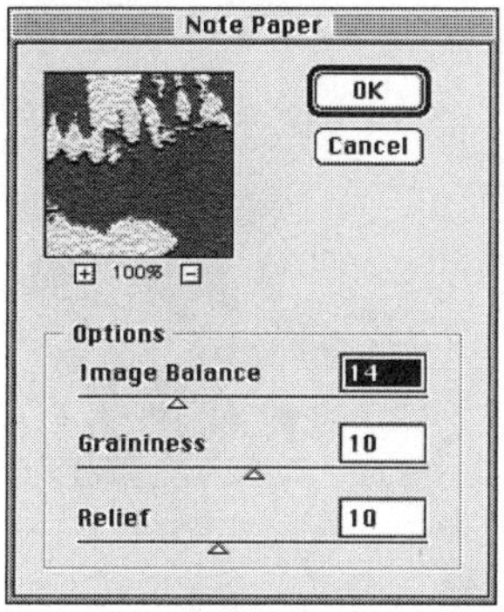

Figure 135

The Note Paper dialog box.

3. Drag the Image Balance to

   The Image Balance setting varies from 0-50. This parameter controls the balance between light and dark areas of contrast. At the extreme settings, you get no detail at all. The Image Balance does best somewhere on one side or the other of the center—depending upon the image itself and the effect that you want. You can think of this setting as creating the Threshold for the image and use it as you would the Threshold command.

4. Set the Graininess to 10.

   The Graininess can vary from 0-20. At 0, the image is smooth. At 20, the grain is a bit too powerful, but still acceptable.

5. Finally, set the Relief to 10.

   The Relief varies from 0-25. At 0, there is no illusion of 3D. At 25, the illusion is destroyed because there is too much black in the grain. If the Graininess setting is low, the image can tolerate a higher Relief setting.

6. Click OK. Figure 136 shows the result.

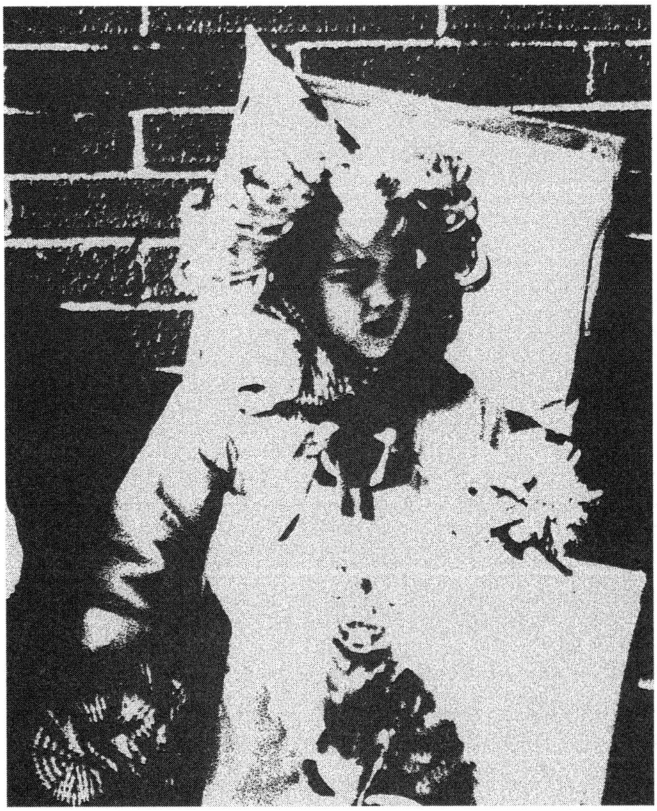

Figure 136

The Note Paper filter applied to an image.

Filter type	Category	Supported Color Modes	Preview type	Data Dependent	Color Dependent
Parameter	Stylizing Filter	RGB, Grayscale	Small Filter Preview	No. This filter adds texture to a blank image.	Yes. The Foreground/Background settings are the effect colors.

Photocopy

The Photocopy filter finds the areas of greatest contrast in the image and creates a duotone from the major shapes that it finds. It can help simplify complex images and looks good when used on text. The Photocopy filter is suitable for Web output, as it reduces the colors in the image to about 6, but the filter still can retain enough detail on a small image to see the original subject. The Photocopy filter is a very attractive and useful filter for stylizing images.

Try it:

1. Open the image "Clown.Psd." Duplicate the image (Image➡Duplicate➡OK).
2. Open the Photocopy dialog box shown in Figure 137 (Filter➡Sketch➡Photocopy).

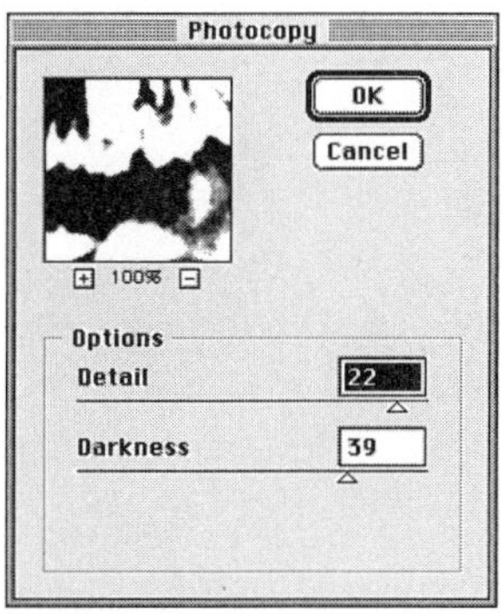

Figure 137

The Photocopy dialog box.

3. Drag the Detail to 22.

   The Detail setting varies from 1-24. This parameter controls the amount of detail that the filter finds. If Detail and Darkness are both 0, you are out of toner. Even if Detail and Darkness are at the maximum, however, you get a usable image.

4. Set the Darkness to 39.

   The Darkness can vary from 1-50. This controls the depth of the lines that the filter produces as it outlines each major shape.

5. Click OK. Figure 138 shows the result.

Figure 138

The Photocopy filter applied to an image.

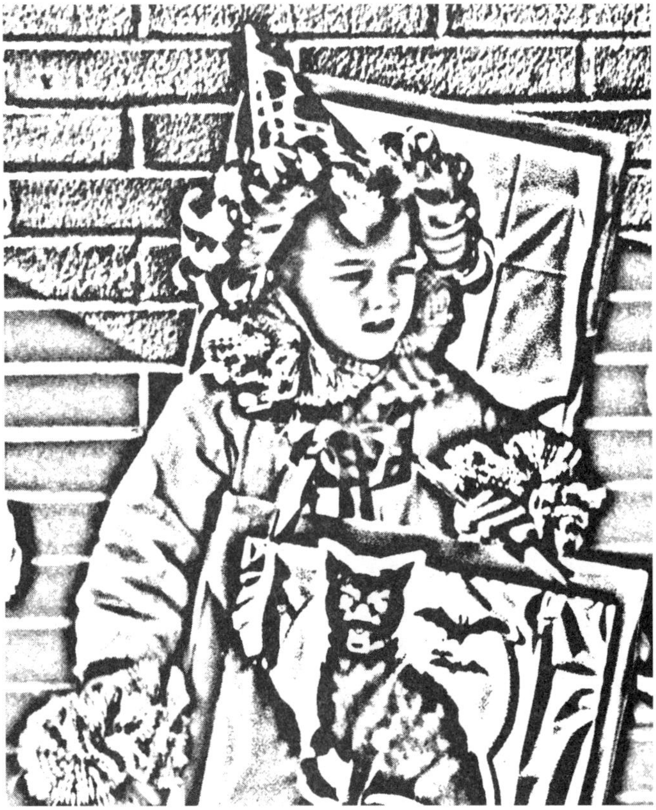

Filter type	Category	Supported Color Modes	Preview type	Data Dependent	Color Dependent
Parameter	Stylizing Filter	RGB, Grayscale	Small Filter Preview	Yes. A blank image produces a blank—though colored—filtered image.	Yes. The Fore-ground/Back-ground settings are the effect colors.

Plaster

The Plaster filter can help simplify complex images and looks good when used on text. It is not only sensitive to the Foreground and Background colors, but it considers their values into the effect. The Foreground color is used for the main image details (the areas that would show up as black if you applied the Threshold command). However, the filter then shades the elevation of the effect by blending dark and light. If your Foreground color is dark, the effect looks indented. If the Foreground color is light, the effect is raised (almost like an image negative).

Try it:

1. Open the image "Clown.Psd." Duplicate the image (Image➡Duplicate➡OK). Select two browns from the image as your Foreground and Background colors. Make the darker shade the Foreground color.
2. Open the Plaster dialog box shown in Figure 139 (Filter➡Sketch➡Plaster).

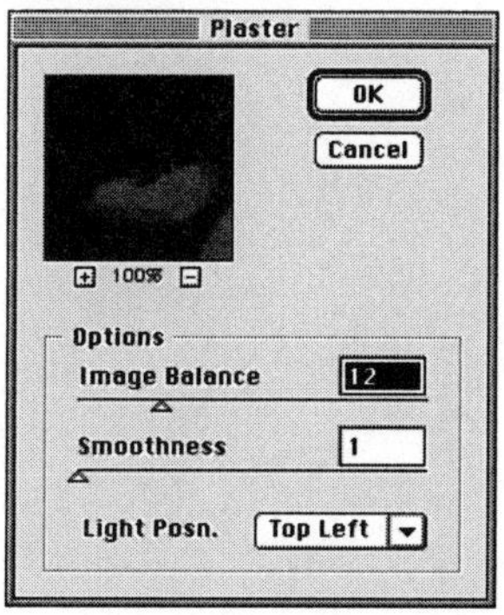

Figure 139

The Plaster dialog box.

3. Drag the Image Balance to 12.

   The Image Balance setting varies from 0-50. This parameter controls the Threshold level of the image. A good way to pre-set this control is to try the Threshold command on the image and find a good level. Threshold runs from 0-255, and this control runs from 0-50. To convert one to the other, divide 255 by the desired Threshold amount. Then divide 50 by that result. Use that number as the Image Balance. Remember, though, just as with Levels, at either end of the scale, you get a solid, blank, image.

4. Set the Smoothness to 1.

   The Smoothness can vary from 1-15. You can have rough plaster (1) to very smooth plaster (15).

5. Finally, set the Light Position to Top Left.

   The Light Position varies from Bottom, Bottom Left, Left, Top Left, Top, Top Right, Right, and Bottom Right.

6. Click OK. Figure 140 shows the result.

Figure 140

The Plaster filter applied to an image.

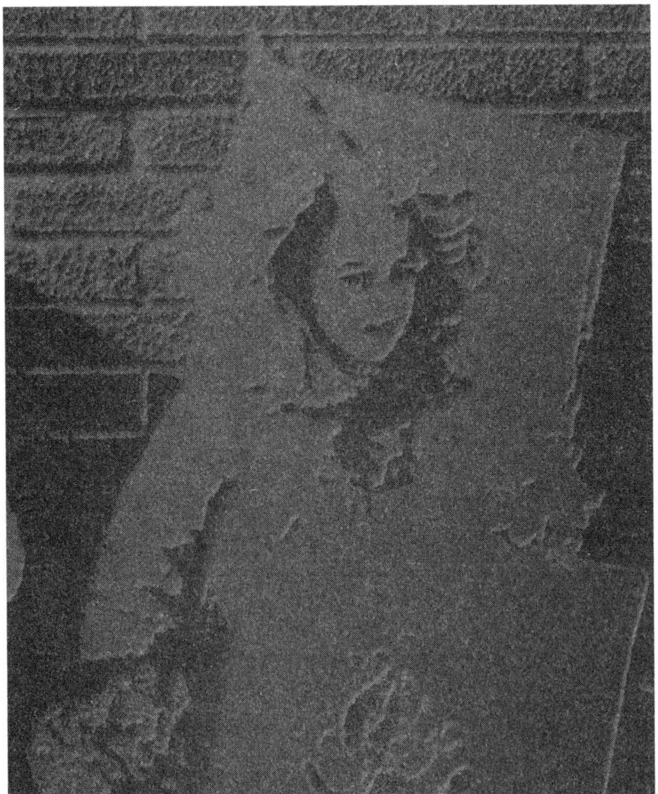

Filter type	Category	Supported Color Modes	Preview type	Data Dependent	Color Dependent
Parameter	Stylizing/ 3D Filter	RGB, Grayscale	Small Filter Preview	Yes. A blank image produces a blank filtered (but colored) image.	Yes. The Foreground/Background settings are the effect colors.

Reticulation

The Reticulation filter can help simplify complex images. It is essentially a graytone Mezzotinting filter that uses contour mapping to report the results. At extreme settings (no Density and maximum black and white), the Reticulation filter renders the image in black and gray (or whatever colors you have selected) with a tiny bit of elevation. It is not performing a Threshold, so you do get different areas than you would using the Plaster filter.

Try it:

1. Open the image "Clown.Psd." Duplicate the image (Image➥Duplicate➥OK). Press D to set the colors back to the default of black and white.
2. Open the Reticulation dialog box shown in Figure 141 (Filter➥Sketch➥Reticulation).

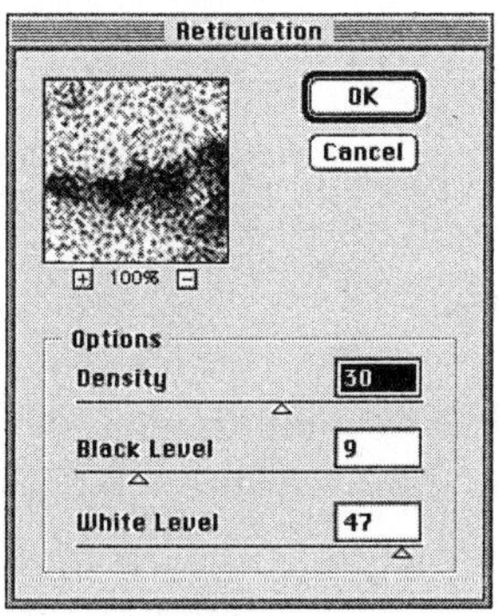

Figure 141

The Reticulation dialog box.

3. Drag the Density to 30.

   The Density setting varies from 0-50. This parameter controls the contour mapping and dot density. At 0, the image looks like a series of grayscale contour maps on top of each other. At 50, the mapping is reversed and the background color is dominant and mottled. At 25, there is a balance and the image almost looks flat. In between, the image is dotted towards either foreground (1-24) or background (26-49).

4. Set the Black Level to 9.

   The Black Level can vary from 0-50 and is controlled by the Foreground color. This carries the image detail. If the level is low, then there will be more detail in the image. As this number gets higher, the results become more abstract.

5. Finally, set the White Level to 47.

   The White Level varies from 0-50. The White level is controlled by the Background color. As this number gets higher, the results become more solid in tone with fewer gray values.

6. Click OK. Figure 142 shows the result.

Filter type	Category	Supported Color Modes	Preview type	Data Dependent	Color Dependent
Parameter	Stylizing Filter	RGB, Grayscale	Small Filter Preview	Yes. A blank image produces a blank filtered, but colored, image	Yes. The Foreground/Background settings are the effect colors.

Stamp

The Stamp filter can help simplify complex images and looks good when used on text. It is a good choice for Web images as it can retain a lot of detail with few colors. The Stamp filter is very similar to the Photocopy filter, but it can produce a 2-color image where Photocopy cannot. It can be both sharper or softer than the Photocopy filter because of the Smoothness option that controls the edge detail and the number of edges found. A large Smoothness setting removes most of the detail from the image but leaves very soft, curved shapes.

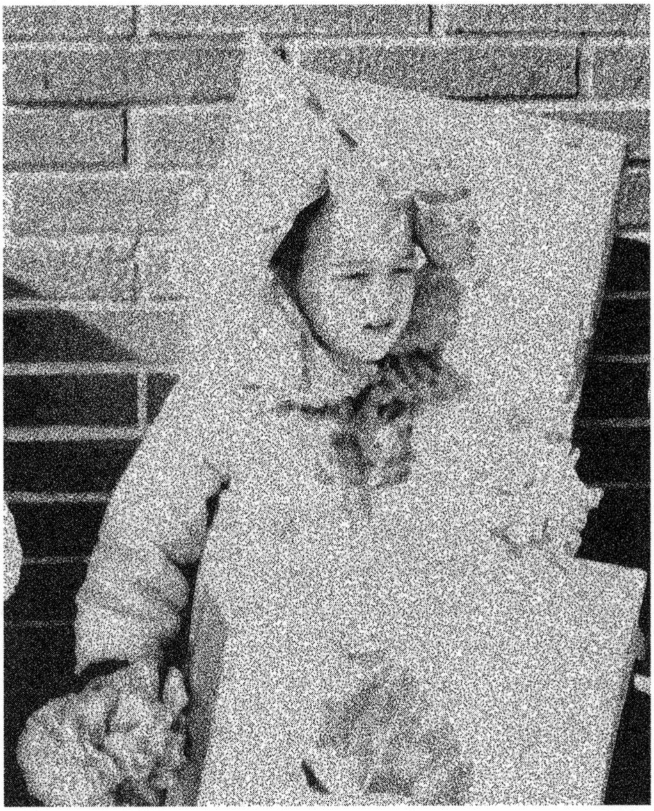

Figure 142

The Reticulation filter applied to an image.

Try it:

1. Open the image "Clown.Psd." Duplicate the image (Image➡Duplicate➡OK).
2. Open the Stamp dialog box shown in Figure 143 (Filter➡Sketch➡Stamp).
3. Drag the Light/Dark Balance to 12.

   The Light/Dark Balance setting varies from 0-50, controlling the Threshold level of the image. A good way to pre-set this control is to try the Threshold command on the image and find a good level. Threshold runs from 0-255, and Light/Dark Balance runs from 0-50. To convert one to the other, divide 255 by the desired Threshold amount. Then divide 50 by that result. Use that number as the Light/Dark Balance.

Figure 143

The Stamp dialog box.

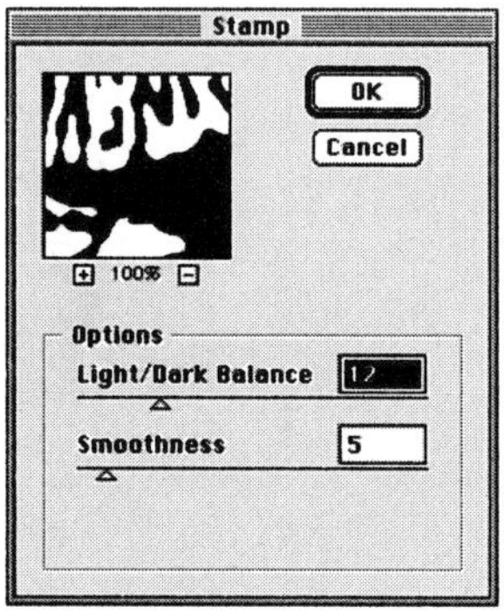

4. Set the Smoothness to 5.

   The Smoothness can vary from 1-50. At 1, there are no anti-aliased edges in the image and as much detail as possible is saved. At 50, there are few shapes, as most of them have been smoothed away (as if you had blurred the sharp version of the image and then used the Levels command to find the smoothest setting).

5. Click OK. Figure 144 shows the result.

Filter type	Category	Supported Color Modes	Preview type	Data Dependent	Color Dependent
Parameter	Stylizing Filter	RGB, Grayscale	Small Filter Preview	Yes. A blank image produces a blank filtered image with a color change.	Yes. The Foreground/Background settings are the effect color.

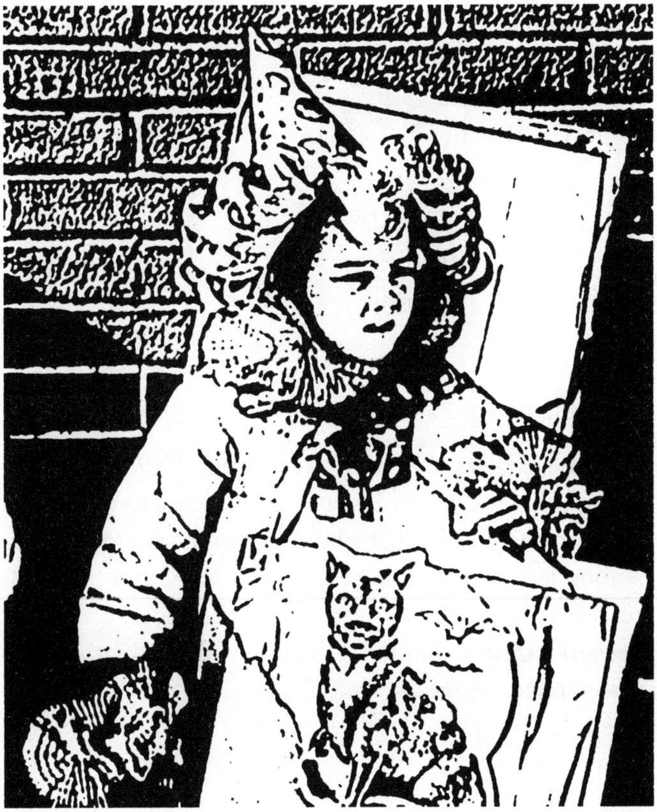

Figure 144

An example of the Stamp filter applied to an image.

Torn Edges

The Torn Edges filter can help simplify complex images and can help enhance a simple line art graphic. This filter looks good when used on text. The Torn Edges filter is a close relative to the Plaster filter except that instead of elevation, the filter produces fuzzy edges between the areas of light and dark.

4.0

Try it:

1. Open the image "Clown.Psd." Duplicate the image (Image➡Duplicate➡OK).
2. Open the Torn Edges dialog box shown in Figure 145 (Filter➡Sketch➡Torn Edges).

Figure 145

The Torn Edges dialog box.

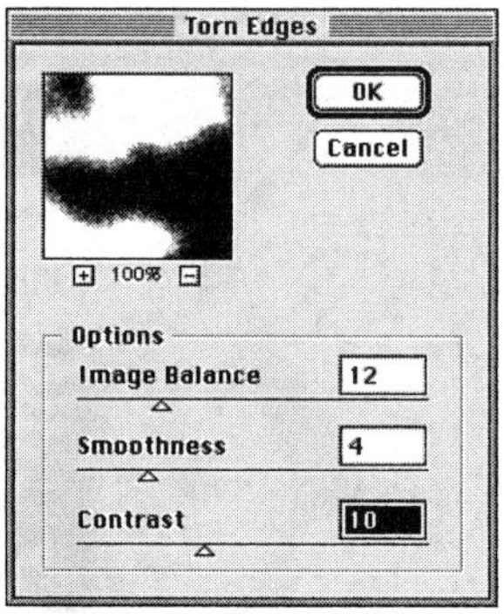

3. Drag the Image Balance to 12.

   The Image Balance setting varies from 0-50, controlling the Threshold level of the image. A good way to pre-set this control is to try the Threshold command on the image and find a good level. Threshold runs from 0-255, and Image Balance runs from 0-50. To convert one to the other, divide 255 by the desired Threshold amount. Then divide 50 by that result. Use that number as the Image Balance.

4. Set the Smoothness to 4.

   The Smoothness can vary from 1-15. At 1, the edges are an attractive, soft speckled blur. At 15, the edges are very crisp and sharp—though not especially smooth (except in the sense that smooth means aliased).

5. Finally, set the Contrast to 10.

   The Contrast varies from 1-25. At 1, the foreground and background colors mix softly in the area where the foreground color dominates (Black areas of the Threshold command). At 25, they speckle in sharp dots within the foreground color area. At 12, the foreground and background colors do not mix at all except at the edges.

6. Click OK. Figure 146 shows the result.

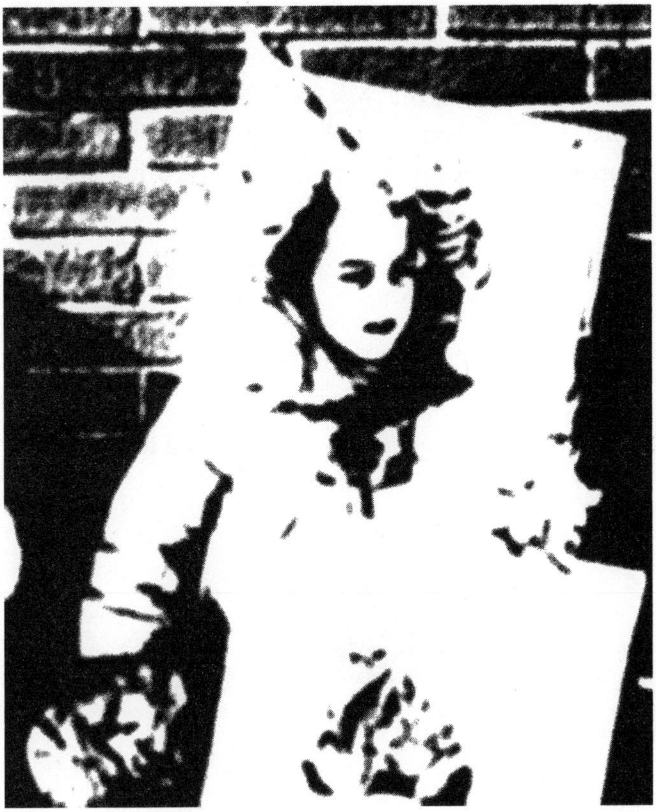

Figure 146

The Torn Edges filter applied to an image.

Filter type	Category	Supported Color Modes	Preview type	Data Dependent	Color Dependent
Parameter	Stylizing Filter	RGB, Grayscale	Small Filter Preview	Yes. A blank image produces a blank filtered—but colored—image.	Yes. The Foreground/Background settings are the effect colors.

Water Paper

The Water Paper filter can help to enhance a simple line art graphic. This filter looks good when used on text. Unlike many filters in this category, however, it does not simplify the colors of the image into two tones. The Water Paper filter makes the image look as if it were placed

4.0

in a pail of water and the paper fibers absorbed the ink. The controls in this filter perform a balancing act. If the Contrast and Brightness are set to either extreme of the scale, the Fiber Length is the most critical determinant of the filter success. It needs to be kept towards the low end of the range or else the image is all water. If the Brightness and Contrast settings are set towards the middle, then the Fiber Length can increase with quite good results.

Try it:

1. Open the image "Clown.Psd." Duplicate the image (Image➡Duplicate➡OK).
2. Open the Water Paper dialog box shown in Figure 147 (Filter➡Sketch➡Water Paper).

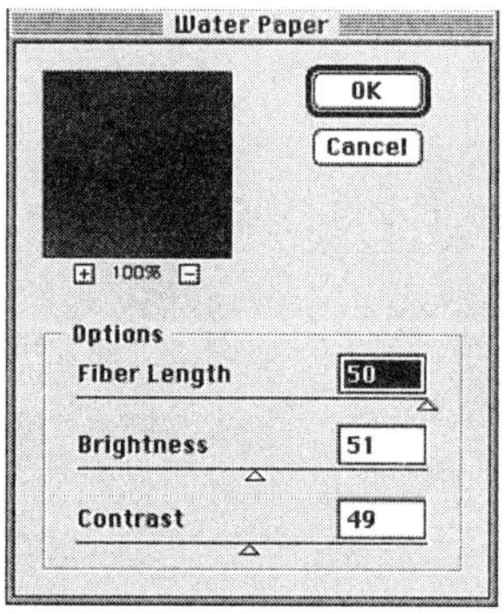

Figure 147

The Water Paper dialog box.

3. Drag the Fiber Length to 50.

   The Fiber Length setting varies from 3-50. This parameter controls the wetness of the effect as well as the length of the strokes. If the fiber length is long, unless the Brightness and Contrast are near the middle, the image will look very soft and blurred with no sharpness to it.

4. Set the Brightness to 51.

   The Brightness can vary from 0-100. At 0, if all of the other controls are low, the image looks as if the ink washed away.

5. Finally, set the Contrast to 49.

The Contrast varies from 0-100. When Contrast is lower than Brightness, the fibers are not well-defined. If Contrast is too much higher than Brightness, the image becomes too dark.

6. Click OK. Figure 148 shows the result.

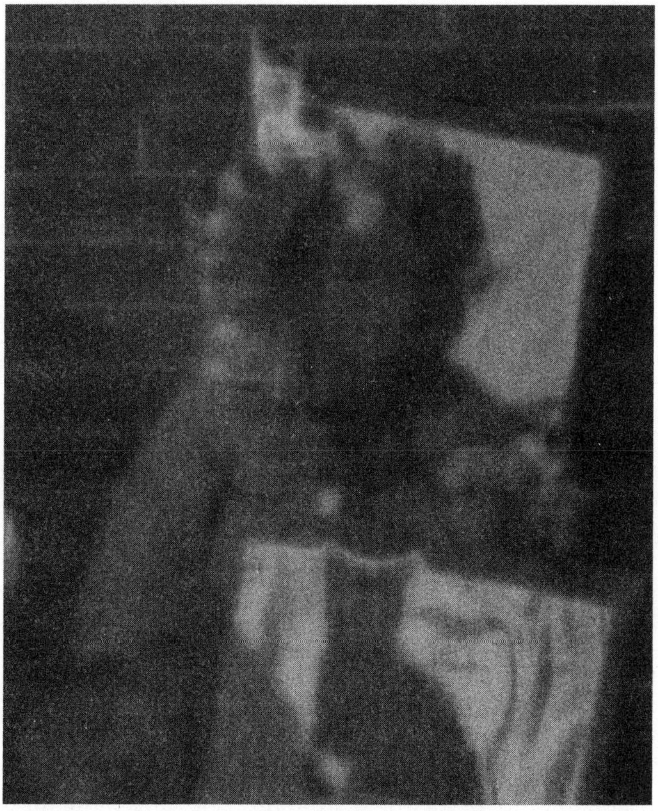

Figure 148

The Water Paper filter applied to an image.

Filter type	Category	Supported Color Modes	Preview type	Data Dependent	Color Dependent
Parameter	Stylizing Filter	RGB, Grayscale	Small Filter Preview	No. A blank image produces a subtly textured image.	No. The Foreground/Background settings have no effect.

PHOTOSHOP'S NATIVE FILTERS—STYLIZE

The Stylize filters are among the most commonly used of the special effects filters. They abstract the image being filtered by changing colors, finding edges, or moving pixels around.

Diffuse

The Diffuse filter dithers the edges of color in the selected area.

Try it:

1. Open the image "Cherry.Psd." Duplicate the image (Image➡Duplicate➡OK).
2. Open the Diffuse dialog box shown in Figure 149 (Filter➡Stylize➡Diffuse).

Figure 149

The Diffuse dialog box.

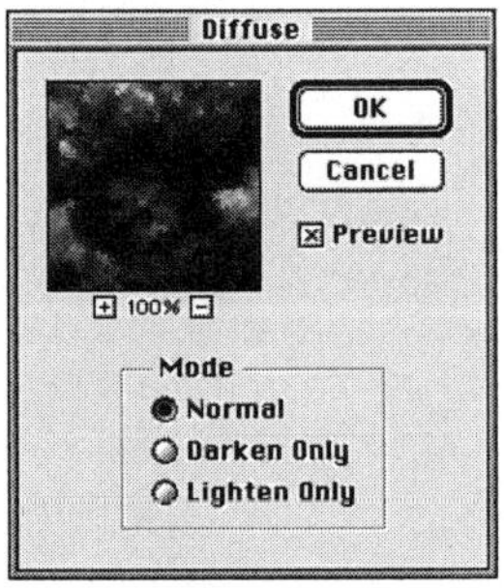

3. Select Normal as the Mode.

   In Normal mode, the pixels are diffused in all directions. In Lighten Only mode the scattered pixels only show up when they are lighter than the pixel on which they land. In Darken Only mode, it is the opposite.

4. Click OK. Figure 150 shows the result.

Filter type	Category	Supported Color Modes	Preview type	Data Dependent	Color Dependent
Parameter	Stylizing Filter	RGB, Grayscale, CMYK, Lab	Small Filter Preview	Yes. A blank image produces a blank filtered image.	No. The Foreground/Background settings have no effect.

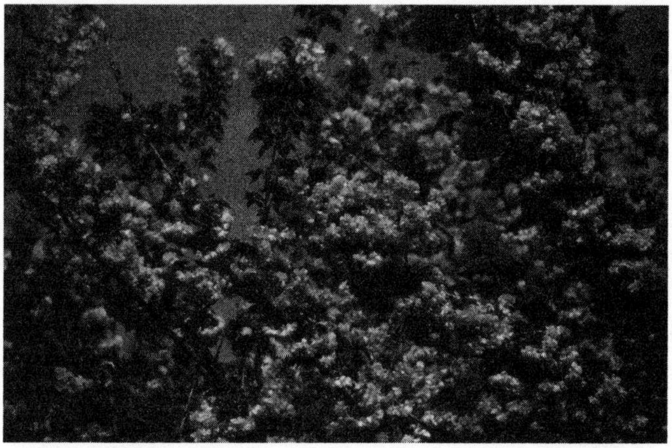

Figure 150

The Diffuse filter applied to an image.

Emboss

The Emboss filter is used to give an image a 3D look—as if it is coming up out of the background (or was stamped into it). The Emboss filter turns the entire image gray, except to trace colors that occur if you use high settings. If you need to return color to the image, you can filter the background Layer and place a copy of the color image in the top Layer for compositing in Color mode (or one of a number of other modes that work). The Emboss filter is frequently the start of many texture and channel effects.

Try it:

1. **Open the image "Cherry.Psd." Duplicate the image (Image➡Duplicate➡OK).**
2. **Open the Emboss box shown in Figure 151 (Filter➡Stylize➡Emboss).**
3. **Drag the Angle to 141 degrees or type in the number.**

   The Angle setting varies from 0-360 (though it gives minus readings if you drag the pointer backwards). This parameter controls the direction of the light.

4. **Set the Height to 3.**

   The Height, varying from 1 to 10, sets the elevation of the effect.

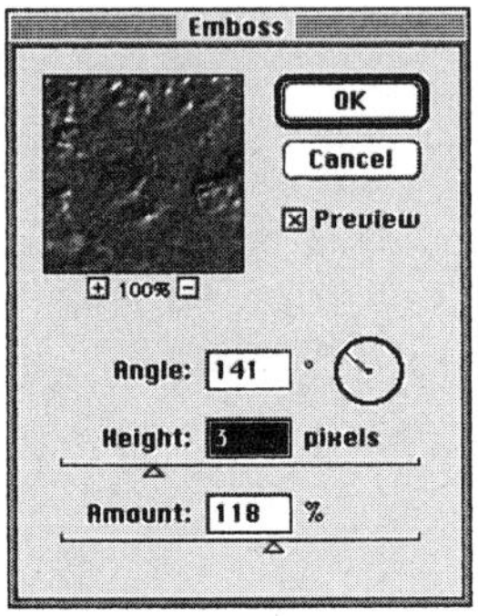

Figure 151

The Emboss dialog box.

5. Finally, set the Amount to 118%.

   The Amount varies from 1-500 and controls how much detail the filter sees to emboss. At low settings, almost nothing is raised up. At high settings, the filter sees edges to emboss everywhere in the image. Your best results occur at the lower end of the scale (to about 300% maximum).

6. Click OK. Figure 152 shows the result.

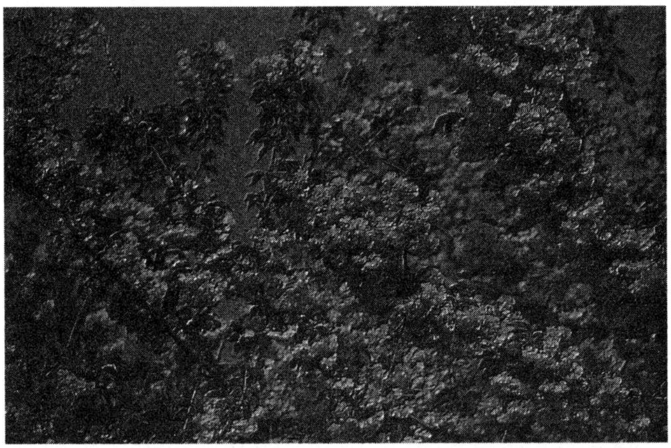

Figure 152

An example of the Emboss filter applied to an image.

Filter type	Category	Supported Color Modes	Preview type	Data Dependent	Color Dependent
Parameter	Stylizing/ Special Effects/3D Filter	RGB, Grayscale, CMYK, Lab	Full Image Preview	Yes. A blank image produces a blank filtered image.	No. The Foreground/Background settings have no effect.

Extrude

Extrude is a bit of an odd filter. It can definitely destroy the content of your image, or it can minimally abstract it. The Extrude filter could make a good basis for charting a photograph for counted craft techniques such as knitting or needlepoint. It can also add cracks to the image. The Extrude filter can make your image look as if it was pulled up into the air as a series of blocks or pyramids.

Try it:

1. Open the image "Cherry.Psd." Duplicate the image (Image➡Duplicate➡OK).
2. Open the Extrude dialog box shown in Figure 153 (Filter➡Stylize➡Extrude).

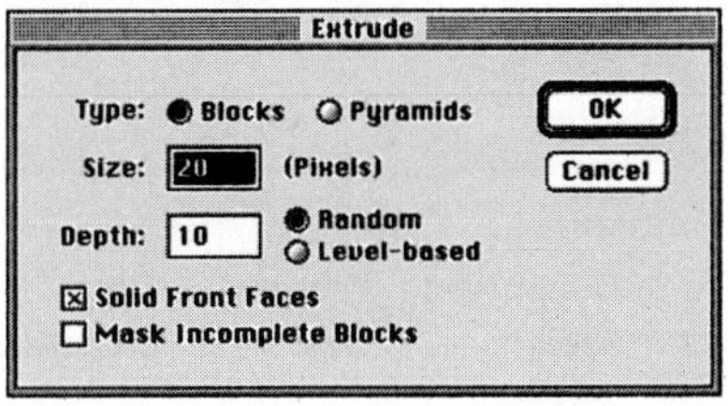

Figure 153

The Extrude dialog box.

3. Drag the Type to Blocks.

   The filter extrudes either Blocks or Pyramids.

4. Set the Size to 20.

   The Size of the extruded forms can vary from 2 to 255. Larger sizes contain only huge blocks—all image content is lost.

5. Next, set the Depth to 10.

   The Depth varies from 1-255. This controls the distance in space that the extrusion seems to travel.

6. Select the "Random" radio button. The other control, Level-Based, creates a more orderly extrusion.

7. Check "Solid Front Faces" to make each block a color based on the image. When not checked, you see the image itself with darker shades to show the intersections.

8. Do not check "Mask Incomplete Blocks." When checked, you see no blocks that extend beyond the edges of the image. If a block cannot be completed, it does not appear at all.

9. Click OK. Figure 154 shows the result.

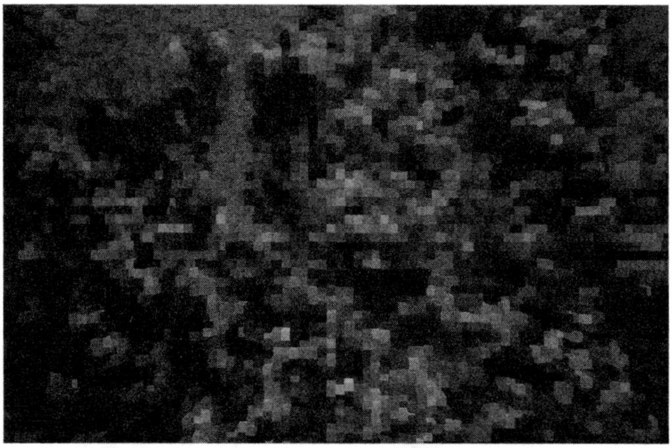

Figure 154

The Extrude filter applied to an image.

Filter type	Category	Supported Color Modes	Preview type	Data Dependent	Color Dependent
Parameter	Stylizing Deforma-tion Filter	RGB, Grayscale, CMYK	None	No. A blank image can be filtered.	No. The Fore-ground/Back-ground settings have no effect.

Find Edges

The Find Edges filter is one of the most useful of the Photoshop filters even though it is a special effects filter. It is an active participant in many texture-creation "recipes" and can create edge interest in an image when applied in Multiply or Screen in a layer over the original image. As a One-Step filter, however, Find Edges gives you no control over the results. Your only way to influence the identification of "edges" is to run the High Pass filter on the image first. You can then desaturate the edges or use the Threshold command on them to selectively change the edges to black. In versions of Photoshop prior to 3.0, the Find Edges filter inverted the result. Seeing the edges in the image against black can be very attractive. To re-create the effect, you need to select the Invert command after the filter is applied.

Try it:

1. Open the image "Cherry.Psd." Duplicate the image (Image➡Duplicate➡OK).
2. Apply the Find Edges filter (Filter➡Stylize➡Find Edges) to see the image shown in Figure 155.

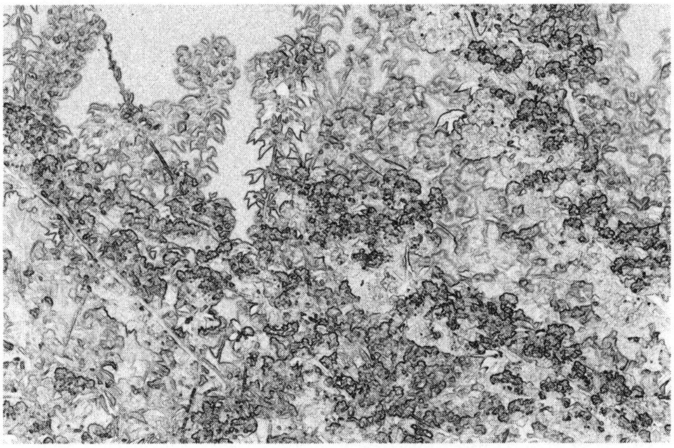

Figure 155

The Find Edges filter applied to an image.

3. Invert the image (Command-I)[Control-I]. Figure 156 shows the result.

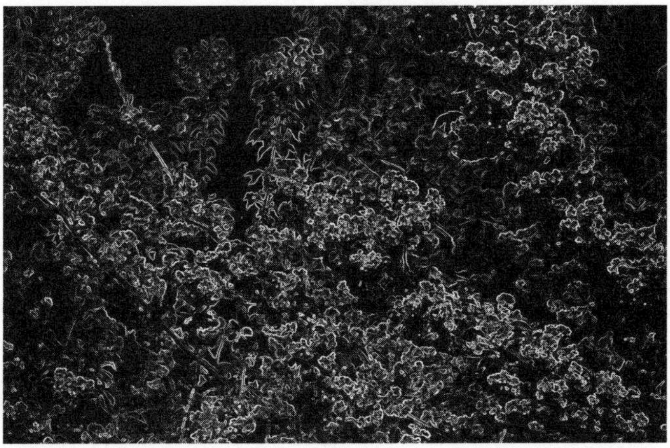

Figure 156

The Find Edges filter inverted.

Filter type	Category	Supported Color Modes	Preview type	Data Dependent	Color Dependent
One-Step	Stylizing/ Distressing Filter	RGB, Grayscale, CMYK, Lab	None	Yes. A blank image produces a blank filtered image.	No. The Foreground/Background settings have no effect.

Glowing Edges

4.0

The Glowing Edges filter is a super-set of the Find Edges filter. It automatically does a "find edges and invert." In addition, you can select the size of the edge and the amount of edges found. The filter looks good when used on text.

Try it:

1. Open the image "Cherry.Psd." Duplicate the image (Image➡Duplicate➡OK).
2. Open the Glowing Edges dialog box shown in Figure 157 (Filter➡Stylize➡Glowing Edges).

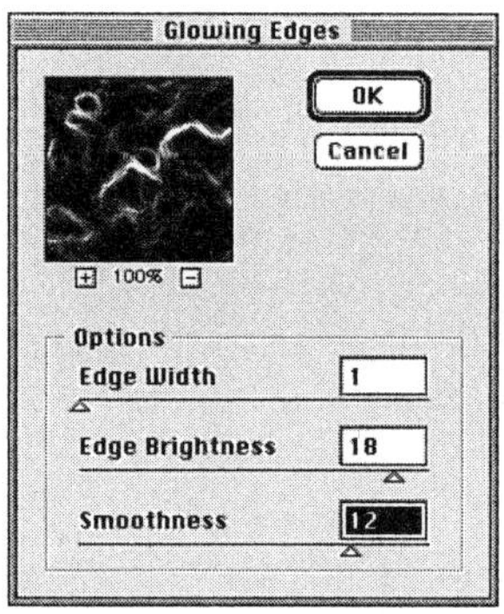

Figure 157

The Glowing Edges dialog box.

3. Drag the Edge Width to 1.

   The Edge Width setting varies from 1- This parameter controls the size of the line drawn around the edges.

4. Set the Edge Brightness to 18.

   The Edge Brightness can vary from 0-20. This controls the intensity of the edge color.

5. Finally, set the Smoothness to 12.

   The Smoothness varies from 1-15. The Smoothness determines how many edges the filter "sees." A high Smoothness setting sees many fewer edges than does a small setting. The edge is therefore longer and less jagged.

6. Click OK. Figure 158 shows the result.

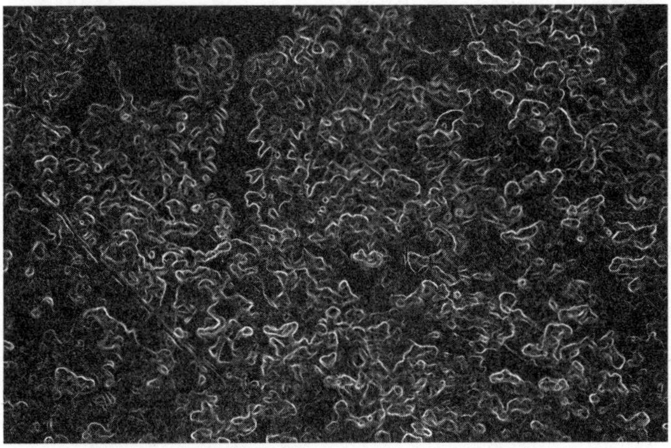

Figure 158

An example of the Glowing Edges filter applied to an image.

Filter type	Category	Supported Color Modes	Preview type	Data Dependent	Color Dependent
Parameter	Stylizing/ Distressed Filter	RGB, Grayscale	Small Filter Preview	Yes. A blank image produces a blank filtered image.	No. The Foreground/Background settings have no effect.

Solarize

The Solarize filter creates an other-worldly color change on an image by changing the Curves of the image so that values lighter than 50% are reversed to black. The effect is a digital re-creation of the photographic technique by the same name that blends a positive and a negative image.

Try it:

1. Open the image "Cherry.Psd." Duplicate the image (Image➡Duplicate➡OK).

2. Select the Solarize filter (Filter➡Stylize➡Solarize) to see the results shown in Figure 159.

Figure 159

The Solarize filter applied to an image.

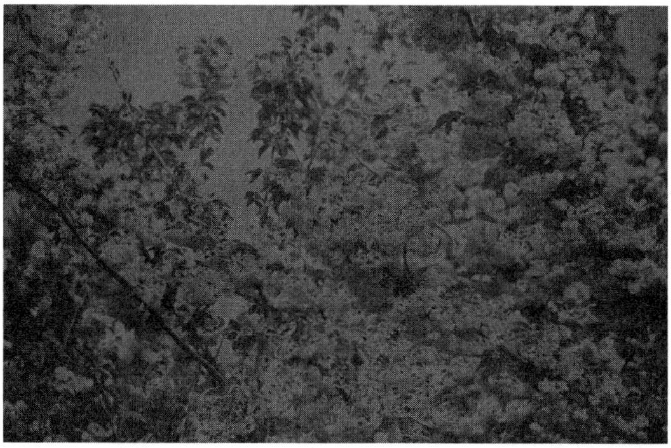

3. Figure 160 shows the Curve that is actually being applied.

Figure 160

The Solarize filter Curve.

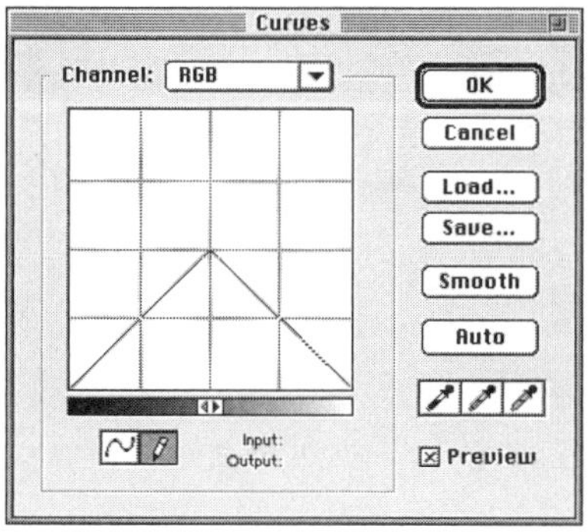

Filter type	Category	Supported Color Modes	Preview type	Data Dependent	Color Dependent
One-Step	Stylizing Filter	RGB, Grayscale, CMYK	None	No. It may invert the original color.	No. The Foreground/Background settings have no effect.

Tiles

The Tiles filter is a relative of the Extrude filter. Think of it as Extrude's 2D cousin. Tiles fractures your image into a user-specified number of blocks across. Each block contains a section of the original image, offset from its original position by a random, maximum amount. You can select how you want the image *between* the blocks to appear. If you select the unaltered image, then you see the filter only as pieces of the image moved from where they belong (almost like viewing it through a major hangover). Tiles is, obviously, a special effects filter.

Try it:

1. Open the image "Cherry.Psd." Duplicate the image (Image➥Duplicate➥OK).

2. Open the Tiles dialog box shown in Figure 161 (Filter➥Stylize➥Tiles).

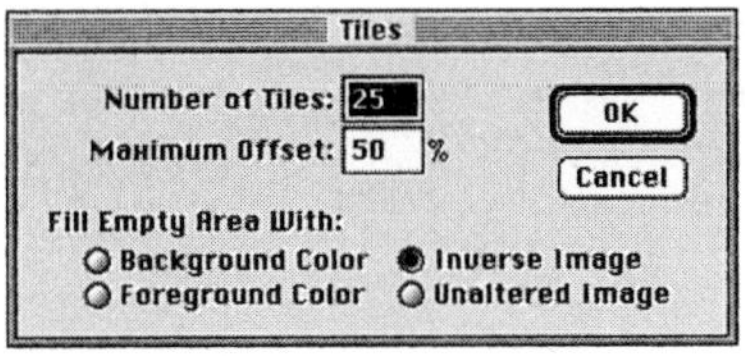

Figure 161

The Tiles dialog box.

3. Drag the Number of Tiles to 25.

   The Number of Tiles setting varies from 1-99. This parameter controls the number of tiles created in each row.

4. Set the Maximum Offset (%) to 50%.

   The Maximum Offset (%) can vary from 1-99%. This indicates the maximum amount that each piece of the image can be moved from its original location.

5. Finally, set the Fill Empty Areas With to "Inverse Image."

   Your other options are Background Color, Foreground Color, and Unaltered Image. This sets the method for filling in the gaps between the offset blocks.

6. Click OK. Figure 162 shows the result.

Figure 162

The Tiles filter applied.

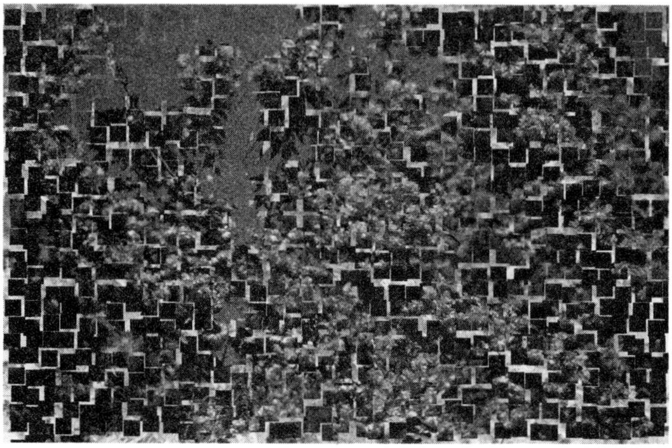

Filter type	Category	Supported Color Modes	Preview type	Data Dependent	Color Dependent
Parameter	Stylizing/ Displace-ment Filter	RGB, Grayscale, CMYK, Lab	None	No. Settings other than "Unaltered Image" pro-duce results.	No. The Fore-ground/Back-ground settings can have an effect if you wish.

Trace Contour

The Trace Contour filter can be used to find shapes in an image. It is similar in concept to Find Edges, but it finds areas of contrast and renders them to each channel. You can get interesting compositing effects by merging the contours with the original image. The contours are not usually all that useful by themselves. Good results are possible by offsetting the image slightly from the original. A simple image will use this technique better than a complex one (like our example image).

Try it:

1. Open the image "Cherry.Psd." Duplicate the image (Image➡Duplicate➡OK).
2. Open the Trace Contour dialog box shown in Figure 163 (Filter➡Stylize➡Trace Contour).

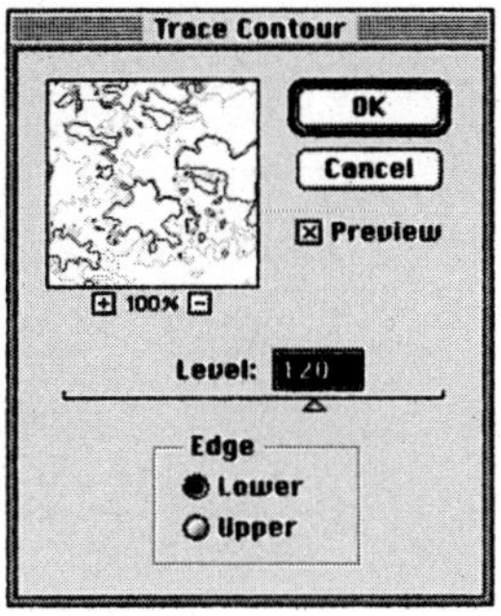

Figure 163

The Trace Contour dialog box.

3. Drag the Levels to 120.

   The Level setting varies from 0-255. This parameter controls the areas (values) in the image that will be seen by the Trace Contours filter.

4. Set the Edge to Lower.

   Edge, which can be Lower or Upper, controls the specific shape of the contour generated by the Level setting. Lower Edge indicates the color values that fall below the Level setting. Upper Edge indicates the color values that are above the Level setting.

5. Click OK. Figure 164 shows the result.

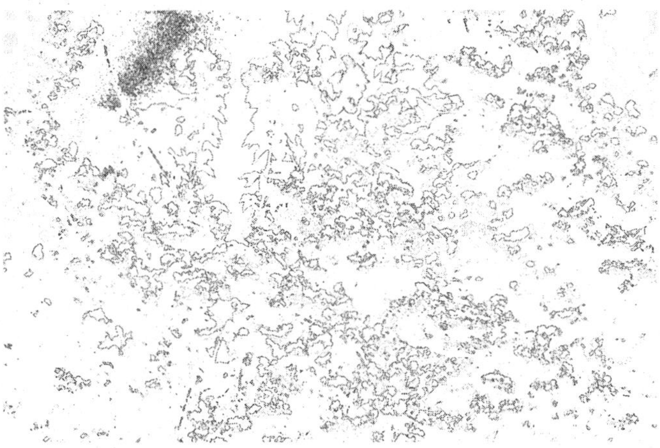

Figure 164

The Trace Contour filter applied to an image.

Filter type	Category	Supported Color Modes	Preview type	Data Dependent	Color Dependent
Parameter	Stylizing/ Distressed Filter	RGB, Grayscale, CMYK, Lab	Small Filter Preview	Yes. But blank image produces a white filtered image.	No. The Foreground/Background settings have no effect.

Wind

The Wind filter shoots a burst of air at the pixels in the image and sweeps them from their accustomed position in a horizontal manner (if you want the image filtered vertically, rotate the image before applying the filter). The Wind filter is a special effects filter but it is very useful for helping to create textures or when used on a shadow behind text. This is a good filter to apply multiple times because you cannot control the amount of the effect applied.

Try it:

1. Open the image "Cherry.Psd." Duplicate the image (Image➡Duplicate➡OK).
2. Open the Wind dialog box shown in Figure 165 (Filter➡Stylize➡Wind).

Figure 165

The Wind dialog box.

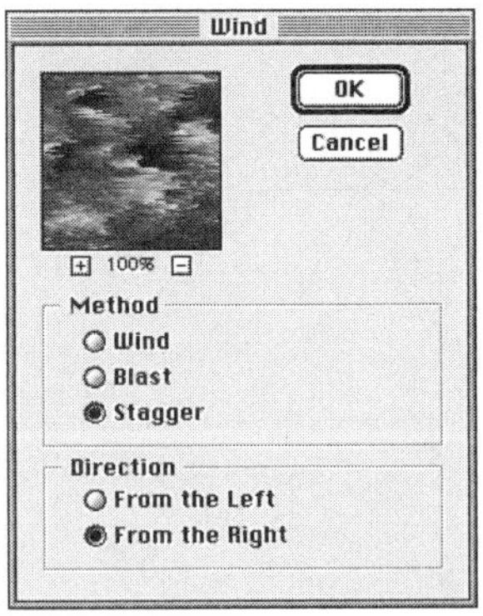

3. Set the Method to Stagger.

   The Method controls the technique used to filter the image. You can have Wind (sprinkles of pixels in a blast line), Blast (straight, long, horizontal lines), or Stagger (short and long lines).

4. Set the Direction to "From the Right."

   You can make the wind blow from the Right or Left.

5. Click OK. Figure 166 shows the result.

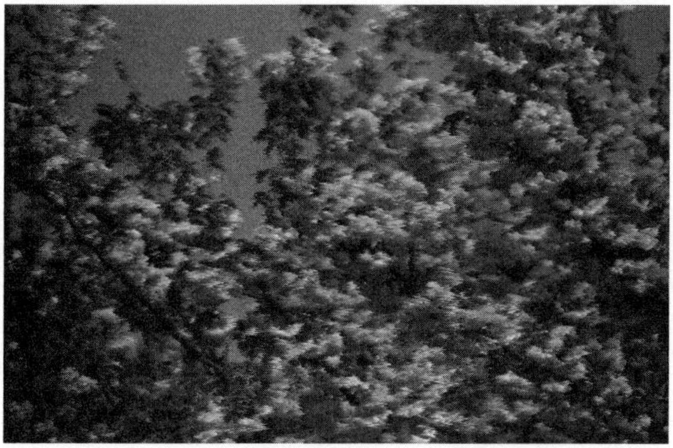

Figure 166

The Wind filter applied.

Filter type	Category	Supported Color Modes	Preview type	Data Dependent	Color Dependent
Parameter	Stylizing/ Distressed Filter	RGB, Grayscale, CMYK, Lab	Small Filter Preview	Yes. A blank image produces a blank filtered image.	No. The Foreground/Background settings have no effect.

PHOTOSHOP'S NATIVE FILTERS—TEXTURE

The Texture filters are all taken from the Adobe Gallery Effects filter sets. They add some type of texture to your image—usually either a grain or an embossing—and all of them work in a blank document to create interesting textures. When applied to a photographic image, the Texture filters abstract and stylize it.

Craquelure

The Craquelure filter looks good when used on text or other simple objects and makes wonderful textures in blank images. A number of ways exist, however, to make this effect look awful—usually by setting the controls too near to either end of the sliders. This filter is designed to make an image look as if it is a very old watercolor that has cracked from age.

Try it:

1. Open the image "Roses.Psd." Duplicate the image (Image➥Duplicate➥OK).
2. Open the Craquelure dialog box shown in Figure 167 (Filter➥Texture➥Craquelure).

Figure 167

The Craquelure dialog box.

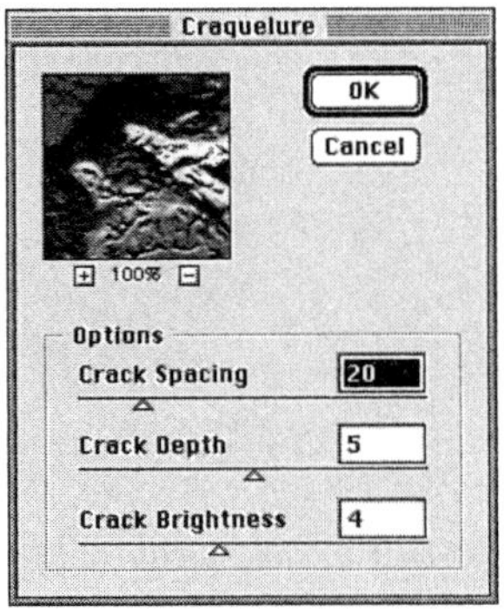

3. Drag the Crack Spacing to 20.

   The Crack Spacing setting varies from 2-100. This parameter controls the distance between cracks. The cracks are fine but infrequent when the control is set to 100. A setting of 2 produces a blank, darkened image, however, because the cracks are so close together that there is no image.
4. Set the Crack Depth to 5.

   The Crack Depth can vary from 0-10. At 0, the effect is subtle; at 10 it is too black to sustain the illusion. Keep it somewhere in-between.
5. Finally, set the Crack Brightness to 4.

   The Crack Brightness varies from 0-10. Surprisingly, the higher settings are not really better because they are too bright to set off the cracks as well. At 0, the cracks are black—maybe not the best idea. Somewhere in-between is the best balance.
6. Click OK. Figure 168 shows the result.

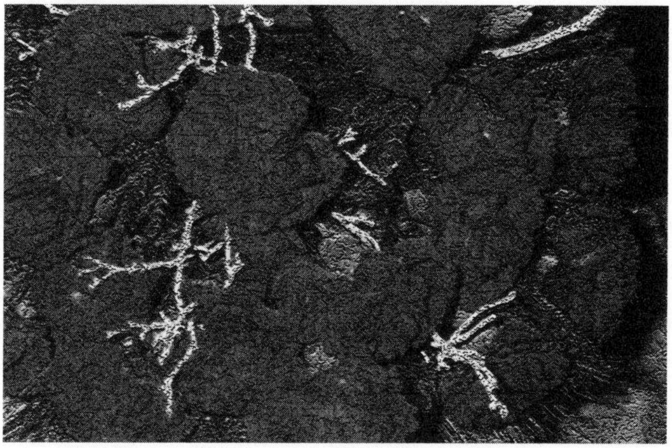

Figure 168

The Craquelure filter applied to an image.

Filter type	Category	Supported Color Modes	Preview type	Data Dependent	Color Dependent
Parameter	Texture Filter	RGB, Grayscale	Small Filter Preview	No. This filter adds texture to a blank image.	No. The Foreground/Background settings have no effect.

Grain

The Grain filter is a super-set of the Add Noise filter. It adds a variety of noise to your image and uses a variety of methods to do so. Settings that work with one type of noise (the example below uses Clumped noise) will not work well with other Grain types (such as Normal or Sprinkles). In addition, some of the methods use the Foreground and/or Background color to create the grain. This filter can be used in texture "recipes" just as you would use the Add Noise filter. The Grain filter makes a wonderful start to a variety of effects. Check out the image file GrainGrd.Psd. The same settings were used in it as in this example, except that each grid square received a different Grain Type (in order from left to right, top to bottom) from the Grain Type menu. The Layer names explain the image color and the Foreground/Background colors as well.

4.0

Try it:

1. Open the image "Roses.Psd." Duplicate the image (Image➡Duplicate➡OK).
2. Open the Grain dialog box shown in Figure 169 (Filter➡Texture➡Grain).

Figure 169

The Grain dialog box.

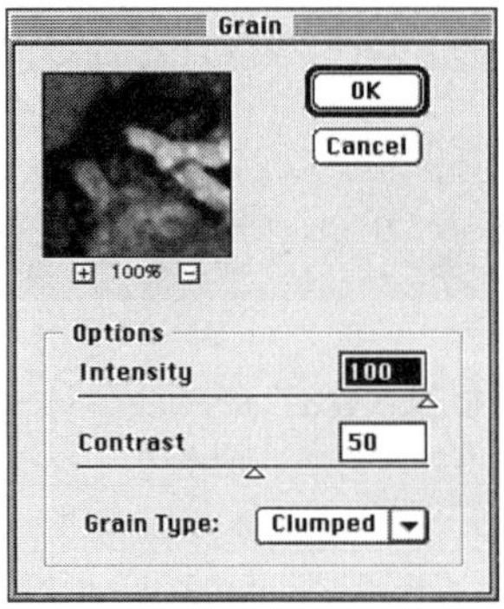

3. Drag the Intensity to 100.

   The Intensity setting varies from 0-100. This parameter is a balance. With some types of grain, you will see no result at either ends of the scale.

4. Set the Contrast to 50.

   The Contrast can vary from 0-100. A setting of 50 keeps it in balance between the lights and darks.

5. Finally, set the Grain Type to Clumped.

   The Grain Type can be Regular, Soft, Sprinkles, Clumped, Contrasty, Enlarged, Stippled, Horizontal, Vertical, or Speckle.

6. Click OK. Figure 170 shows the result.
7. For the sake of trying something different...Select the Fade Grain filter command (Filter➡Fade). Change the Mode to Exclusion and the Opacity to 70%. Figure 171 shows the result.

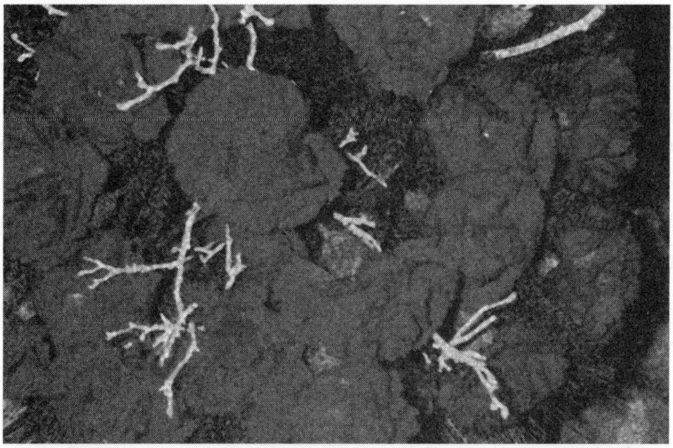

Figure 170

The Grain filter applied to an image.

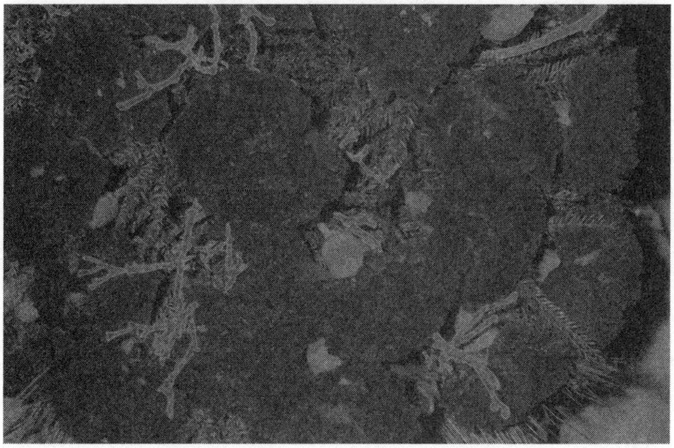

Figure 171

The Grain filter faded in Exclusion Mode.

Filter type	Category	Supported Color Modes	Preview type	Data Dependent	Color Dependent
Parameter	Texture Filter	RGB, Grayscale	Small Filter Preview	No. This filter adds texture to a blank image.	Yes. The Foreground/Background settings do affect the Sprinkled and Stippled Grain Types.

Mosaic Tiles

The Mosaic Tiles filter is a close relative of the Craquelure filter. It produces, however, irregularly-contoured squares at regularly-spaced intervals. The Mosaic Tiles filter does not really resemble mosaic. However, it is an interesting-enough look for you to be able to find something to do with it. It could also make an interesting treatment for image-filled text.

Try it:

1. Open the image "Roses.Psd." Duplicate the image (Image➡Duplicate➡OK).
2. Open the Mosaic Tiles dialog box shown in Figure 172 (Filter➡Texture➡ Mosaic Tiles).

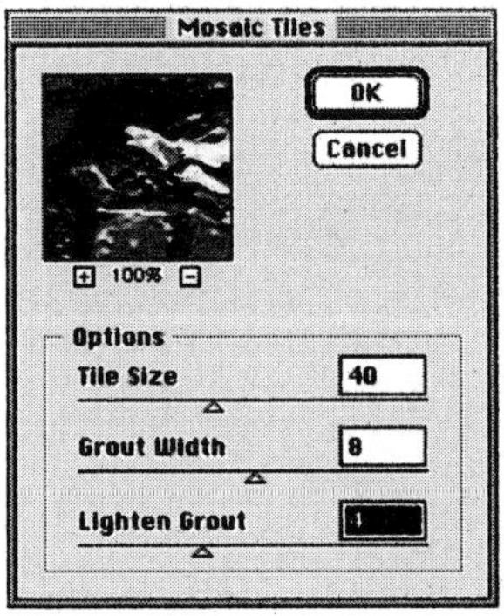

Figure 172

The Mosaic Tiles dialog box.

3. Drag the Tile Size to 40.

   The Tile Size setting varies from 2-100. Even when the tile size is small, it produces useful results. The small sizes are almost more interesting because when they overlap, no tile is produced. This creates an irregularity missing at larger sizes.

4. Set the Grout Width to 8.

   The Grout Width can vary from 1-15. It should, however, be smaller than the tile size.

5. Finally, set the Lighten Grout to 4.

The Lighten Grout varies from 0-10. When this setting is high, you do not see the effect very much. This setting does a fairly subtle embossing that highlights edges but no longer looks like grout at high settings. Keep this below 5.

6. Click OK. Figure 173 shows the result.

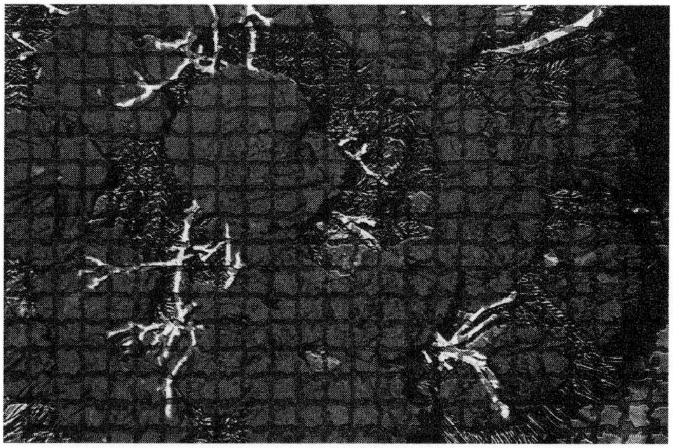

Figure 173

An example of the Mosaic Tiles filter applied to an image.

Filter type	Category	Supported Color Modes	Preview type	Data Dependent	Color Dependent
Parameter	Texture Filter	RGB, Grayscale	Small Filter Preview	No. This filter adds texture to a blank image.	No. The Foreground/Background settings have no effect.

Patchwork

The Patchwork filter is really what you might expect the Mosaic Tiles filter to be. It is basically the Mosaic filter (Filter➡Pixelate➡Mosaic) with elevation added. The Patchwork filter, however, adds a few twists at the end of the ranges that give totally different and unexpected results (try a Square Size of 0 with a Relief size of 0 or 25). It works best on images that have clearly defined color differences. The roses in the example image are too flat. A way to change that will be shown.

Try it:

1. Open the image "Roses.Psd." Duplicate the image (Image➡Duplicate➡OK).
2. Use the Select➡Color Range command to select just the red roses in the image (you do not need to be extremely precise).
3. Open the Patchwork dialog box shown in Figure 174 (Filter➡Texture➡Patchwork).
4. Drag the Square Size to 6.
5. Set the Relief to 10.

   The Relief can vary from 0-25. Even a Relief of 0 is visible, whereas a large Relief seems to shoot the tiles up in space a bit (somewhat like the Extrude filter).
6. Click OK. Notice that is image is very flat.

Let's try it again—with a few changes.

1. Open the image "Roses.Psd." Duplicate the image (Image➡Duplicate➡OK).
2. Drag the icon for the Background layer to the New Layer icon (the center icon at the bottom of the Layers palette) *twice*. Make the Background copy (the middle Layer) the active Layer and turn the Eye icon off the top layer.
3. Use the Select➡Color Range command to select just the red roses in the image (you do not need to be extremely precise).
4. Equalize the selection (Image➡Adjust➡Equalize➡Selection Only). Deselect (Command-D)[Control-D].
5. Open the Patchwork dialog box shown in Figure 174 (Filter➡Texture➡Patchwork).
6. Drag the Square Size to 6.

   The Square Size setting varies from 0-10. A tiny square size looks like large sprinkles.

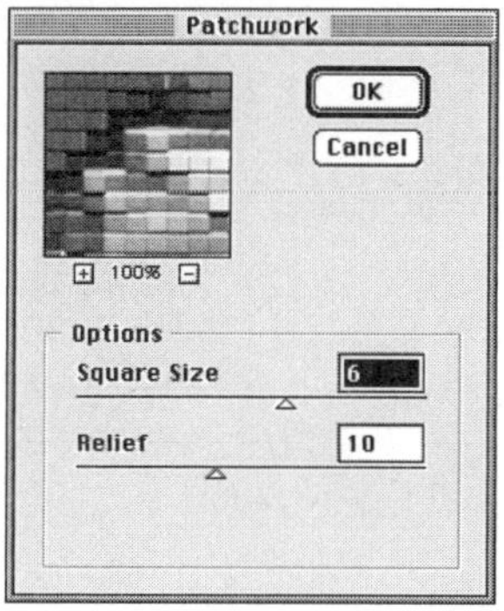

Figure 174

The Patchwork dialog box.

7. Set the Relief to 10.

   The Relief can vary from 0-25. Even a Relief of 0 is visible, while a large Relief seems to shoot the tiles up in space a bit (somewhat like the Extrude filter).

8. Equalizing the roses made them exhibit much more difference between the adjacent tiles, but it also turned them pink. Make the top Layer both visible and active. Apply the Patchwork filter to it at the same settings (Command-F)[Control-F].

9. Notice how flat the roses are. Change the Blending mode to Color, and you will get the red back into the roses but retain the altered values of the tiles. Figure 175 shows the result.

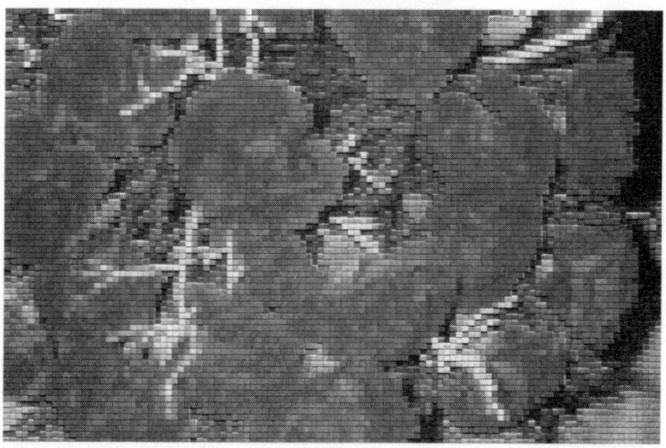

Figure 175

The Patchwork filter applied to an image.

Filter type	Category	Supported Color Modes	Preview type	Data Dependent	Color Dependent
Parameter	Texture Filter	RGB, Grayscale	Small Filter Preview	No. This filter adds texture to a blank image.	No. The Foreground/Background settings have no effect.

Stained Glass

4.0

The Stained Glass filter is another mosaic-tile wannabe. This may actually be the closest one to real mosaic tiles. It looks, however, nothing at all like stained glass. The Stained Glass filter is a crystallize filter with grout and more intensity.

Try it:

1. Open the image "Roses.Psd." Duplicate the image (Image➡Duplicate➡OK).
2. Open the Stained Glass dialog box shown in Figure 176 (Filter➡Texture➡Stained Glass).

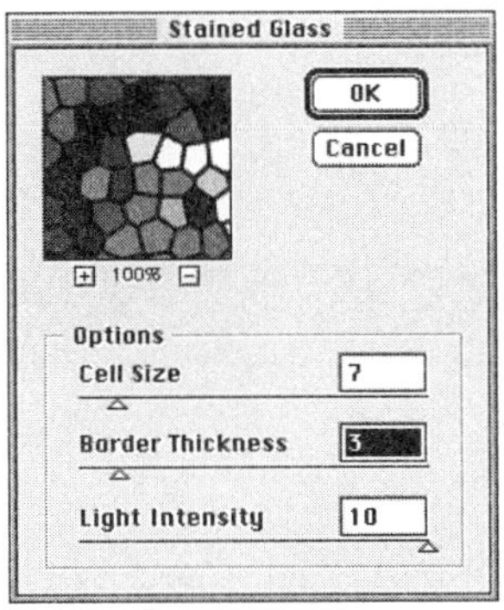

Figure 176

The Stained Glass dialog box.

3. Drag the Cell Size to 7.

   The Cell Size setting varies from 2-50. When this parameter is high, you create an image that has two colors—one on each diagonal half of the tile. The cell size is proportional to the image size, so you do not need to select a larger cell size when you are working on a large (in pixels) image. Keep the tile size fairly low to retain any detail in the image.

4. Set the Border Thickness to 3.

   The Border Thickness can vary from 1-20. It should be less than the Cell Size. This control uses the Foreground color setting.

5. Finally, set the Light Intensity to 10.

   The Light Intensity varies from 0-10. The light shines directly in the center of the image and radiates out. A setting of 0 does not shine anything; a setting of 10 causes the center of the image to white out.

6. Click OK. Figure 177 shows the result.

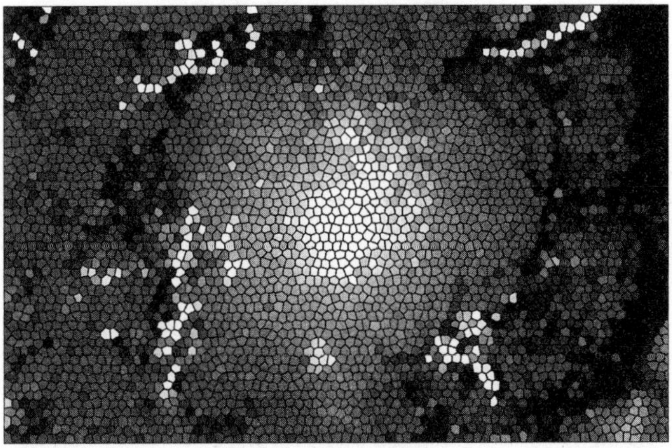

Figure 177

An example of the Stained Glass filter applied to an image.

Filter type	Category	Supported Color Modes	Preview type	Data Dependent	Color Dependent
Parameter	Texture Filter	RGB, Grayscale	Small Filter Preview	No. This filter adds texture to a blank image.	Yes. The Foreground color is the grout color.

Texturizer

The Texturizer filter looks good when used on text. This filter is actually the precursor of the Lighting Effects filter. Until the advent of that filter in Photoshop 3.0, using the Texturizer filter was the only way to easily add embossed textures and bump maps to images (other than to bring them into Painter). It is still an easier filter to use than the Lighting Effects filter, but it gives you less control. The Texturizer filter is similar to other filters in the Gallery Effects set that let you add texture as part of the filter. But in this case, the only thing that this filter does is add texture.

Try it:

1. Open the image "Roses.Psd." Duplicate the image (Image➡Duplicate➡OK).
2. Open the Texturizer dialog box shown in Figure 178 (Filter➡Texture➡Texturizer).

Figure 178

The Texturizer dialog box.

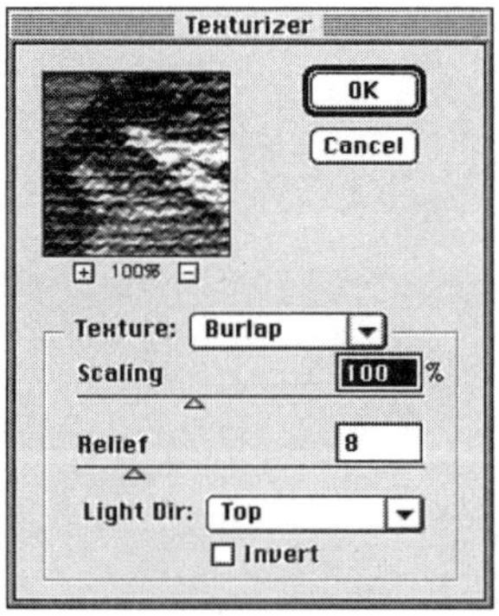

3. There are a number of settings that concern the texture to be applied. Set the Texture to Burlap.

   The Textures included are Brick, Burlap, Canvas, and Sandstone, but you can load your own texture from a Photoshop file.
4. Set the Scaling to 100%.

   Textures can be scaled from 50-200%. At 100%, you are using the original size of the texture-pattern.
5. Set the Relief to 8.

   You can set Relief to values of 0-50.

6. Select Top as the Light Direction. You can select from any 45-degree angle. You may also invert the texture if you wish to reverse the embossing (don't for now).
7. Click OK. Figure 179 shows the result.

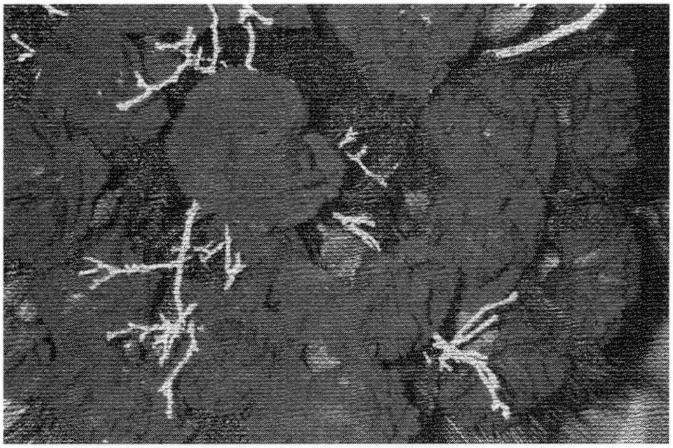

Figure 179

The Texturizer filter applied to an image.

Filter type	Category	Supported Color Modes	Preview type	Data Dependent	Color Dependent
Parameter	Texture Filter	RGB, Grayscale	Small Filter Preview	No. This filter adds texture to a blank image.	No. The Foreground/Background settings have no effect.

PHOTOSHOP'S NATIVE FILTERS—VIDEO

These two Video filters are used to prepare images for writing to a videotape and to help fix images imported from videotape.

De-Interlace

The De-Interlace filter is used to help remove the jitter and fuzziness from an image imported from a video source—either a tape, still, or motion video. Because most video images are created by interlacing—

showing the odd and then the even scan lines onscreen—they can be very noisy when brought into the computer. This filter helps to remove some of that jitter by either building new odd or even lines based on the image (interpolation) or by simply repeating the line above it. You can also use this as a special effects filter with a little extra work as shown below.

Try it:

1. Open the image "TuRed.Psd." Duplicate the image (Image➡Duplicate➡OK).
2. Drag the icon for the Background layer to the New Layer icon (the center icon at the bottom of the Layers palette).
3. Open the De-Interlace dialog box shown in Figure 180 (Filter➡Video➡De-interlace).

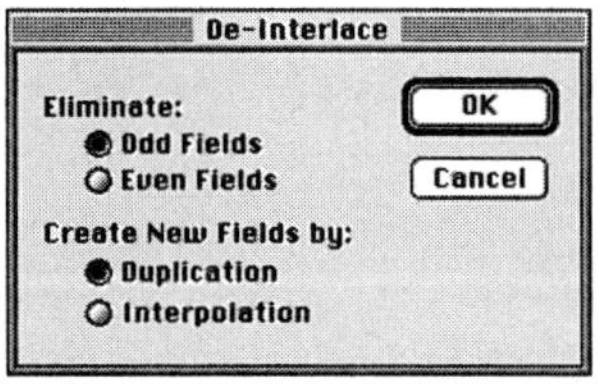

Figure 180

The De-interlace dialog box.

4. Set Eliminate to Odd Fields.

   You can eliminate either the odd or even scan lines.

5. Set the "Create New Fields by" setting to "Duplication."

   You can also interpolate between the odd or even lines that surround the line being removed.

6. Click OK.
7. Set the Blending mode to Difference and Flatten the image.
8. Use the Auto Levels command (Image➡Adjust➡Auto Levels). Figure 181 shows the result. This action actually shows the changes that the filter has made to the image.

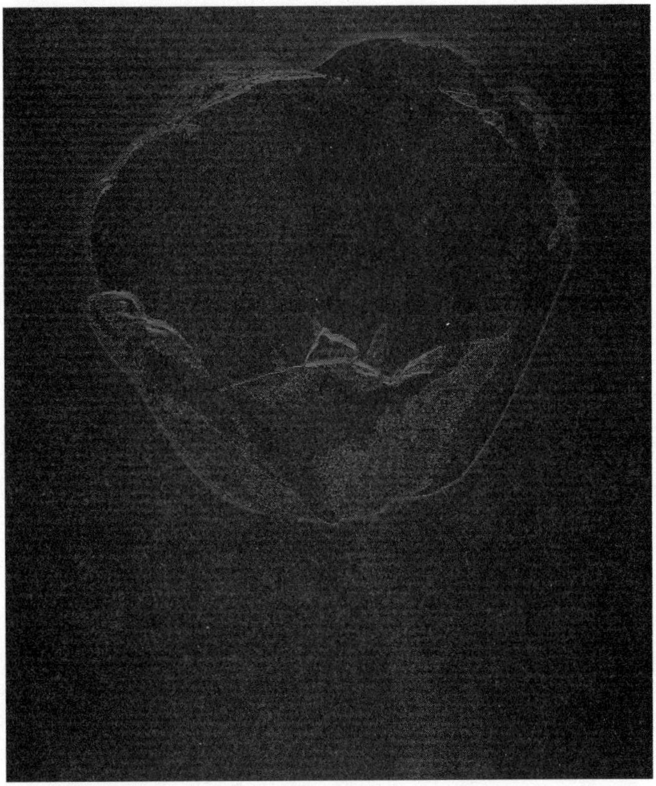

Figure 181

The De-Interlace filter applied to an image.

Filter type	Category	Supported Color Modes	Preview type	Data Dependent	Color Dependent
Parameter	Production (and Special Effects) Filter	RGB, Grayscale, CMYK,	None	Yes. A blank image produces a blank filtered image.	No. The Foreground/Background settings have no effect.

NTSC Colors

The NTSC Colors filter changes the colors in the image to colors that will display on a video screen without vibrating and bleeding into other scan lines. It does this by moving the "unsafe" color to the nearest legal color.

Try it:

1. Open the image "TuRed.Psd." Duplicate the image (Image➡Duplicate➡OK).
2. Apply the NTSC Colors filter (Filter➡Video➡NTSC Colors) to see the result shown in Figure 182.

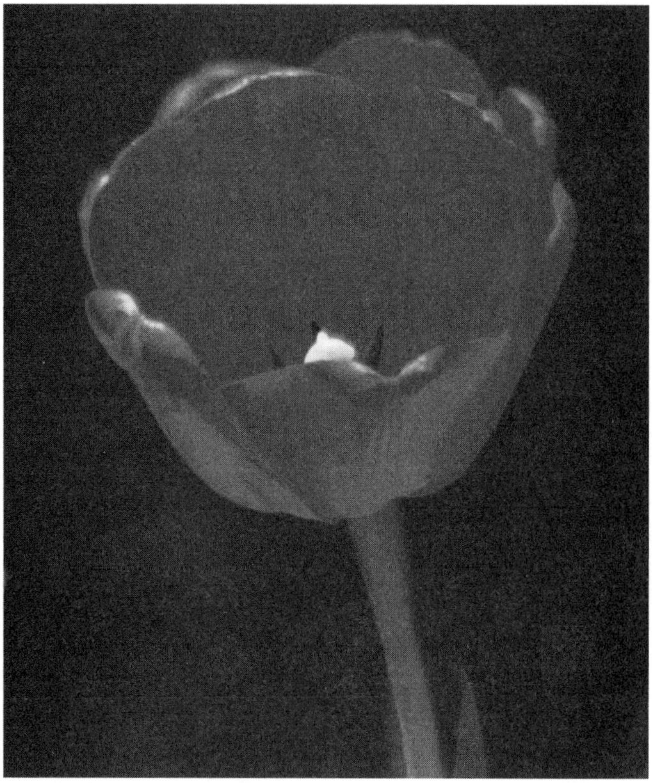

Figure 182

The NTSC Colors filter applied to an image.

Filter type	Category	Supported Color Modes	Preview type	Data Dependent	Color Dependent
One-Step	Production (Color Change) Filter	RGB only	None	No. It will find a legal solid color.	No. The Foreground/Background settings have no effect.

PHOTOSHOP'S NATIVE FILTERS—OTHER

The "Other" category of filters contains a variety of workhorse filters that do not seem to fit under any other category.

Custom

The Custom filter is one of the more complex filters and a major time-consumer—once you know enough theory to "play" with it. This filter is really an engine that enables you to create a number of different effects numerically on an image. You can load different settings and save settings as well. The saved settings are called Convolution Kernels because the Custom filter performs a convoluted form of math on a matrix (Note: groan at my pun if you wish—but don't believe my reason for calling these Convolution Kernels!). The filter, however, *does* use a 5×5 grid matrix to obtain its results. For each pixel in the image, the filter multiplies the center matrix value with the brightness value of the current pixel and uses the other values to calculate the brightness values of nearby pixels. The filter divides the sum of the total brightness amounts by the scale value and adds in the offset amount. It then repeats this process for every other pixel in the image. Whew!

What can you do with the Custom filter? The basic effects that you can achieve are those of sharpening, blurring, edge detection, and embossing. In addition, you can perform certain types of color changes. If the complexity of this filter completely frustrates you, you can also purchase KPT Convolver from MetaTools, which does the same thing but in a much more user-friendly way!

There is a trick to this filter, however. You almost always get some type of usable result so long as the sum of the numbers in the matrix divided by the Scale amount is equal to 1.

Try it:

1. Open the image "TuRed.Psd." Duplicate the image (Image➡Duplicate➡OK).

2. Apply the Custom filter (Filter➡Other➡Custom). Your dialog box may not look like Figure 183 when it appears. It contains either the default settings or last settings used. The numbers shown in this dialog box produce no change in the image at all.

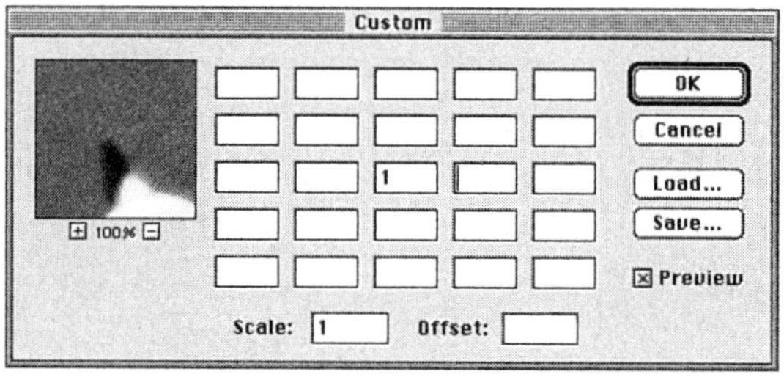

Figure 183

The Custom dialog box.

3. Change the numbers in the Matrix so that they are the same as the values shown in Figure 184. Notice that when you add up all of the positive and negative numbers, they add up to 1.

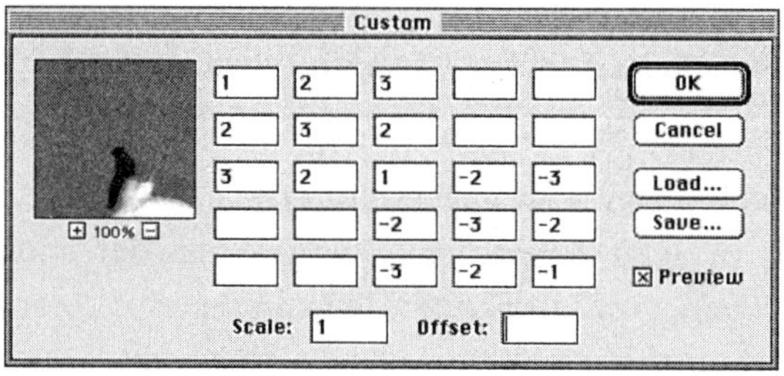

Figure 184

The Custom dialog box showing new settings.

When divided by the Scale amount of 1, the result is still 1. These settings start to produce an embossing effect as you can see in Figure 185.

4. Now, add an offset amount of 128. This makes many of the values in the image a neutral gray and emphasizes the embossing effect. Figure 186 shows the finished image.

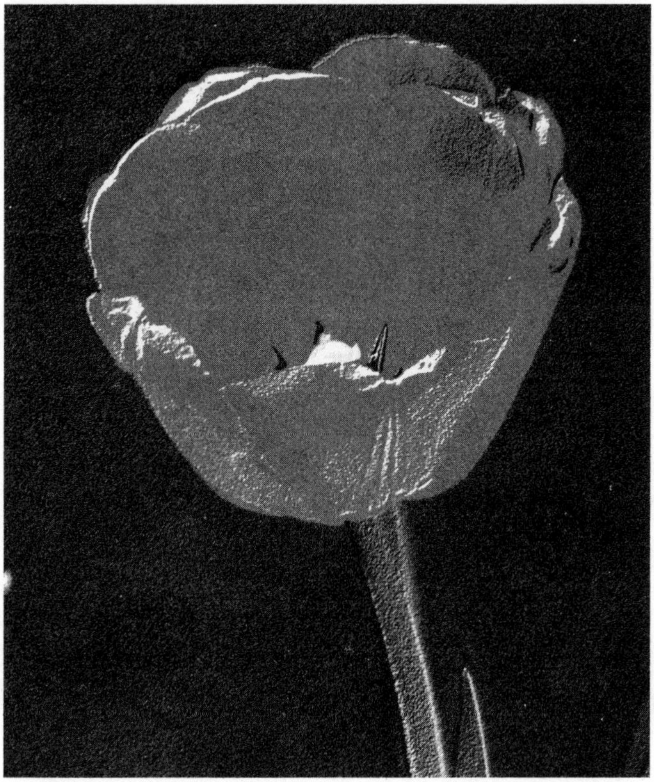

Figure 185

Filtered image with no offset amount.

You can get very creative with this filter. Just remember to try to make the numbers come out to 1. Sometimes it does not matter, but if you vary too far afield, you end up with an image that is all white or all black—an effect that is not especially useful. Try arranging the matrix symmetrically and non-symmetrically. See what different results you can get.

Filter type	Category	Supported Color Modes	Preview type	Data Dependent	Color Dependent
mini-app	Special Effects	RGB, Grayscale, CMYK, Lab	Full Image Preview	Yes. A blank image produces a blank filtered image.	No. The Foreground/Background settings have no effect.

Figure 186

The filtered image with offset of 128.

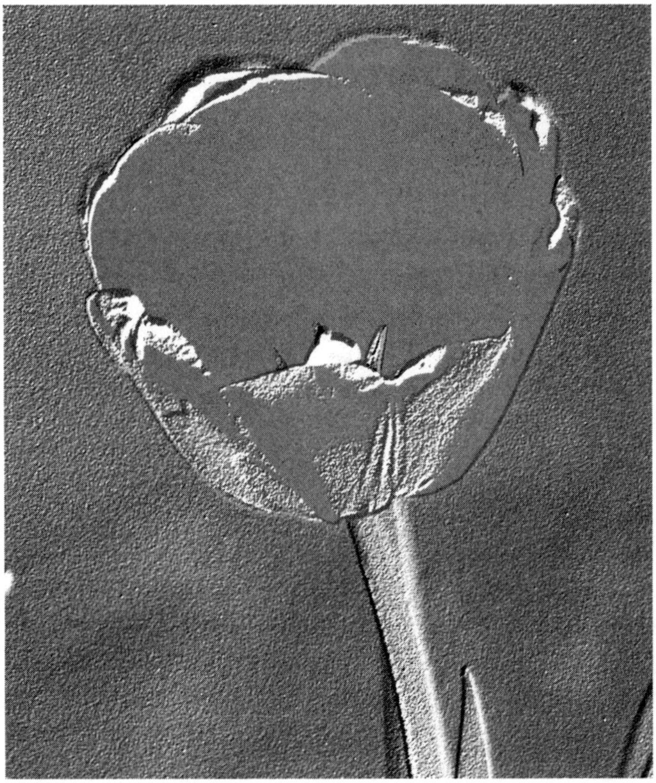

High Pass

The High Pass filter reduces the contrast in an image. It is very useful for simplifying an image prior to finding edges or applying the Threshold command. The High Pass filter can also be a good starting point for developing a mask or selection. Though it is not especially attractive as its own filter (the High Pass filter in Painter is much prettier), it is very useful for creating woodcut effects.

Try it:

1. Open the image "TuRed.Psd." Duplicate the image (Image➡Duplicate➡OK).
2. Drag the icon for the Background layer to the New Layer icon (the center icon at the bottom of the Layers palette).
3. Open the High Pass dialog box shown in Figure 187 (Filter➡Other➡High Pass).

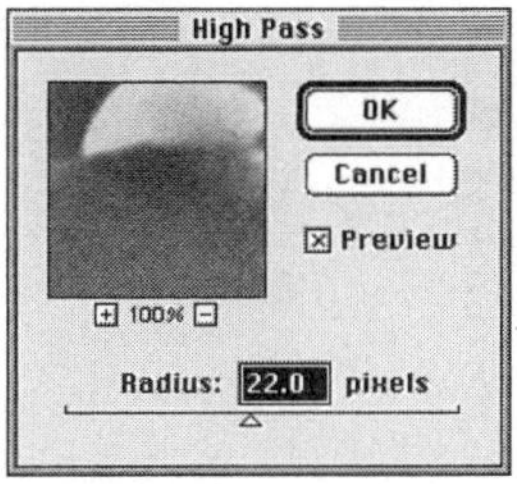

Figure 187

The High Pass dialog box.

4. Drag the Radius to 22.

   The Radius setting varies from 0.1-250. This parameter controls the distance in pixels that the filter looks as it applies the effect. A setting of 1.6 produces a very fine woodcut look. The setting of 22 gives a solid outline.

5. Click OK. Figure 188 shows the result.

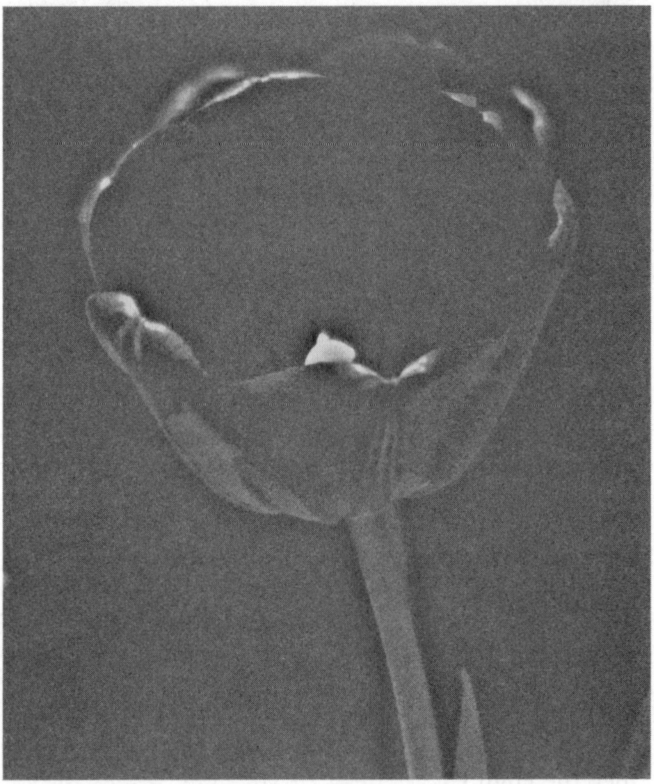

Figure 188

The High Pass filter applied to an image.

6. Select the Threshold command (Image➡Adjust➡Threshold) and drag the slider to 121. This leaves only the strongest blacks in the image.
7. Set the Blending mode to Multiply. Figure 189 shows the result.

Figure 189

The Woodcut look achieved.

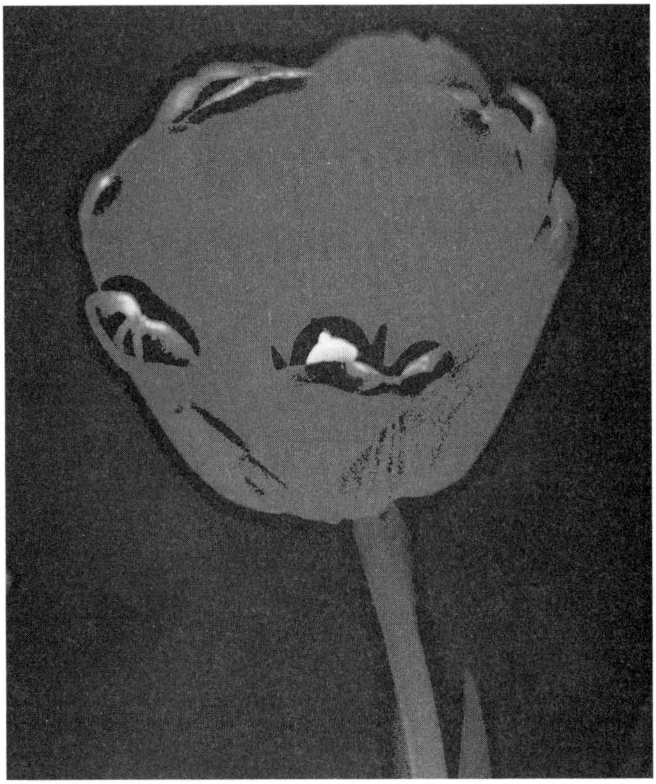

Filter type	Category	Supported Color Modes	Preview type	Data Dependent	Color Dependent
Parameter	Production/ helper filter	RGB, Grayscale, CMYK, Lab	Full Image Preview	Yes. A blank image produces a blank filtered image.	No. The Foreground/Background settings have no effect.

Minimum

The Minimum filter emphasizes the dark pixels in an image. This filter is most useful for working in channels where you want to reduce a selection. It can also be used to choke-trap areas of a channel if you are working in spot colors.

Try it:

1. Open the image "TuRed.Psd." Duplicate the image (Image➥Duplicate➥OK).
2. Open the Minimum dialog box shown in Figure 190 (Filter➥Other➥Minimum).

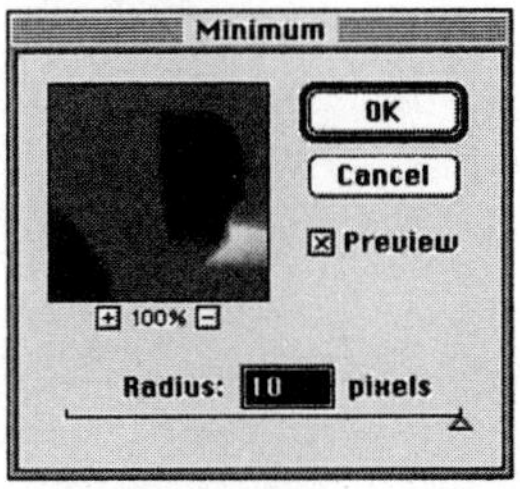

Figure 190

The Minimum dialog box.

3. Drag the Radius to 10.

   The Radius setting varies from 1-10. This parameter controls the distance from each pixel that the filter uses to see the darkest pixel value.

4. Click OK. Figure 191 shows the result.

Filter type	Category	Supported Color Modes	Preview type	Data Dependent	Color Dependent
Parameter	Production/ Helper Filter	RGB, Grayscale, CMYK, Lab	Full Image Preview	Yes. A blank image produces a blank filtered image.	No. The Foreground/Background settings have no effect.

Figure 191

The Minimum filter applied to an image.

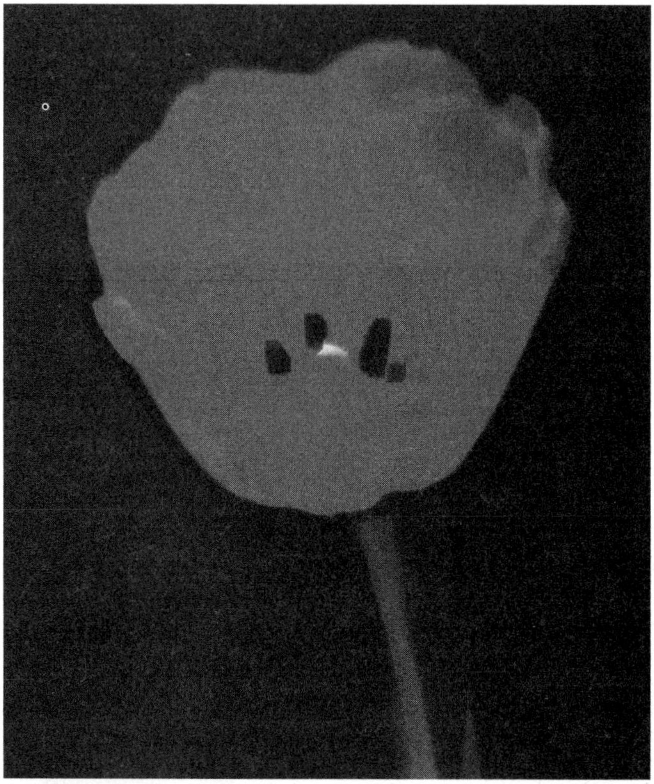

Maximum

The Maximum filter emphasizes the light pixels in an image. This filter is most useful for working in channels where you want to enlarge a selection. The Maximum filter can also be used to spread-trap areas of a channel if you are working in spot colors.

Try it:

1. Open the image "TuRed.Psd." Duplicate the image (Image➥Duplicate➥OK).
2. Open the Maximum dialog box shown in Figure 192 (Filter➥Other➥Maximum).

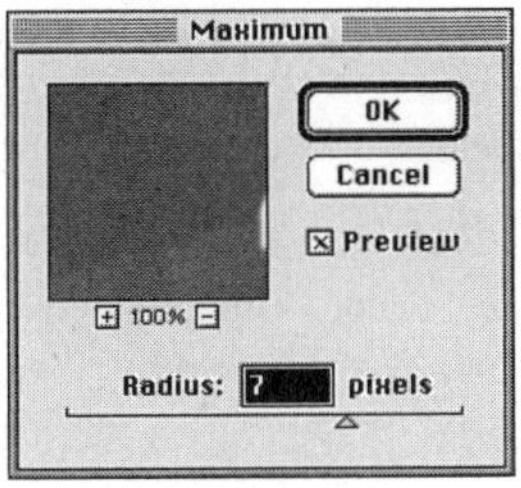

Figure 192

The Maximum dialog box.

3. Drag the Radius to 7.

   The Radius varies from 1-10. This parameter controls the distance from each pixel the filter uses to see the lightest pixel value.

4. Click OK. Figure 193 shows the result.

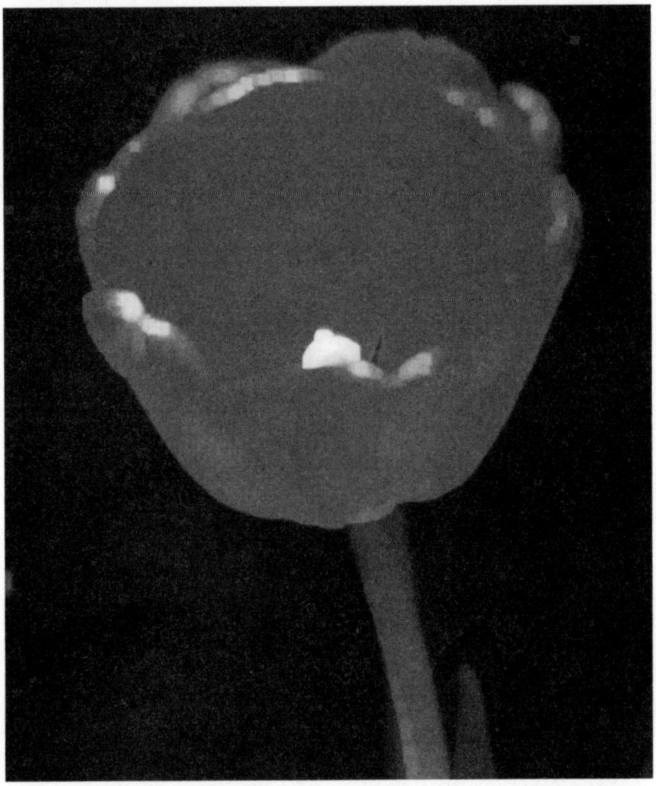

Figure 193

The Maximum filter applied to an image.

Filter type	Category	Supported Color Modes	Preview type	Data Dependent	Color Dependent
Parameter	Production/ Helper Filter	RGB, Grayscale, CMYK, Lab	Full Image Preview	Yes. A blank image produces a blank filtered image.	No. The Foreground/Background settings have no effect.

Offset

The Offset filter is incredibly useful for making patterns. It enables you to move part of an image from one location in the image to another and wrap the pixels that "fall off the edge" to the other side. Let's see how it can be used to create a seamless brick pattern repeat from the TuRed.Psd image.

Try it:

1. Open the image "TuRed.Psd." Duplicate the image (Image➡Duplicate➡OK).
2. Use the Image Size command (Image➡Image Size) to reduce the image to 100 pixels wide and 121 pixels high.
3. Drag the icon for the Background layer to the New Layer icon (the center icon at the bottom of the Layers palette).
4. Press D to set the colors back to the default of black and white.
5. Use the Canvas Size command (Image➡Canvas Size) to change the size of the image to 100 pixels wide by 242 pixels high (anchor in the top center box).
6. Open the Offset dialog box shown in Figure 194 (Filter➡Other➡Offset).
7. Type in 50 for the Horizontal (pixels) right.

   The Horizontal (pixels) setting varies from -30,000 to 30,000. A setting of 50 pixels in a 100-pixel wide image offsets the image by half.
8. Set the Vertical (pixels) to 121.

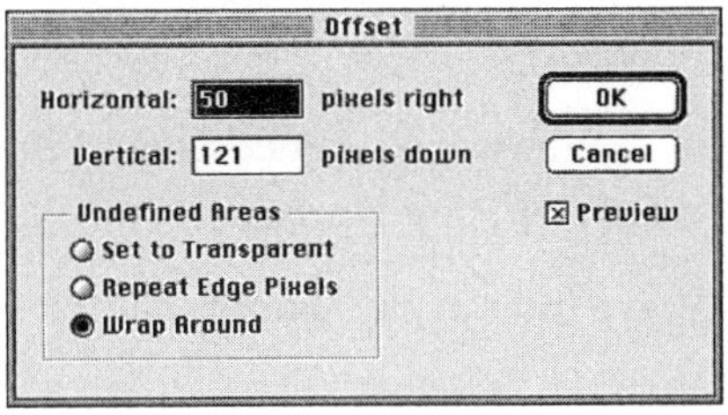

Figure 194

The Offset dialog box.

The Vertical (pixels) can vary from -30,000 to 30,000. This parameter controls the distance, in pixels, towards the bottom (positive number) or top (negative numbers) that the image will move.

9. Select Wrap Around to make the pixels move from one edge onto the other. Your other options are to repeat the edge pixels, or, if you are filtering in a Layer, set to transparency (or background color if not in a Layer).
10. Click OK. Figure 195 shows the result.

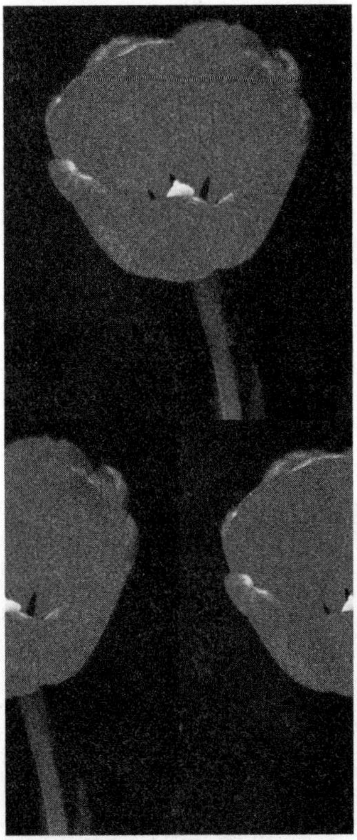

Figure 195

The Offset filter applied to an image.

11. Flatten the image.
12. Use the Lasso to draw a Marquee around the area where the seams meet. Feather it by 10 pixels.
13. Apply the Wave filter at the settings shown in Figure 196. Click OK.

Figure 196

The Wave filter settings.

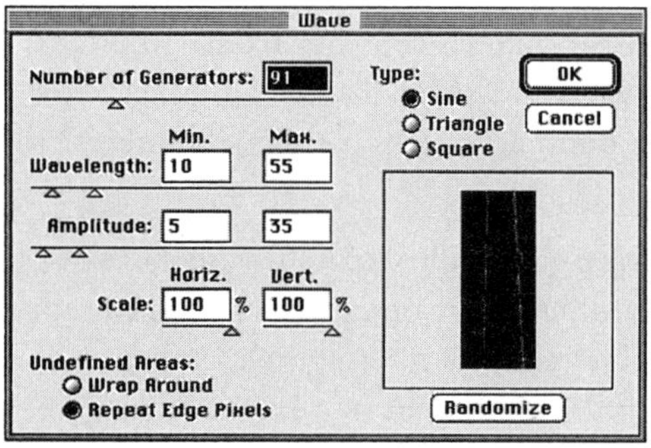

Apply the Offset filter again, at 50 pixels right, 121 pixels down, Wrap Around. This puts the image back to show the other set of seams. Select those as you did in Step 8. Feather this by 10 pixels.

15. Apply the Wave filter at the same settings. Click OK.
16. Select the entire image (Command-A)[Control-A]. Define this as a pattern (Edit➥Define Pattern).
17. Create a new document (Command-N)[Control-N] 1,000×1,000 pixels.
18. Fill the image with the pattern (Shift-Delete➥Pattern, 100 percent opacity, Normal). Figure 197 shows the result.

Figure 197

The Offset filter pattern applied to an image.

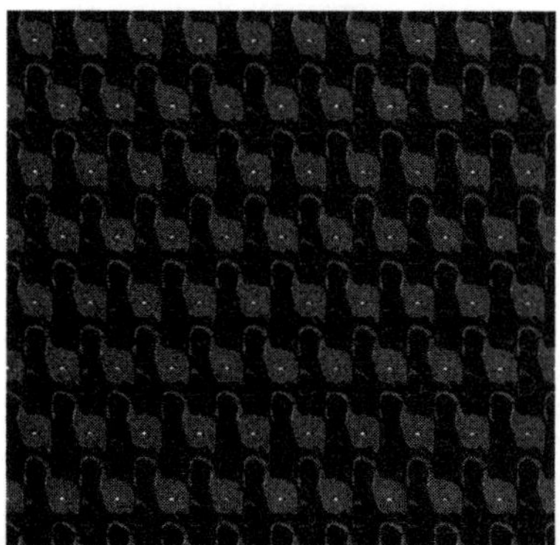

Filter type	Category	Supported Color Modes	Preview type	Data Dependent	Color Dependent
Parameter	Production/ Helper Filter	RGB, Grayscale, CMYK, Lab	Full Image Preview	Yes. A blank image produces a blank filtered image.	No. The Foreground/Background settings have no effect.

WATERMARKING IMAGES

Photoshop 4.0 also contains a filter set that helps you to protect and copyright your images. These filters, the Embed Watermark and Read Watermark filters, appear below all of the native Photoshop filters in the menu. These two filters were developed by Digimarc and are being included by Adobe as a way to help prevent unauthorized copying of images.

Watermarking is an old process. In traditional printing, a watermark was a stamp or logo applied to paper to identify the maker. It acts as both a certificate of authenticity and a means of identification. It is subtle enough not to detract from the printed page but visible if you know to look for it.

The electronic watermark is very similar—except that you need a specialized program to see if it is present because it should not be apparent to the naked eye. The Digimarc Embed Watermark filter works by adding a user-controllable amount of noise to an image. The noise is actually a pattern that contains the identifier of the artist who created the image; an identifier that must be "rented" from Digimarc for $150 per year.

The watermark is designed to survive rough handling. Even if the image is printed, the watermark is still there and can be recaptured by scanning the printed piece back into the computer. Blurring or sharpening the image does not remove the watermark, nor does cropping.

Warning

Once you have put a water mark on a file, you cannot remove it. Always save a copy of the original file before you water mark it in case you need to revert to that file.

You need to obtain a personal ID before you can embed anything other than a demo watermark in your images. You can obtain the ID by accessing the Digimarc Web site on the Web (`http//www.digimarc.com`).

Try it:

1. Open a copy of any of your own images (unless you have your own ID, you do *not* want to brand your only copy of an image with a demo ID).
2. Open the Embed Watermark dialog box (Filter➥Digimarc➥Embed Watermark). The dialog box shown in Figure 198 appears.

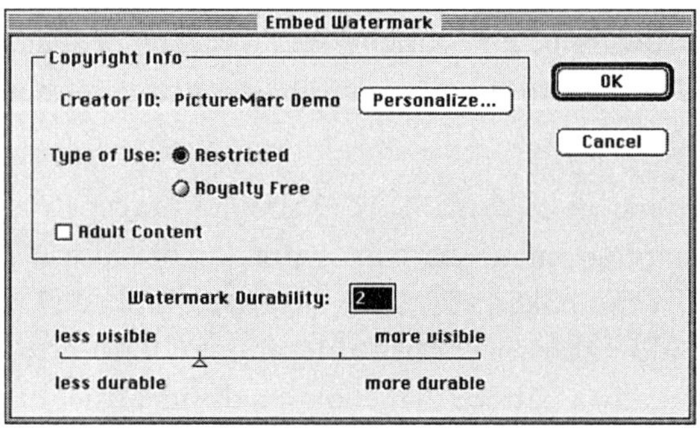

Figure 198

The Embed Water mark dialog box.

3. You may place your image in the public sector or make it available as a restricted-use image only only. You may also brand the image as "Adult Content."
4. Finally, select the strength of the watermark that you desire. Remember, the stronger and more durable the watermark, the more likely it is to detract from the original image.
5. Click OK.

Viewing a Watermark

If you'd like to see the watermark that you've embedded, follow these steps to make it visible.

1. Drag an unmarked copy on top of the watermarked copy (with the Shift key pressed to make the images align).
2. Change the Blending mode to Difference.
3. Duplicate the 2-layered image and flatten it.
4. Invert the result. You will see only the added noise that carries the watermark.

Reading a Watermark

Every time you open an image into Photoshop, if the Read Watermark filter is present, it scans the image to see if it can find a watermark. If it does, it displays the copyright symbol after the name of the image. If you wish to use this image, you need to check Digimarc's database to see who owns it and then contact the artist for permission to use the image.

To read a watermark that has been embedded in an image, choose Read Watermark from the Digimarc submenu of the Filters menu (see Figure 199).

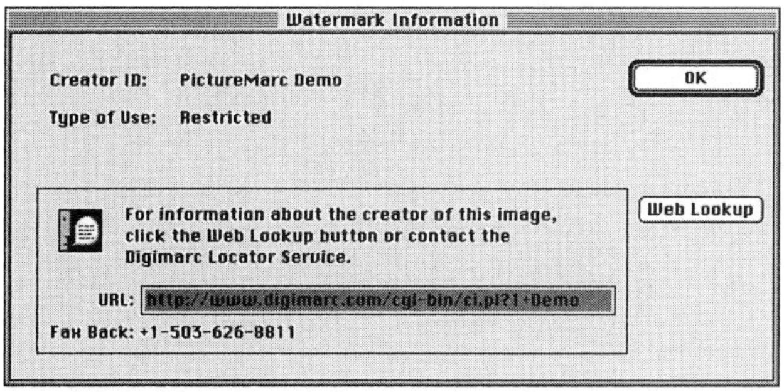

Figure 199

If this watermark had been embedded by someone with a Digimarc ID number, you could click on the Web lookup button to locate the artist's name and other information at the Digimarc Web site.

Index

Symbols

A

B

E

F

G

H - I

L - M

N

O

P

R

S